Tell Me Something,

She Said

By David Raether

To: Alexandra, Marisa, Claire, Cristian,
Constantin, Saskia, Mariangela and Juliette.

Prologue

In the 26 years we were together, whenever the house got quiet and it was just the two of us, Marina would say to me: "Tell me something." And then I would. It would be a story about my day, often told just after the dinner plates were cleared and everyone had gone off to study or play the piano or watch TV. And then, with just the two of us at the table: "Tell me something," she would say.

Chapter 1: "The Assistant Director, the Philandering Healer and the Golf Ball Scuba Diver"

We were standing in the parking lot of the Burger King just off the 5 Freeway on the Lyons Road exit in Valencia, California, waiting for Isaac. I suppose there are drearier spots in the world than this, I thought, places more bereft of any sense of esthetics, wonder, awe, joy, spontaneity or life, but I would be hard-pressed to come up with one now. Maybe the basement of a Lutheran church in Minnesota a couple hours after a winter funeral. No, even that has the vague smell of food in it. A Burger King parking lot doesn't smell of food. It smells like nothing, really. Just nothing.

Isaac would be the fourth passenger on the ride. That was all we knew about him: his first name and that he was going north. We were hours behind schedule, and still Isaac was late. So we knew that about him as well. And that's why we were waiting. And waiting. It was yet another delay in one of my most misbegotten Craigslist Rideshare journeys. It was August 2011, and I decided to go up to Berkeley to visit Annie for the weekend. Annie is a woman with whom I had been involved in a misbegotten and faltering romance. She is an essayist and critic and has a Ph.D. in clinical psychology and is an expert on autism and to be honest I don't know what she saw in me. I'm fairly certain she was beginning to ask herself the same question.

I have begun this tale, dear reader, "in media res," in the middle of things. I am starting here in the Burger King parking lot in Valencia on a hot August afternoon in 2011, and we will get to Berkeley soon enough, and then we'll go backwards several decades, and then forward to today. This will be the story of my life, and all of it is true, but not all of it I will tell. Some things will remain secret in my heart, but I will endeavor in all ways to be honest with you in the stories that I do tell.

I will tell you how I fell in love in my 20s with Marina, a beautiful Serbian poet, and had been married to her for 26 years, and how we had eight children, and how I had been a hugely successful comedy writer. And I will also tell you how I lost all of that, and had been homeless for a time and then began to rebuild my life, and then fell in love again in my 50s with Annie. This is the tale that is to unfold in the pages that follow.

So here we are, in the middle of things, in the Burger King parking lot in Valencia, California on a hot August Friday afternoon with three souls as equally disheveled as mine, traveling from Los Angeles to San Francisco.

David was our driver. He was sixty-one or so, a retired Assistant Director/Unit Production Manager/PR Consultant. He looked like Sigmund Freud, if Freud had given up his Viennese propriety and wool suits and moved out into the desert east of Palm Springs and let his thinning hair grow into a ponytail and wore mismatching floral rayon shirts and floral cotton pants and flip flops from Target.

He drove a silver 1997 Chrysler minivan, the exact same model as the one I had lived in for five months a few years earlier, except mine was green. The silver and matching trim set gave this a slightly more elegant look than the green model. Keep in mind, this is quite a low bar I'm talking about here when I say David's silver 1997 minivan was slightly more refined than my long-gone green 1997 minivan. But when I first climbed in, it had the warm feeling a familiarity, including the mountain of clutter in the back. It took me back to when I had all my possessions in this same model, and lived in it, parked as it was in the lot behind the FedEx Kinko's store on Colorado and Lake in downtown Pasadena, California.

Back to the Burger King parking lot in Valencia, however. When we had arrived at the Burger King parking lot, we all decided to go in and pee. I went in first, and was coming out when David and the other passenger, Michael, came walking toward me with grim looks on their faces.

"What's going on?" I asked.

"I locked my keys in the car!" said David.

I looked at Michael, who shook his head in disbelief.

"Can anything else go wrong on this trip?" I asked.

"Plenty," said David. "We're only in Valencia."

It was a little after five o'clock on a baking August afternoon in Southern California. I had left my apartment at ten a.m. in South Pasadena to meet a different Rideshare in Hollywood for a ride up. I had spoken to David earlier in the day, and had agreed to meet him, but he seemed a bit of a flake. He said he was driving from Palm Springs to Oakland and could stop in Pasadena and pick me up. He was leaving Palm Springs at about noon, so he could meet me at "one or one-thirty." That seemed like an optimistic time frame, because Palms Springs is way, way, way more than sixty minutes east of Pasadena.

I figured I needed a back up ride, and found what seemed to be the perfect one. A guy leaving Hollywood at noon was headed to Berkeley. We didn't talk, just texted each other. I hopped on the Gold Line in South Pasadena and texted him when I got to Union Station downtown that I was about to get onto the Red Line subway and would be able to meet him at the Hollywood and Vine Station in about twenty minutes. The communications that go on in setting up a Craigslist Rideshare usually are pretty minimal. I've been on many where I didn't even know the person's name before getting in the car. Rideshare was basically hitchhiking, which I had done a lot in my early 20s. My children and friends were appalled when I told them I did it on a regular basis. But what did they know? Rideshare is always worth it, sometimes if only for the people you meet.

"No rush," this sensible guy texted back. "I'm running a little behind. See you around one-thirty."

Well, no big deal, I thought. Only a ninety-minute delay. Gives me time to have some lunch. I considered getting a Jalapeno Cheese Dog at the Wetzel's Pretzels in Union Station in downtown Los Angeles, but passed. There probably would be a good Armenian dive to eat at in Hollywood. Hollywood and West Hollywood are full of Armenians and Russians now. There had to be some good food there. I'd wait.

I took the Red Line subway over to Hollywood and wandered around until I found what from the outside appeared to be an Armenian chicken restaurant. One of the important things I had learned in my twenty years of living in Los Angeles was this: Armenians know how to make chicken. In my opinion – and I don't believe I'm alone in this -- a roasted Armenian chicken right off the spit is up there with Mozart's "Jupiter Symphony" in being among the greatest creations of the human race.

But when I went in this joint, something was off. It was very nice – brightly lit with sunlight from the large street-facing windows, architecturally designed with wainscoting made of glass tiles, well-conceived mixed media paintings on the walls and flowers on the tables. The staff wore polo shirts and were smiling and polite.

And those weren't the only things wrong.

The place didn't reek of garlic and cucumbers, and they didn't have the meat on display so you could see them slicing it off the spit to put in your pita. There were no posters commemorating the Armenian Genocide, no fading photos of the harbor of Beirut, no uncomfortable plastic tables and chairs. There were no angry-looking, overweight staff members wearing ratty, too-small, tee shirts and barking at each other.

I really started to doubt whether this was a legitimate Armenian chicken restaurant at all. Where was the bored niece of the owner slumped over the counter looking at her pedicure while she talked to her boyfriend in Armenian on the phone and acting remarkably put upon when you asked if you could order?

I scanned the menu. No babaghanouge. I asked the smiling young Chinese man named Terry behind the counter if they had any babaghanouge.

"No," he said, still smiling. "We don't have that!"

"Hmmm," I said. "I had really hoped to have some babaghanouge for lunch."

I walked out. I hadn't really wanted any babaghanouge for lunch. It's just the whole premise of this restaurant bugged me. The very idea of a clean and friendly-looking Chinese guy named Terry in a polo shirt standing behind the counter in an Armenian chicken restaurant, asking me politely if he could help me. There was something wrong with the whole thing. So I got out.

That was a close one, I thought, as I walked along Hollywood Boulevard. I had nearly eaten at a fake Armenian chicken restaurant. Oh, the shame of it all. No worries. I wasn't that hungry anyway. I could grab my usual trail mix and Gatorade on the road.

I texted my ride that I would be waiting for him on the west side of Hollywood Boulevard, directly across from the Pantages Theater and in front of the W Hotel. I'll be waiting by a bike rack.

Fifteen minutes later I texted again. It's 1:30. How are things coming with you?

His nearly immediately response: "I'm on the 405. Will be there in a few mins."

Hmmm... I thought. He lives in Hollywood. What is he doing on the 405? That's nowhere near here. That's gonna be more than "a few mins."

And then silence from him.

At 1:50 I texted again: "Are you close?"

No response.

At 2:15 I texted once more: "Still here! Just checking to see how close you are."

Again, no response. And then the phone rang. It was David, the flaky guy from Palm Springs whom I had hoped I wouldn't have to ride with.

"Hey, man," he said. "This is my official 'I'm late' call. I'm in San Bernardino. I should be in Pasadena in an hour."

"Okay," I said. "See you then."

I hung up. God, I hope it doesn't come to this that I have to go with David, I thought. And how come no matter where he is, everything is an hour away? No way do I want to go with him.

But this Hollywood guy definitely was flaking on me. It's a problem that shows up every once in a while: you make an arrangement for a Craigslist Rideshare, and the driver or rider just never shows up. They flake. One time I'd made an arrangement to meet a guy in the San Fernando Valley near the 405, which is not particularly easy to get to from Pasadena using mass transit in LA. I took the Gold Line downtown, then the Red Line out to North Hollywood and then the Orange Line to the Sepulveda Station. And sat there and sat there and sat there.

Finally, after an hour I got a hold of him.

"Hey," I said. "I'm here. Where are you?"

"Oh, man," he said. "Look, I'm bumming out about my car."

"What do you mean you're bumming about your car?" I said.

He explained something about it seeming to overheat and that this was bumming him out.

"Really?" I said. "You're bumming out about your car? Because here's what I'm bumming about. I'm bumming that I just spent more than an hour getting here by train, subway and bus and then sat at a bus station in some god-forsaken part of the Valley and now have to go back home!"

"Dude, I'm sorry, man," he said. And then he hung up. It was your classic Rideshare Flakeout.

And this Hollywood guy had all the earmarks of being another one. I texted the Hollywood guy again at 2:32: "Just let me know if you're coming or not, okay?

I began to think I should just give up on the whole idea of going to Berkeley. Just forget it. The Hollywood guy was flaking out on me, and David just seemed too screwball to trust. Should I really go back to Pasadena to meet him? Or should I stay here a bit longer?

At 2:45 I sent my final text to Hollywood Guy: "Please let me know if you're coming."

Nothing.

Maybe I should just go home and forget about this visit, I thought. Then, a second later, no. I hadn't seen Annie in three weeks. I wanted to get out of L.A. and see her, if only for a day or so. In fact, I *had* to get out of L.A. and see her, if only for a day or so. Things were tentative enough between us as they were. Calling her up this late and telling her I wasn't coming up to see her because of a classic Rideshare Flakeout really wouldn't wash. I mean, come on. I could just see her in her lovely little house in the Berkeley Hills overlooking the San Francisco Bay and the Golden Gate Bridge after that conversation ended and sighing to herself and saying: 'Seriously, I'm a beautiful, educated woman of 54. Is this guy the best I can do?' I didn't even want to think about the answer to that question.

At 2:50 I gave up and called David. "Hey," I said. "Could I meet you at the North Hollywood Red Line Station? That's a lot easier for me."

"No problem," he said, amiably. "I'm in Irwindale right now. I should be in North Hollywood in about half an hour." A breakthrough in our relationship! He was going to be someplace faster than an hour! (Now, the fact that he could actually make it from Irwindale to North Hollywood in half an hour was ludicrously implausible, but at least David was making the effort to bring new life to a relationship that had gone stale since earlier that morning.)

I went back down into the subway and made the ride up to North Hollywood. I came up the stairs, and the heat of the west end of the San Fernando Valley hit me. The temperature was in the upper 90s and the air was dry as paper.

And there was David, across the street, "reorganizing my shit," as he called it. He had pulled out various items from the back of his minivan and was evaluating their merit-worthiness. Only one item didn't make the cut: a leafless stick from some kind of tree.

"Don't need this anymore," he said definitively as he chucked it into a garbage can.

And at what point did you need that stick? I wondered.

"The other guy is going to be here soon," David said, as he finished reloading his reorganized shit back into the minivan. "His name is Michael and he's from Hawai'i. He said he'd be wearing a white shirt and a fedora."

"A white shirt and a fedora?" I asked.

"That's what he said."

"Does he own a plantation or something?" I said. "I mean, what kind of an outfit is that?"

David was bemused. He started digging into a bag.

"You want a sandwich?" he asked me.

"Nah," I said. "I'm good."

"I made it myself," he said. "Lettuce, tomato and avocado."

"I'm not that hungry."

"It's a really good sandwich," he said.

"I'm okay," I said, getting a little testy. "I really don't need a sandwich right now."

"Whatever, man," he said, and pulled it out and began chomping on it. And I want to underscore that. David didn't eat the sandwich; he chomped on it.

The other thing about this sandwich is that it was lettuce, tomato and avocado. That was it. No bread. In fact, it wasn't really a sandwich. It was more of a handheld salad.

Time passed. No Michael. We were both starting to get antsy. It was now 4:15. On a Friday. We were now going to be heading north into the beating heart of Los Angeles traffic. The whole genius scheme of leaving at midday to avoid the traffic and make great time: gone. Ahead of us now lay the prospect of traveling twenty miles per hour for the next hour in a sea of cars, trucks and buses.

Just when it seemed I would never get out of Los Angeles, Michael came rolling up. He hopped out of the car, and clearly was no corrupted Hawaiian plantation owner. He was about 5'9", slender, with an untucked white dress shirt that had an image of a dragon wrapping around the body on it. The fedora wasn't really a fedora. It was small-brimmed and dusty. He had a ponytail, making him the second member of our three-person party to have a ponytail. He also had an enormous untrimmed beard of the type monks wear on Mt. Athos in the remote monasteries in Greece. His eyes were blue and seductive and he and the woman he rode to the station with were kissing passionately on Chandler Boulevard as he readied to leave.

It should be noted that Chandler Boulevard, which is named for the family who owned the Los Angeles Times for many decades and had played a key role in building Los Angeles and the career of Richard Nixon, is among the least romantic boulevards in the world. In fact, how it got to be called a boulevard at all is a bit of a mystery to me because it's just a wide street that runs through the Valley and on to Burbank, thudding its way into the 5 Freeway. I don't know about you, but to me a boulevard is about a mile long, and has a center island with trees and is lined with art museums and cafes and bookstores and spies drinking absinthe at little tables and college professors riding by on bicycles. A boulevard shouldn't have forty five-year-old hippies in dragon shirts making out with their girlfriends across the street from a body shop and a nail salon. That is NOT a boulevard. That's just a busy street named after a family of increasingly forgotten plutocrats.

Regardless, there we were, loaded and finally on our way out of Los Angeles.

"Just one stop to make," David announced as we slipped into the traffic inching its way northward on the 5 Freeway.

"We have another stop?" I asked.

"Yup," he said. "We're picking up a guy named Isaac in Valencia. Then we're on our way straight up to Berkeley."

"That's cool," I said. "All four of us are going to Berkeley."

"Isaac isn't going to Berkeley," David said. "We're dropping him off in Stockton."

"Stockton?!" I was furious.

"Yeah, why not?" David asked.

"Stockton's way the hell out of the way," I said.

"Really?" he said.

"I'm telling you, you cannot take him all the way to Stockton," I said.

"Let me check the map," he said.

He started to dig around for a map while he drove. I told him to pay attention to the road since we were in tremendously heavy traffic on the 170 Freeway, nearing the juncture with 5.

"Go ahead and steer while I look for this," he said. He gestured for me to grab the wheel. So I did, leaning over. It was a long lean for me, and it was at this point I remembered why the '97 Chrysler minivan was such an excellent shelter for me for those many months: it's very roomy vehicle. You can almost sleep sideways in it. So, there I was sprawled across the front of the car, steering from the passenger seat while David studied a map of California.

"Holy Christ, you're right," he said.

"I told you," I said. "Stockton is way out of the way."

"Nah, we're not going to Stockton," David said. "We'll figure someplace to drop him on the 5 or the 580. His girlfriend is coming down from Sacramento to meet him anyway."

I was relieved that we gotten that settled before we pulled into the Burger King parking to meet Isaac. Because you don't want to get into that kind of discussion during the drive. On a Craigslist Rideshare, the driver gets to set the terms up front. We got out and were stretching our legs and I went to pee and it was then that David noticed his keys were locked in the car.

We went back into the Burger King and asked to speak to the manager. A few moments later, a cheerful and completely proper-looking sixty-something bald man in a short-sleeve button down shirt and striped tie came out.

"How can I help you?" he asked us across the counter.

"We need a coat hanger," said David.

The manager's face turned nervous and he gave us a look suggesting he suspected a trio of seedy-looking itinerate abortionists had just wandered into his Burger King. Man, this would not go over well at Burger King world headquarters.

"I'm sorry," he said. "We don't have coat hangers here."

Of course they didn't. Why would a Burger King in Valencia, California, carry a supply of coat hangers? People don't wear coats in Valencia, California. It's 106 degrees out most days of the year. It was a ridiculous request, and he seemed glad to see us go. David and Michael decided to hit the nearby gas stations to see if they had coat hangers. I decided to just sit and feel crappy about my life while they searched for a coat hanger.

David showed up a few minutes later with a sign frame made of thick, stiff wire. It was all that gas station had. We wrestled with it for five minutes, trying to make a suitable long hook to pull up the door lock. I was starting to get really depressed. Why hadn't I just gone with my earlier instinct and gone back home for the day and come up on Saturday morning? In fact, why did I find myself in my mid-50s, once respectable and living in a large house in a wealthy Los Angeles suburb now taking a Rideshare anyway? What the hell was wrong with me? The answer: just about everything.

David and Michael finally broke in and reclaimed the minivan. We had been in the parking lot now for twenty minutes and still no Isaac. Dark thoughts were filling me, so I decided to talk, which is what I do best.

"So, what do you do for a living, Michael?" I asked him. He had a preternaturally calm and peaceful nature. Maybe he knew something that was worth sharing.

"I'm a healer," he said.

Nope, he didn't know anything I wanted shared with me. Healer! What kind of a job is that? For God's sakes, man! Look at you in the beard and hat and untucked shirt with a dragon design on it. I mean, I'm a disaster as a person, a complete failure as a father and a husband, but at least I'm not self-deluded. I didn't ask any more questions. I just stood there and let the nothingness of a Burger King parking lot in Valencia, California, swallow me up.

Moments later, Isaac arrived. He was in the back seat of a rust-colored, beat-up 1983 Toyota Land Cruiser driven by a short, surly, sweaty man, in a grimy, off-white (or unwashed) tank top. Sitting next to the driver was a short woman with black safety glasses, and, in the backseat with Isaac, sat a mixed breed, black, scraggly dog that barked a lot.

In New England, there is a class of people known as "Swamp Yankees." The Swamp Yankee is the person who drives a forty-year-old car (usually a station wagon) that is filled with old newspapers, clothes, tools, laundry baskets, knick-knacks and other items just too valuable to throw away because you just never know when you might need one of them. Swamp Yankees are pale-skinned and generally quiet except when yelling at their kids in the supermarket: "Shut the fuck up, Bobby! I'm not buying you any more licorice." or "Fine, get some popsicles, I'm tired of arguing with you." They don't live in town, but out in the country – often near swamps -- in rundown houses with dogs tied to tires in the front yard, and they usually keep large appliances, such as refrigerators or washing machines, on the front porch.

I met a Swamp Yankee once at the hardware store in my town. I told him I had been to Boston the prior night to see a Red Sox game.

"Boston," he said. "Yeah, I was there once about eleven years ago."

Boston was forty-seven miles away. It was the only time he had ever left New Hampshire.

This couple was the Southern California version of the Swamp Yankee. Except out here they are called Desert People. Like the Swamp Yankee, they emerge from the staid, well-kept world of old New England towns or neatly-swept California subdivisions in beat-up cars and unkempt clothes, carrying an "I-don't-give-a-shit-about-you-and-your-ordered-lives-cause-this-is-where-I-live-too" attitude.

Isaac fit that bill. He was covered in tattoos and wore cheap running shoes and ill-fitting socks. A cigarette hanging from his mouth, he started unloading his stuff to transfer it into David's minivan.

After the third suitcase and the second plastic tub, David said we were going to have to tie some of it to the roof. And the stuff kept coming: a guitar, several large boxes of cans of tuna, a scuba tank, three loose pairs of shoes and two backpacks. It took awhile, but David and Isaac eventually got everything stuffed in or tied down. We were just one dead grandmother sitting in a rocking chair from being the Joad family in "The Grapes of Wrath."

I have to give Isaac this: he was cheerful and good-natured and liked to talk. He was a fallen-away Mormon with a pregnant girlfriend in Sacramento and twin daughters there, and had spent the past several months down in Los Angeles looking for work to no avail.

"What do you do for a living, Isaac?" I asked.

"I scuba dive for golf balls," he said.

"That's what I figured," said David.

Wait a minute, David, I thought. There is no way that is what you figured Isaac did for a living. Who dives for golf balls? That isn't a job. That's something thirteen year-olds do for quarters.

Turns out, however, that it is actually a legitimate job. Isaac had signed on with a golf ball diving agency and was going to start working for them on golf courses in Northern California and Oregon. He made $.08 per ball, and earned between $300 and $600 a day. He was certified to be an underwater plumber, but the BP oil spill in the Gulf of Mexico had resulted in a shutdown of a lot of off-shore oil work and cost a lot of diver/plumbers their work, so now he dove for golf balls.

It was nearly seven p.m. by the time we came down the Grapevine and into the Central Valley. I had left the house ten hours earlier and managed to travel just seventy-five miles. We had at least four more hours in the valley. It was hot and the air conditioning in the minivan was out of freon.

Dear God, this is your faithful servant, I said to myself. If you could please explain what I have done to deserve this ride, I'd be very interested to hear it.

It was a typical dry, dusty, shit-smelling August day in the Central Valley. And by shit-smelling, I mean it actually does smell like shit. Cow shit to be specific. Used as fertilizer. Or just piling up in one of the immense feedlots that cling to the 5 Freeway and make you overcome with sorrow and nausea over the idea of eating one of those pathetic beasts. (But not that overcome because, hey, I'm not turning down an In 'N Out Burger anytime soon.) Because we had no air conditioning, the windows were open, blowing hot, dusty, shit-smelling air into the minivan. This was going to last for hours.

Isaac broke the ice on the smoking front. "Would it be okay with you guys if I smoked?" he asked in an oddly polite but thoroughly Mormon upbringing way. Within moments, the other two guys were smoking. Which left me sitting there, longing with all my heart for a cigarette.

No, I can't smoke, I thought to myself. I've quit. Annie will be furious with me if I smoke. She worries about me dying from smoking and says my mouth tastes terrible. But it's only one cigarette and I won't see her for hours and I can get some breath mints, and, you know what? If she were sitting in this minivan with no air conditioning, a golf ball diver, a healer and Sigmund Freud's gone-to-seed grandson, she'd have a cigarette too.

Many hours later, we were nearing the 5 and 580 juncture and looking for a place to dump – I mean, drop off – Isaac. His angry pregnant girlfriend was driving down from Sacramento to meet him and was none too happy that we weren't taking Isaac all the way to Stockton. Isaac was willing to let us drop him in the darkness in the middle of the freeway because he figured she could find him, but David and I were adamant we find some well-lit place to drop him.

David pulled out a laminated foldout map and told me to steer again while he studied it. He was going eighty-five miles per hour, and I was leaning over and steering while he looked at the map with a magnifying glass and found the perfect spot – Chrisman Road. It was about two miles north of the juncture that connected the 5 and the 580. My heart was racing – and probably not just because of the terror of steering for a guy who was going eighty-five and not looking at the road but because I had smoked a few cigarettes and that made my heart race and I knew I was in trouble.

We got to the exit and there it was: a lone 76 station in the middle of the darkness. We unloaded Isaac, and he sat down with his luggage and plastic tubs and cans of tuna and air tank and pulled out his guitar and started softly to play and sing a pretty and very old folk song.

"Fox went out on a chilly night/

And prayed to the moon for to give him light…

For he has many a mile to go tonight

Before he reaches the town-o, the town-o, the town-o…"

Isaac was gonna be okay. His girlfriend would be there soon and in a couple hours or so, he'd be home. He had that on me, and I didn't begrudge him it at all. He seemed to have seen enough sorrow and confusion in his 28 years to deserve to be going home. We pulled away into the dark August night.

It was nearly midnight as we came into a seedy part of Berkeley to drop off Michael. He had found a woman to stay with for the night. He said it was his girlfriend. I guess he hadn't mentioned to her the woman he was making out with on Chandler Boulevard in North Hollywood. Or maybe he had. Maybe being a healer meant you got to have several girlfriends.

The clock was turning to midnight as we made the left turn onto Shattuck Avenue to head toward the Downtown Berkeley BART station where Annie was waiting for me. As we drove through intersection, the car started to shake.

"Oh, fuck!" said David.

"What is it?" I asked.

"We're out of gas," he said.

I was two miles from Annie and we had run out of gas. I hopped out of the minivan, pulled out my phone and called her.

"I'm not making this up," I said. "I'm at the Ashby BART station and we just ran out of gas."

"Just stay there," 'Annie said. "I'll come over to get you."

It was 12:15 a.m. when she pulled up. I had left my apartment in South Pasadena fifteen hours earlier. I was frazzled, exhausted, and dusty from the road. She rolled down the window.

"Hey babe," she said, with a sleepy, happy smile on her face.

I leaned down and kissed her through the window. She pulled away from the kiss.

"Who smoked?" she said.

Chapter 2: "Prelude No. 7 in A Major by Shostakovich"

On Christmas Day, 2001, I sat down at my Yamaha G2 grand piano, set up my metronome and opened up a book of Shostakovich's "Preludes."

It was late afternoon, and the warm, orange light of the fading Southern California winter's day poured into the piano room of my five-bedroom house in San Marino, California, a wealthy suburb of Los Angeles. All of my eight children were still at home, including the eldest, who was a senior in high school. They were doing things children do on Christmas break: watching television, reading, and gathering in the kitchen talking to their mother while she made dinner. I was entering my eleventh year as a television comedy writer, a career that had included 111 episodes of "Roseanne." I had just sold a romantic comedy pilot to Fox Family. As I began learning one of my favorite pieces by Shostakovich, Juliette, our youngest, walked into the piano room. Almost three, she was wearing a red and black checkered dress.

"I like when you play the piano, David," she said.

I looked at her, and she took my breath away with her long curling hair, black and white dress patent leather shoes she was inexplicably wearing around the house while the rest of us were something only slightly more presentable than pajamas and bathrobes.

"And I love everything about you," I said, as I kissed her on the forehead.

She pulled up a little chair she kept in the room and looked at her picture books while I played the piano. The sun set and the house was filled with the comforting smell of a Christmas turkey cooking a few rooms away.

****

On Christmas morning, 2008, I woke up on the floor of the 1997 Chrysler minivan I was living in, parked behind the Kinko's at Colorado and Lake in Pasadena, California, just two miles from my old house in San Marino. It was raining, and I was cold, even though I had slept in three layers of clothes. It was one of those blustery storms that regularly whoosh down from the Gulf of Alaska and pummel Los Angeles during the winter. I climbed out of the van and walked to a Starbucks five blocks away. Although I didn't have any money, in my pocket I had the Sunday Los Angeles Times crossword puzzle I had scavenged from another coffeehouse a couple days before. The Starbucks baristas didn't mind me sitting there quietly for several hours every day getting warm and killing time.

Five months earlier, Marina, Juliette, and her immediately older sister by two years, Mariangela, had moved in with two of my eldest daughters in a cramped apartment in San Francisco while I tried to find work, an apartment and some new kind of future. Constantin, who we called Coco and Saskia, our two remaining children still in high school and who were living with friends in San Marino, had gone to San Francisco for Christmas break.

I was neither a drug addict nor an alcoholic, nor was I a criminal. But I had committed one of the more basic of American sins: I had failed. In eight years, first my career had vanished, then my savings, and then our home. The family had broken apart. I was alone, hungry and defeated.

Between 2007 and 2011, five million American families (that's 5,000,000) lost their homes to foreclosure. Some of them certainly were able to find alternative housing: renting an apartment, moving in with other members of their families, etc. But not all of them.

Many American families broke apart during this time. Mine was one of them. And I was one of the people who ended up homeless.

This, however, is not the story of five million American families. It's not the story of that young man I saw crawling out of his car in the Kinko's parking lot every morning, then go inside, brush his teeth and wash his armpits in the men's room, and then change into a suit and got to work. Nor is it the story of the mother and her two children sleeping in a Volkswagen in a Public Storage parking lot. Nor is it the story of millions of others like them. This is just my story.

It was Christmas. I stared out the Starbucks window at the rain. God, help me. I had said this prayer a thousand times, and would say it a thousand more. I had to find a way back to my life.

And over the course of the next four years I would do just that. I would do it with the pure, unquenchable, unrelenting — some might say naïve — belief that things would just work out. And I would do it with Craigslist, the omnifariously oddball website that has nearly destroyed the newspaper industry by taking over the classified advertising business. But it would be Craigslist that would help me find my way back.

People say you can find just about anything you need on Craigslist.

You might even find your life again.

Chapter 3: "Let's Get Lost"

Marina had been in Tunisia with her boyfriend.

I looked at the photos of her that she had posted on Facebook, and she looked as beautiful as she ever had; her fine-featured, elegant face and her now long, graying hair touching lightly on her shoulder. And she was smiling. She was happy. There was a great and contented happiness on her face, especially in the photo of her sitting in his arms on a Tunisian beach.

It was the kind of smile I remember from a night we had spent together 30 years earlier in a noisy, smoky bar on Mihailova Street in Belgrade filled with gypsy music from a band at a nearby table.

We had finished dinner and it was past midnight.

"What do you want to do now?" I asked. The street was full of singing and gypsy bands and crowded cafes. It was only a Tuesday night, but we had walked for blocks along the cobbled street to find an empty table. Dinner was over and I wanted to go to every place on that night, to smell the sweat and the food cooking on open grills and hear the singing and the tamburica and the trumpets and feel the life that throbbed in this chaotic and muscular city.

"Let's just sit and talk," she said.

And she smiled that beguiling smile of hers and said to me something she would say to me thousands of times over the years of our marriage, late at night in bed or in the morning drinking coffee together or while we were out walking.

"Tell me something," she said.

"Okay," I said. "How about I tell you again the story of how we met."

She smiled. Yes, she said. Tell me that story again.

The genius scheme had been this: Brian and I would move to New Zealand and become New Zealanders. As far as genius schemes goes, it was a fairly average one. I would rate it considerably below the development of the color television but considerably above sub-prime mortgages.

It was 1980, and I was 24 and a newspaper editor in northern Minnesota and Brian was 26 and finishing his senior year at the University of Minnesota's Institute of Technology. We were both anti-American at that time, which was a relatively easy position to take for an American coming of age in the 1970s. We had decided in a drunken evening at a dive bar in Minneapolis called The Tempo that the best country for a pair of young anti-American Americans was New Zealand because they didn't have nuclear weapons.

And that was the extent of our thinking on the matter.

At roughly the same time Steve Jobs and Steve Wozniak were in a garage in Palo Alto, California, inventing Apple Computer and Bill Gates and Paul Allen were in a strip mall in Seattle, Washington, creating Microsoft, Brian and I were drinking cans of Grain Belt beer in a dive bar in Minneapolis, Minnesota, plotting a move to New Zealand to do what? Nothing really. Just be New Zealanders.

We were on the low end of our generation's dreams for a greater future.

Now it so happened that the University of Minnesota had a program for engineering students during the summer prior to their senior year – you could be placed with an engineering firm anywhere in the world for the summer. Just pick a country. Brian, of course, picked New Zealand. The plan was he would go down there that summer and find a place to stay and a job for me and then I would move down there that fall and he would come back, finish at the U, and then join me the following summer and we would be New Zealanders and not have nuclear weapons of any kind.

Brilliant, right?

One small catch: you had to pick a second country just in case your first country didn't have any summer job openings. As a joke, Brian picked the most obscure country he could think of in Europe: Yugoslavia. But no worries. We had to be the only anti-American guys in their 20s who dreamed of moving to New Zealand. Right?

Brian called me up one day at my job as Managing Editor of the International Falls, MN, Daily Journal.

"Hey, I found out where I'm going for the summer internship," he said.

"Great!" I said. "What is it, Wellington? Christchurch? Auckland? It's Auckland, isn't it?"

"Nope," he said. "I'm going to Yugoslavia."

Silence. I was furious.

"Good job, Brian!" I said, angrily. "You have completely ruined our genius scheme! Yugoslavia? I don't even know what language they speak there!"

I ranted for a few more minutes, but it was to no avail. He was going to Ljubljana, Yugoslavia, where, it turns out they spoke something called Slovenian and used the dinar as their currency. Who knew Slovenian was even a language? And how could you live in a city with an unpronounceable name and used money that was sounded like something pirates lost at sea? This is just great! Our genius scheme of moving to New Zealand is ruined!

Brian went to Yugoslavia, however. And while he was there he wrote to me about a beautiful Yugoslavian medical student he met there named Lidija who lived in Germany but was working at the hospital in Ljubljana for the summer. He said it was supposedly the best hospital in Yugoslavia, although Tito later died there a few months earlier, so how good could it be?

When Brian returned home I was eager to see photos of this beautiful woman he had fallen in love with, and when he finally got the photos developed the first one on the stack was of a dark-haired, intelligent-looking woman who was beautiful indeed.

"Is that Lidija?" I asked.

"No," he said. "That's her awful twin sister, Marina. She's a poet."

"Well, she's very beautiful," I said.

"She's pure evil," said Brian.

He didn't really explain it, but she didn't look pure evil. She looked like the kind of woman I have always been drawn to: skinny, nervous, brilliant and somewhat troubled. I was determined to meet her.

A year later, I did. I decided in the summer of 1981 I would go to Europe. I was 25 and I wanted to go somewhere. For a while I considered hitchhiking up to Hudson's Bay in the summer to see polar bears. I studied maps of the trip for some time and looked into travel arrangements, and then I realized: well, I go all the way up there and see the polar bears and then what? What do you do then?

I changed my mind and decided to go to Europe instead. My main plan was to go to Vienna. It's lost from my memory now exactly why I wanted to go to Vienna, but there probably was no good reason. It just seemed like a good place to go. I had been corresponding with Lidija for a while, and told her that I would be arriving in Germany in early August, and wanted to stop by and see her.

She was living in Bonn at the time, finishing medical school. After a day of me, Lidija was bored and announced she was going to take me up to see her family in Bottrop, Germany. Her twin sister, Marina, had just returned from three months in Rome studying

Italian, and maybe she could dump me off on Marina, with whom she had a contentious relationship. I figured I would go up there with Lidija; spend a day or so there, and then head on to Vienna.

Marina and I took an immediate liking to each other. I wasn't, as she said, "just another of Lidija's stupid boyfriends." I knew about poetry and books, and we talked and talked and talked. Marina was the unfocused daughter. Lidija was nearly done with medical school and was then starting a course of study in radiology, which would lead her to a career in radio-oncology. Marina, on the other hand, had attended three different German universities, had tried to move back to Belgrade, and then lived for a while in Dubrovnik. She had completed less than two years of university studies, and had recently been studying Slavic languages at the University of Germersheim. In addition to Serbian and German, she was also fluent in Russian and French, and had published two books of poetry and several short stories, and was utterly unlike any of the women I met in Minneapolis.

She was funny and cynical and highly opinionated and improvisational and didn't seem to have much of a plan for her life. It was just happening, unfolding day by day. She had been to America once, three years earlier, with an eccentric Polish professor of sports psychology and had visited New York, St. Louis, and Dallas. She had been captivated by Americans and their easy way of just doing things, of putting their hands in their pockets and laughing loudly and yelling on the streets. America was a noisy, lively place, not the stifling and properly prosperous world of stable West Germany.

I mentioned my plan to go to Vienna.

"Ach, Vienna, don't go there," she said.

"Why not?" I asked.

"It's awful," she said. "Austrians are awful."

This view of Austrians was something she has stuck with all her life, a view that was only reinforced by the misdeeds of Arnold Schwarzenegger.

"What did I tell you about Austrians?" she said, decades later when news came out of his secret fatherhood of a boy by his housekeeper. "He's a brute like all Austrians."

It should be pointed out that her attitude about Austrians was not unique among the Serbs I've met, and probably should have been communicated to the Archduke Ferdinand in 1914 before he visited Sarajevo. What I did not know about Marina at the time and came to learn was that many of her opinions were received opinions that were reinforced by experience. She had heard that Austrians were brutes, then looked for – and generally found – evidence to support that view. And it wasn't just Austrians. It was Romanians (thieves). It was Chinese acupuncturists (utterly trustworthy) or Mexican gardeners (they butcher plants) or American politicians (craven philanderers).

Her suggestion as an alternative to Vienna: I should go with her and her mother to Belgrade. Her mother was suing someone in Belgrade and didn't want to drive there by herself. Marina, of course, had nothing to do, so she was asked to come along. The idea of spending a month in Belgrade with her mother, aunts, uncles and cousins all grilling her for not doing anything with her life was not that appealing, so she asked me to join her.

Marina had tried to immigrate back to Belgrade a year earlier. She had been born there, and lived there until she was eight, and was, from all her self-reporting, happy there. Her parents were not. Her father was a urologist and a highly regarded surgeon, but was from the minor Serbian aristocracy. Royalists, they were deemed. And, as a result, they were on a ten-year waiting list for an apartment. In the meantime, they lived in a room (Marina, Lidija, and her parents) in the grandmother's apartment in Zemun, a suburb of Belgrade on the far side of Danube. The apartment also had other aunts, uncles, and cousins living in it, and it was no way to conduct a married life. Marina, as a little girl, didn't mind it at all. It was noisy and people laughed loudly and yelled at each other. It was alive.

Her father got a job at a hospital in Germany, and moved away for a year. At the end of the summer, he came home and announced the family was moving to Germany. And a week later they did. She was eight, and hadn't seen it coming. Suddenly, she was in a new country, and not only did she not speak the language, she didn't even know the alphabet it was written in.

"I remember riding on the train and looking out the window at the streets in Germany and thinking, 'Where is all the garbage?'" she told me once. "And everything was so quiet."

She never liked Germany. She became fluent enough in its language to write poetry in it. But she never liked it. She did, however, come to respect it for its strengths: the sense of order and propriety. When Germans decided to do something, they did it the right way. There wasn't shabbiness or people living on the streets or disorder. It was a liberal democracy with a benevolent state that protected its citizens from the buffeting of economic or personal disasters. Things were taken care of, and in a proper manner. It was an admirable country. Not a warm or lively country where you felt alive like Serbia or the America she had visited, but Germany was something good on its own: it was comfortable and predictable.

Germans didn't invent jazz; they invented the Mercedes.

But it wasn't home for her. She had tried to move back to Belgrade, and found that that wasn't home anymore either. After living sixteen years in a country like Germany, she found Belgrade impossible. It was too dirty. It was too disorganized. At first it's funny, then it starts to wear you down and eat at you: from shopping for groceries in stores with half-empty shelves, or dealing with the government to find a place to live, or trying to ignore the men shouting and whistling at you on the street, or the aunts and uncles and cousins and neighbors spying on you about a date you had with the dentist over in Belgrade. It was impossible to live there.

She had tried Rome, under the ruse of studying Italian, but that was unsatisfactory too. She was 25 now, headed toward 26, and her life was fluttering around like an empty plastic bag on an afternoon wind. She was at that point in her life where she wanted to meet a man and fall in love and have a family. But it couldn't be a German because they're too stiff. Or a Serb because they are too combustible.

Enter, stage left: David, The American. Who laughed loudly, and put his hands in his pockets, and knew about books and seemed open and happy and full of life. Which I was in those days. I was open and happy and full of life. As I write this, thirty years have passed since the day I met Marina. I am still open and happy and full of life. Perhaps not as quite as open as I used to be, nor quite as happy, nor quite as full of life. But I still have a large measure of all those qualities that Marina originally fell in love with. And she is to me still as she was then: beautiful, mysterious, and complicated.

I am not revealing much when I say that we fell in love, made a family, soared, and then crashed. She fell out of love with me, and, eventually, I with her. We both failed at the single greatest task of our lives: to love, honor and cherish each other until death did us part.

But that's getting ahead of the story at hand. First, we had to go to Yugoslavia.

Dame Rebecca West wrote one of the great books of the 20th century about a pair of trips she took to Yugoslavia just before the start of World War II. The prologue of "Black Lamb, Grey Falcon" ends with a passage in which she frets to her husband about her desire to return to Yugoslavia:

"'Is it so wonderful there?' he asked. 'It is more wonderful than I can tell you,' I answered. 'But how?' he asked. I could not tell him at all clearly. I said, 'Well, there is everything there. Except what we have. And that seems very little.'... The thing I wanted to

tell him could not be told, however, because it was manifold and nothing like what one is accustomed to communicate in words. I stumbled on. 'Really we are not as rich in the West as we think we are. Or rather, there is much that we have not got which the people of the Balkans have got in quantity. I must go back to Yugoslavia. In spring. In time for Easter.'"

We left Bottrop, which is a pleasant but eerily soulless suburb of Essen in the Ruhr Valley of Germany, in the morning and drove south and east. Marina's imperious mother, Mirjana, was at the wheel. By late afternoon, we were in Austria, and I have to tell you it was not at all the horrible place that Marina described it. I found it to be breathtakingly beautiful.

We stopped briefly in Klagenfurt for a very late lunch. Klagenfurt is the hometown of both Schwarzenegger and Robert Musil, the author of the dreamy modernist novel "Der Mann Ohne Eigenschaften" ("The Man Without Qualities"). It is more than 1,000 pages long, and concerns the decline of the Austro-Hungarian Empire as seen through the eyes of an eccentric and hermit-like Viennese mathematician named Ulrich. Musil never finished the book, but was nominated for a Nobel Prize regardless. Marina considers having read that book one of the great accomplishments of her life. She may be on to something there. I tried it once in English. I got about three pages in and threw up my hands in despair. This was an impossible book to read.

From Klagenfurt, we drove into Yugoslavia. This part of the country is now the independent nation Slovenia, and it was then, and is now, the wealthiest and most orderly part of that misbegotten country. I was immediately happy. Things were a little shabbier, drivers passed you on the side of the road, when you rolled down the windows of the car in a village, you smelled food. We made it to the capital city of Ljubljana and had dinner. The plan was to put the car on a train to Belgrade and ride there rather than drive. Mirjana did not trust gas stations to have gas and the thought of getting stranded without gasoline in a village in Croatia was not particularly appealing to her.

Marina was sent to the train station to buy tickets and arrange for the car to be put on the train. We arrived at the ticket counter where a crowd had gathered. There was a fat man behind the counter in a mustard yellow polo shirt, blithely ignoring the increasingly angry crowd of people trying to buy tickets. He reached under the counter and pulled out an enormous glass of beer, took a long drink, put the glass back and then said he was ready to work.

"Ach! It starts again," Marina said, disgusted and angry. It was a weary sound she had in her voice, the sound of someone who just was reminded that she was back in the country where things didn't run properly, where the trains didn't run on time and people didn't do what they said they were going to do and had an irritated attitude about actually having to work. We were imposing on this guy's evening beer by forcing him to sell tickets for the train company that paid his salary. He clearly had better things to do than sell tickets -- even though his job was selling tickets -- and he wanted to make sure we all knew that.

I was enchanted.

The train rattled its way across Slovenia and Croatia and part of Bosnia-Herzegovina and arrived in Belgrade the next morning. It was night, so I didn't see any of these places, other than as dim lights as we passed through. It was all so exotic, I thought. Such an adventure I'm on. Look at me. I'm glad I didn't go to Vienna. I can do that some other time.

We disembarked at the central station in Belgrade and it hit me.

The place was messy, and crowded and filthy. There was a man washing himself in the fountain. People were yelling at each other, and kissing each other and there was garbage everywhere and no garbage cans. I pointed out the man washing his feet in the fountain to Marina.

"Gypsies," she said with utter disgust. She hated gypsies, like her mother and most other people in Belgrade and most everywhere else that gypsies lived. Unvarnished and freely expressed racist attitudes were alien to me, growing up in liberal and sensible Minneapolis. If anyone said anything racist out loud there, everyone got a little nervous and comfortable. Not here. The people of the Balkans are among the most openly racist people I have ever met. They don't have any hang-ups about their attitudes. We're the best, everyone else is disgusting. By the mid-1990s, without an authoritarian regime squashing actions on these attitudes, the country devolved into a tragic but entirely predictable civil war.

One day, during the height of the civil war in around 1995, I pointed out an article I had noticed in the Los Angeles Times about an atrocity in Montenegro. Marina looked at the article and turned away. "I learned how to swim in the lake in that village when I was a little girl," she said. She threw the paper away. "Don't tell my anything more about what's going on over there. I don't want to know. I hate all of them." She was inconsolably sad.

Inconsolable sadness was the central feature of her character. I think in part it stemmed from the fact that she never felt at home anywhere. The country of her childhood fell apart in horrific violence. She considered herself a "Yugoslav" because her mother was Slovenian and her father a Serb and she had grown up in Yugoslavia. So she considered herself something that did not exist. There are no Yugoslavs because Yugoslavia disappeared, becoming an obsolete country, like the Belgian Congo or Burma. Germany and the Germans were really not a solution either. She didn't like them or their country. It was a fine country and all, and even though she has a German accent, she is the least German person I have ever met.

And then there was the incomprehensible cipher of America and Americans. Everything was just too nutty here. Things came and went, institutions and businesses rose and fell and nobody seemed surprised. You couldn't put your hands on anything permanent in America because tomorrow it might be gone or reinvented or destroyed or utterly changed. That was the nature of America and Americans, and it was completely antithetical to her. For Marina, things were, are, and will be. For Americans things maybe were once, maybe, probably aren't what they seem today, and likely will not be eventually. It's just all too ambiguous a country for her.

Regardless of all that (and much of it I did not know at the time and it wouldn't have mattered if I had) we fell in love on our second night in Belgrade. We were standing on the tiny balcony of her childhood apartment, overlooking a dark courtyard two stories below where they had butchered chickens when she was a girl, looking west as the sun set. The dying light was on her angular and intelligent face and her eyes softened as we looked at each other. I pulled her close and kissed her.

"Oh, Marina," I said, making a sound like I was giving into something, "I love you."

She smiled.

"David," she said. "I love you."

She said it in a tone of voice that was not like her usual tone. It was a warm and soft tone, passionate, happy and content. We kissed again and I pulled away and looked past her to the window of the kitchen. Her 93 year-old great aunt Fina was standing in the window looking at us and smiling. A great happiness came over all three of us. Outside was the sound of traffic and people shouting in the night and the smell of cooking slipping up through the courtyard, and I was as perfectly happy as a person could be in life. And so was Marina. For utterly chance and completely implausible reasons, we had met. And then we had fallen in love.

The next morning we went to Dubrovnik.

Marina had lived in Dubrovnik several summers earlier. She had gotten a job as a tour guide for Germans on package tours of the area. In many ways, she was the ideal person to hire. Her German is perfect, and her Serbo-Croatian is perfect as well. She met the groups at the airport, got them on the bus into town and settled into the hotel. Part of her job was to sell small day trips. There are some Roman ruins near Dubrovnik, and she sold most of the group of middle aged-Germans on the trip. Okay, so this was 1978, and most of the Germans were in their 50s and 60s. So you do the math on how old they were during the early 1940s and you speculate as to what, exactly, they were up to during those years.

Anyway, the plan for this day trip was for everyone to assemble at 8:45 a.m. The bus would arrive at 9:00 and leave promptly afterwards for the tour. The German tourists all arrived promptly at 8:45. The bus, however, did not. This was Yugoslavia. The bus driver wasn't going to be there at 9:00 a.m. He was going to show up when he was ready to show up. Time passed; it was 9:15, then 9:30. Still no bus. The Germans were getting really unhappy and restless. Finally, one of them, a man Marina described as being in his late 60s said in a loud voice: "You know this country would run efficiently if we were in charge."

Marina turned to him and glared.

"Yes," she said, in an equally loud voice. "We saw your efficiency during the war!"

There was a gasp and then silence. Now it was a ridiculous thing to say. Marina hadn't been there to personally witness their efficiency during the war. She wasn't born for another ten years. But she had effectively shut them up. The bus showed up a few minutes later, and she took them on the tour. Silence as they got on the bus, silence during the tour. No questions. No discussion. Silence as she explained everything about the ruins. Silence as they got off the bus on their return. Later that afternoon, she was called into the office of the manager of the tour company and was fired.

We stayed in a private room in Dubrovnik, and the window opened to the city and the sea. During the day we walked around the town or went to a rocky beach and ate. One afternoon, she walked me to a quiet part of the city and showed me a small apartment building.

"That's where Fina lived until the war," she said. Fina, or Josefina, was the younger sister of Mirjana's mother, Stefanija. Fina married late, in her 30s, to a pleasant and quiet man who was an attorney for the national railroad. He had been transferred to Dubrovnik and they lived in a small apartment there for several years. They did not have children. When the Nazis invaded Yugoslavia, the Yugoslavs took that as an opportunity to have a civil war with themselves at the same time. It made perfect sense. Basically, there were four parties at war with each other: the royalist Serbs, the nationalist Croats, the Communists and the Germans. They were all fighting each other in the sort of incomprehensible madness that the people of the Balkans specialize in.

At one point, the Communists – or Partizans – under their brilliant and, later, incredibly corrupt, leader, Josip Broz Tito, swept into Dubrovnik and claimed it. They rounded up political prisoners, including Fina and her husband, who were the most apolitical people ever. As the Germans moved in on Dubrovnik, the Partizans fled into the mountains, bringing their prisoners with them. It was winter. They began executing the prisoners, holding firing squads for the other prisoners to watch. Among the people executed was Fina's quiet and soft-spoken husband, an enemy of the people for serving as a lawyer for the national railroad. She was forced to watch his execution.

A few days later, Fina overheard two guards talking about the plan to kill the rest of the prisoners because food was running short and they were constantly on the run from the royalists or the Germans and the prisoners were too much trouble. She escaped that night, wearing only the light winter coat she had when they were rounded up. She wandered in the mountains for a day or so, and found a road. As she walked on the road, she saw a soldier in the distance, riding on a horse. She did not know what Army he served in, any one of which might be disposed to kill her. As he approached, she kneeled in the road, put out her hands and looked up. The soldier, whom it turned out, was an officer in the Germany Army, a Nazi, actually, took pity on her, gave her food, and hid her in a barn for a couple days until he could put her on a train back to Dubrovnik.

By the time she got back to Dubrovnik, the Nazis were in control. She came to her street, which had been called The Street of the Jews. It had been renamed Dubrovnik Street. All her old neighbors were gone. They had been rounded up, and put on trains.

There was nothing left for her in this beautiful little walled city by the sea. She made her way back to Belgrade. She never remarried. And she never returned to Dubrovnik.

The original plan Marina gave her mother and aunts and uncles and cousins and a neighbor when she left Belgrade with me to Dubrovnik was that she was going to return after few days. We spent several days in the old city, staying in a room that had a window that overlooked the town and the sea beyond. During the day we walked around or went to the beach or drank coffee or just sat and looked at the Adriatic. Marina knew many people in the town because she had lived there several years earlier, and so we met them for dinner or coffee. Finally, it was time to leave and she booked me a ticket on a boat that was sailing up the coast to Rijeka.

And then she booked herself a ticket.

We were in love, of the truly, madly, deeply variety. And not yet ready to say goodbye. It didn't feel like a summer romance. It felt like a collision of two large and irrepressible souls.

The trip up the Dalmatian Coast was awful. Being a Yugoslav enterprise, the boat was ridiculously overbooked and filthy. The ship was built to carry about 75 passengers, uncomfortably, but with basic accommodations of beds and bathrooms. Jadrolinja, the state-owned line that operated the ship, had booked approximately 250, however.

Virtually all of them were drunken high school students. All night long they were singing, fighting, talking, and vomiting. Finally, Marina and I went up to the main deck and decided to just stand there and watch the sea go by. A school of dolphins passed us, then the sun began to rise. I can still see her now, standing on the deck of the ship, the rising sun at her back, smiling a warm half smile, her arms folded, leaning against the railing of the deck, looking at me. I sometimes think I imagined how much she was in love with me at that point, had invented the whole thing. But, no, it was true, as she told me later. "I loved you with my whole soul once, David," she told me, sadly, one day not long before we split up.

We ended up going on to Venice and stayed in a house there for several days not far from the main piazza, and then by train on to Florence, and then north through the Alps to Munich and finally back to Bonn. The night before I left to return to America, we agreed to marry. We had known each other for three weeks.

It all seemed like a dream at the time, but it was true. It had all really happened. I had met her and we had fallen in love and traveled around Europe together and got married and lived a passionate life together for years and years and had a large and lively family.

And, 30 years later, it was good to remember these sorts of things as true. In the ensuing years, we would marry, have eight children, buy a couple of houses, build a life together, and then, in an agonizingly slow process, lose the house, break down the life together and gradually say goodbye to that love, let go of it.

So how did it happen? What was this long, sorrowful process? W. H. Auden once observed that no marriage, no matter how dull, is ever as interesting as any love affair, no matter how passionate.

Ours was not a dull marriage. It was an intense and deeply felt marriage, and it broke apart in stages despite the trappings that would seem to make it inseverable. People don't just have eight children together and then fall out of love and end the marriage.

Well, actually, sometimes they do.

Just past the third anniversary of that split, after many angry transcontinental phone calls and periods of no communication at all, I was sitting in my apartment in South Pasadena one day, alone and burst into tears. I could not bear that anger between us any more.

I looked at the photographs on Facebook and decided to call her. We hadn't spoken in several months. The phone rang and my stomach churned. Finally, on the ninth ring, she answered.

"Ja," she said, with that amusing German accent of hers, which is so ironic because she is the least German person I have ever met.

"Marina, it's David," I said.

"Yes," she said.

A brief pause.

"Listen, I was looking at your photos from your trip to Tunisia and I wanted to let you know that you looked very beautiful," I said.

"Oh, thank you," she said. I could hear the smile across the phone line.

"And the other thing I wanted to tell you is that you looked very happy," I said.

"I am happy," she said.

"Well, I'm glad about that," I said. "I like it when you are happy."

We didn't say anything for a moment, just listened to the thousands of miles that separated us now. There she was on the other end, the woman who had borne eight children with me, who I had planned to travel with and host weddings and grow old with and finally be buried next to.

But that, as Christopher Marlowe once wrote: "... was long ago and in another country."

"How about you?" she said. "How are you?"

"You know me," I said with a laugh.

"I wish you weren't so restless," she said.

"I wish it more than you," I said.

She chuckled. And then she said it.

"So... tell me something."

And so I did. I told her about my plans to move to the Bay Area, about the new venture, about Annie, and about the kids, because I speak to them more often than she does. I gave her some gossip about people we knew, I had her laughing as I imitated someone we didn't like, and on and on for more than an hour.

"Well," she said, "I have to get going. When you are ready, send me the divorce papers and let's get that taken care of."

"I will," I said.

And then I didn't do something I had done thousands of times before when the conversation ended. I didn't say, "I love you." I just said 'goodbye.' We would never return to Dubrovnik either.

Chapter 4: "The Demon of the Noonday and of the Sixth Hour"

The Orthodox Christian rite of baptism begins prior to the liturgy, usually with the church nearly empty, and the godparents holding the baby in their arms at the back of the church while the priest recites a series of questions to the baby that the godparents answer. Several of the questions involve Satan, and whenever Satan's name is mentioned, the godparents are required to spit.

The sacrament of baptism is partially intended to offer up protection from Satan, which is a futile hope because Satan -- or some other demon -- it is believed, inevitably infiltrates your life and you engage in a great battle with these demons. It is part of being human.

One of the demons -- in ancient Christianity -- is "the demon of the noonday." There is even a prayer service called the Sixth Hour, which offers up prayers against the demon of the noonday. And what is the Demon of the Noonday?

Quite simply it is an affliction we now know as depression. And Marina was mightily afflicted with it. What I did not realize initially – and, in fact, did not realize fully until much later – was the depth and persistence of it in her life. I only recently found out, for instance, that she had attempted suicide two years before we met and had been hospitalized for a month after that. Had I known that when we met would I have still fallen in love with her, married her, and had eight children with her? Without question I would have. I would have fallen utterly in love with her.

What *was* in question was my understanding of her plight, my ability to deal with it, and her ability to face it. That was what was in question. We both failed on all three of these questions.

Marina was never a sunny person. That was part of her appeal to me. She is cynical, funny, irrational, and unpredictable. Again, these were highly appealing traits to me because they were so unlike the traits of the women I was meeting in Minneapolis. Not long before I decided to go to Europe in 1981, I was set up on a date with a woman. She was the best friend of my best friend's girlfriend. She was a buyer for sportswear for a large department store chain in Minneapolis. Perfectly put together woman, sharply-dressed, ambitious, somewhat humorless, but pretty in a precise sort of way. I know she found me attractive because I seemed a bit on the "dangerous" side (as she told me): I worked as a bartender, was trying to write short stories, and I didn't have what she called "a life plan." (She had one, by the way. It was fairly detailed, and involved a series of well-timed life decisions.)

We agreed to meet at a German restaurant in south Minneapolis. I decided that afternoon to go my parent's house and do some laundry. I ironed my shirt, put on a nice pair of pants and a jacket, and caught the bus back to south Minneapolis to meet this woman at the Black Forest restaurant. I was thinking contentedly about how cool it was to be going on a date with a woman who was so attractive and who had a career and a life plan and was still willing to go on a date with me, despite the fact that I didn't have a career or a life plan. Maybe if I get involved with this woman, she'll straighten me out and get me thinking right about maybe going to law school or getting a Master's in something or other and becoming a professional something or other and… stuff like that. This is gonna be great, I thought. She is really what I need in my life now. Okay, so she was going on and on about how much she admired Ronald Reagan and other political things that sort of set my teeth on edge. But, I thought to myself, maybe she has a point. Maybe Ronald Reagan will be a great President and maybe socialism is evil and maybe I'd come around to her way of looking at things once I got to know her because she was so far ahead of me in terms of getting her life going the right way. I mean, here I was, 24 years old and was bartending and writing short stories, and she was 24 and had a career as a buyer for Donaldson's in the Ladies Sportswear department and had a life plan. I really didn't have much of a leg to stand on. And she, meanwhile, had a couple of awfully nice, long, well-shaped legs to stand on. And looked really good in that sleek black dress she was wearing at the party when we met.

Yup, I'm gonna go for this one. She can help me put together a life plan and things'll be great with our fantastic life plans and her long legs and Ronald Reagan.

I was about halfway to the Black Forest restaurant, just about ready to get married and settle down with her, when I reached back to check something in my wallet and – OH NO!!! – I FORGOT MY WALLET!!!

Well, it was too late at this point to get off the bus, catch another bus back home, get my wallet, catch another bus back to the Black Forest. I would just have to go there and figure something out.

Except I never did figure anything out. I just fumbled my way through this, and snuck away and called my friend Brian and he came over and lent me some money to cover the meal and she figured the whole thing out and refused to see me again. I found out that a week later she went out on a date with an air traffic controller and fell in love and they got engaged and then he went on strike and got fired by Ronald Reagan. I don't know what happened after that. But I did enjoy the idea that her fiancé was fired by a man she admired so much.

And that was the kind of woman I was meeting until I met Marina. She wasn't so much a breath of fresh air in my lungs as a shot of whisky in my throat. She is bracing and it burns a little but I felt excited and in the company of a kindred spirit. She is a difficult person, with a kind of brittle, angry intelligence.

We were living in a small town in New Hampshire and I was working a respectable job with a publishing house there when my old Minneapolis friend, Tom Arnold, called me one day and invited me to write on "Roseanne." Tom and I had met in 1983, not long after Marina and I married. A friend of mine in Minneapolis and I had started a small magazine together, and, of course, we didn't have any money. Normally, this wouldn't have been a problem but I was married now and, well, when you're married it is always advisable to have money, even a small amount.

I got a job bartending at a comedy club in Minneapolis called William's Pub. One of the employees -- and one who would certainly never win Employee of the Month -- was a young comic from Iowa, Tom Arnold. He and I became fast friends, wrote bits together and thoroughly enjoyed ourselves. I even helped him move once -- he loaded all of his belongings into two large Hefty garbage bags and put them into the back of my rusting Chevette, and we drove four blocks from his old shabby apartment to his new shabby apartment.

When Tom offered me the job on "Roseanne," I took it and, as they say, followed my bliss. Over the next 12 years, I was a comedy writer. I worked on 111 episodes of "Roseanne", which is now regarded as one of the best comedies ever produced. I sold pilots, had development deals with studios and rewrote film scripts. It was, when I think about it now, almost as much a dream as when I think now of falling in love with Marina. I was being paid -- and paid handsomely -- to be a wisenheimer, which I was very good at naturally and which, for all my life up to that point, had done for free.

I got out of the smothering little New England town and the smothering little career in magazine publishing and was living the life in Los Angeles, one of the world's great cities.

Marina, however, was deeply opposed to the move to Los Angeles. She was content – I began to type "happy" but then realized that is not a word I ever really associate with her – in the small town in New Hampshire. To say she hated Los Angeles is to really underestimate the depth of her antipathy for it. What made her content there was having a baby. Our three youngest, Saskia, Mariangela, and Juliette, were all born in Los Angeles. The pattern of our life in the late 80s to the late 90s was familiar: she would begin pestering to get pregnant. I would resist. She would become pregnant. I would become furious. The pregnancy would go well and she would feel happy. And then the birth and then the long post-partum spiral of sadness and depression would start up again. Then she would begin pestering me to get pregnant.

By 1998, after she gave birth to Juliette, the depression began to deepen and extend further into her day. Increasingly, she would stay in bed long after the children had gone to school. Her weight was falling. She wasn't hungry. Her eyes grew increasingly sunken and her hair was falling out. She was down to 93 pounds at its nadir.

One day, in 2001, I came home from a meeting at around 5 p.m., and the kids were all milling around in the kitchen, wondering what she was going to make for dinner.

"Where's Mama?" I asked.

"She's upstairs like always," said Marisa, bitterly. Marisa was 16, and didn't mince words.

I went upstairs and Marina was still in bed, in her pajamas and bathrobe, just as she was when I had left five hours earlier.

I told her to get dressed and come downstairs. She said she would. Now, I said. I will, she said. She didn't move.

"Get out of the fucking bed!" I shouted, and pulled the covers off her. "I'm sick of this!"

"Sick of what?" she shouted back.

"Sick of this," I said. "Sick of you just lying in bed all day. You just can't live like this!"

"Ja, well, I'm sick of you!" she said. "You're fat and angry and disgusting! Leave me alone."

"No, I'm not gonna leave you alone," I said, with an anger and fury that surprised me.

Marisa came up the stairs and stood in the doorway.

"Stop yelling at each other," she said. She was sobbing. "We hate this when you do this, David! Don't yell at her! Don't yell at each other!"

And then she ran back downstairs.

It was silent in the house for a long time, upstairs and down. I stood there and looked at Marina and she laid there and stared at the wall.

She did get up and make dinner and then stayed up until 2 in the morning reading and then vacuuming the rugs. I woke up and vowed to myself that I would do something about this.

I would no longer work.

I could no longer work.

I just couldn't. Marina refused to go the psychiatrist with whom I had set up an appointment. She refused to even consider medication. She was just going to get worse. She was going to wither further and more hair would fall out and I just couldn't go on. The career and job I had dreamed of nearly all my life would just have to wait. I had to leave television and stop being the big-time, wise-ass, well-paid comedy writer who spent 16 hours a day in a writing room and barely any time with my wife and our children.

What was I now, in this moment in that room while I was screaming at my wounded wife? I know what I was not. I was not a successful comedy writer with a big career and an enormous income with awards and the respect of my colleagues and peers. In that room, at that moment, I was an arrogant and angry fat man, screaming at a wife who was so incapacitated by depression she couldn't leave her bed and who looked at the wall for much of the day. I was a monster. I was a hideous caricature of myself. She couldn't stay in the bed any longer, but I couldn't stay in television any longer either.

I had to walk away and go back to the original job I had signed up for when I fell in love with Marina on a balcony in Belgrade twenty years earlier: I would have to be a husband and a father. I would stay home. With her. Until she got better.

And I did. I turned down a couple of job offers, and for the next several years Marina and I basically spent every hour of the day with each other. Gradually, the depression began to lift. And that is what depression does when it dissipates. It lifts. Like low, dark clouds receding into the low dark hills in the distance. Marina was still intensely fragile, but she was capable of getting up in the morning, making lunches for the kids, having coffee and reading the paper and talking with me, then running errands, and then making dinner and picking up the house. She wasn't back to writing poetry, or being a perky San Marino mom. But she was Marina again – cynical, dark, funny, irrational.

The house at 1742 Warwick Road was a stolid as they come from the outside. Originally built in 1935, it was a one-storey Spanish Mission-style house with light pink exterior walls and Mexican roofing tile. During our time there, I planted three apple trees, a mulberry, a fig, an apricot tree, three varieties of oranges, a pear tree and a plum tree. It was a thoroughly proper-looking house on a thoroughly proper-looking street in a thoroughly proper town. Parking on the street after 10 p.m. is illegal in San Marino, as is having sports equipment (such as a basketball hoop) in the front of the house.

We were a well-known family in town. I coached Little League and we had children scattered across three of the four schools: Valentine Elementary, Huntington Middle School, and San Marino High School. I was making hundreds of thousands of dollars a year as a comedy writer, and living in a city of doctors, lawyers and bankers.

From the outside, everything looked great. Except from the inside everything was falling apart. In the two years that I left television writing to be with Marina and be a husband and father full time, television changed and situation comedies went through a serious retrenchment.

I was unable to find work when I was ready to return. We had lived cautiously and prudently when I was working and I was able to comfortably take two years off and still stay current on the mortgage. But then we started eating into my savings. First the mutual funds were liquidated, then the life insurance policy was cashed in, then everything else went.

The problem, it turns out now as I think back on it, was I didn't have a life plan. But how do you build a life plan that incorporates demons and the havoc that they wreck?

I had spent twelve years right in the center of my working life "making nonsense," as my mother would say. I was incredibly skilled at writing jokes for imaginary angry, fat, working class housewives. It was a well-paid skill for many years, but not a transferrable one. I was in my late 40s now. I hadn't had a real job for more than a decade.

But what I was doing was a more important job. I had helped Marina defeat the Demon of the Noonday. Other demons now awaited us.

Chapter 5: "Outsmarting Myself"

One of the most vivid images in American film is the scene in John Huston's "The Grapes of Wrath" when the Joad family comes driving into a camp filled with Okies fleeing the dust storms. The camera takes the point of view of the Joads as the family drives through the camp of starving, beaten down families, once decent people with ragged clothes and empty faces.

It is a profoundly brilliant sequence, and in many ways as shocking a sequence of images ever to appear in a mainstream Hollywood movie now. Orgies of violence, eye-popping computer graphics, outrageous physical humor about bodily fluids: no problem, nowadays. (I, by the way, don't have a problem with any that myself – it's the movies. So what?)

But try to imagine a depiction of the sorrows of real American lives in the wake of the worst economic downturn in eighty years? Normal, decent middle class families living on the streets or crammed into cars, the children hungry, the parents beaten down and angry. I can't possibly imagine that source of sorrow ever making it into a single frame of a mainstream American studio movie. Never. Not anymore.

Between 2007 and 2011, millions of American families and individuals lost their homes to foreclosure. When you lose your home to foreclosure, it's difficult to find new housing. A prospective landlord runs your credit and there it is: that big giant foreclosure sitting like a turd on the dining room table.

What happened to my family and me was partially the result of larger forces of the global financial system that don't really bear going into once again. For me, however, when I sit down and truly and honestly assess what happened to me, it boiled down to a series of a decisions, hundreds of them, large and small, that seemed each sensible in the sequence I made them. And, in summary, they ruined us.

I made a good decision to leave television to be with my family, but I arrogantly assumed I would be able to return quickly. I held onto the house and refinanced over and over because each time the market bore the refinance and why sell when the market was continuing upward and equity was still available? Why disrupt the lives of the children when the house was saving us?

In the end each of those decisions, based on best information at the time, proved to be ruinous.

All of it reminds me of an incident I had witnessed in 1979 when I was working on a small weekly newspaper in western Wisconsin. It was my first job out of college, and I had several beats: the courts, the police, a couple of local school boards, a column and, if I could manage it, a weekly feature article.

The publisher suggested to me that an article on the semi-annual visit of the fur buyer would make an interesting feature.

It was a Saturday morning in mid-March, cold, and snow still on the ground in this rural area of western Wisconsin. People here made their living as farmers, loggers and a small iron mine at the edge of town. It was an old-fashioned American rural world, and many men would supplement their income by trapping fox and beaver.

The fur buyer would come a couple times a year to buy their pelts. He set up shop in a garage of a couple living at the edge of town. It was a convivial atmosphere, and the buyer himself was a large personality, wise-cracking, full of tales of visits to New York City and Chicago to resell the pelts he would buy today and other days as he worked this circuit. He smoked, and drank coffee and was as worldly a figure as the people in this town would come across.

On this day, he was telling about a trip he and his wife had made to Italy, to Rome and the Vatican, and the sellers and the hosts listened and were spellbound by his tales of life in the wide world.

The trappers would come in and lay out a skein of their pelts. Typically, he would offer a price for the entire skein, dismissing their quality, complaining he would never be able to resell them, putting on a show of being at enormous risk offering such a high price for pelts of such low or average quality. The deal would be completed, the trapper and the buyer would shake hands, and the trapper would leave with his hundred dollars in cash and the buyer would turn back to the rest of us and continue his tales of his large and sophisticated life.

Late in the morning a young man came in with a skein of what even I could see were very average red fox pelts. No one seemed to know him. He was not much more than 20, had a scraggly beard and drove a rusted 20 year-old car. His clothes were poor and hung on him and he didn't smile and carried a doleful manner as he laid out the pelts.

The buyer offered a price for the skein, but the boy insisted on pricing each one. He fought the buyer on every price on every pelt, squeezing the tiniest extra dollars out of each of his nearly 30 pelts. It was annoying. He seemed so completely unaware of what his offerings were truly worth, but the buyer seemed to be amused by the relentless haggling the boy wanted to do over such paltry sums.

They concluded their business and the buyer gave the young man his cash, and sent him on his way. Just as the young man was about to walk out the open garage, he stopped and turned back.

"I have a few more pelts in the car," he said. "Are you still buying?"

The buyer roared with laughter.

"Show me what you got, kid!" he said.

We all laughed. We were all up for more entertainment as these two haggled over more low-grade pelts.

The young man walked slowly out to his car unlocked the trunk and pulled out a skein of about 20 pelts. He carried them in and laid them down on the table. A gasp went through the garage. These were pelts of the finest quality, many of them virtually perfect.

The buyer was speechless. He looked at the pelts and then at ~~the boy~~ and then back at the pelts and then back at the young man. He smiled.

"Well, look at that," he said softly. "You just worked me over good, didn't you?"

The young man didn't smile. He just took a long drag on his cigarette and stared back at the buyer.

"How much for each of these?" he said, unsmiling.

What the boy had been doing by haggling over all the poor quality pelts was pushing up the price of the good pelts he had in reserve. While the buyer was regaling us with his worldliness and sophistication and tales of Rome and Paris, he had missed what was really going on.

In the end, I was the fur buyer.

I had outsmarted myself.

Chapter 6: "The Day the Sheriff Comes"

For more than a year, I was almost entirely occupied with trying to hold on to a house I could not afford.

And then on Sept. 6, 2006, two deputies from the Los Angeles County Sheriff's Department showed up at our house, along with a locksmith, to make sure we were moving out.

We knew they were coming. It wasn't a surprise.

Still, the sight of two uniformed officers with guns walking across your lawn and checking to make sure that you were actually leaving the house you had lived in for 11 years is more than a little unsettling. I felt like a criminal.

It wasn't our house anymore. Technically, it hadn't been our house for several months after we lost it to the grinding foreclosure process.

You don't immediately vacate when your house is sold at a foreclosure auction. There is some additional legal rigmarole you get to go through and some additional time you can spend fighting it.

But, ultimately, it is no longer yours. It is gone.

Except it isn't really gone. People talk about losing their house. But in reality, the house isn't lost. It's you who is lost. The house is still there. Somebody else buys it, and makes it their home. You and your family, your wife, your children, you are the ones who get lost. You have to find a new place to live.

The school year had started three days earlier. So we were able to claim a San Marino address. Cristian was starting his sophomore year, Coco eighth grade, Saskia seventh,

Mariangela fourth and Juliette second grade. The older three girls were out of the house by then, all in college or about to finish college.

The final summer in the house had been chaotic. We were nearly penniless. At one point, our water was shut off and we couldn't afford to pay the bill for a few days to get it turned back on. Marina, being of Balkan heritage, was able figure out a way around that. Our neighbor to the south was an older widow and she was out of town. The south side of our house faced the north side of hers across the driveway. There was an outside spigot and hose, and at night Marina snuck across the driveway and snaked her hose up through our kitchen window and hijacked enough water to cook pasta and for everyone to have sponge baths.

I was working as a real estate agent in San Marino. It is a genuine testament to my lack of skill at selling anything that at the peak of the housing boom I was unable to sell a house. Everything that came on the market in those days was receiving multiple bids at ludicrously inflated prices. And San Marino, with one of the best school districts in the state of California, was particularly benefitting from this boom.

And yet I couldn't make a single sale.

On the day before the house was to auctioned at foreclosure, I walked to a church a half block from the real estate office where I worked. I went into the office and the church secretary was there.

"Excuse me," I said to her. "I'm wondering if I could go into the sanctuary and pray for a minute?"

"Oh," she said, a bit surprised. "Sure. It's open."

"I won't be long," I said.

"Take as much time as you need," she said.

I went into the sanctuary, and went into one of the pews in the back rows. I made the sign of the cross, bowed my head, and... I couldn't think of anything to say. I sat there for a long time, drawing a complete blank. I had always been told that when you pray, you should ask for something specific. I couldn't think of anything specific I wanted, other than the obvious. And that seemed too obvious to ask for.

Then: "Just get us all through this."

Whatever that meant.

I sat there some more for a long time and didn't say or think anything. Just sat there. Well, this may have been a waste of time, I thought. I don't feel any better. I got up and walked back to the church office.

"All done," I said to the secretary, as if I had finished some kind of procedure to fix a car.

"Okay," she said. "I hope it helped."

I smiled weakly.

A few weeks later, the eviction process was completed and the move-out date was set. That's the moment when you realize it is over.

The kids were in the living room watching TV. I came in and stood by the front window, and looked at them.

"Okay, everyone, I have some bad news," I said. "Mama and I have been trying to hold onto the house for a long time and we just have been unable to refinance the mortgage anymore. So... we have to move out. So what I need all of you to do is pack up your stuff. Your clothes and other stuff. You can put your clothes into suitcases and I'll get boxes for you to put your other stuff like trophies and books and toys in."

I explained that my friend Greg was going to help us rent an apartment in Pasadena and that it had a pool and was a nice place for now. But tomorrow, while you're at school, we are moving out. Our friend Kim was going to help us pack while you all are in school. We will spend tomorrow night at a hotel in downtown Pasadena while we get the new apartment ready, and that's where you will spend the night tomorrow.

There was silence for a moment.

And then Cristian yowled and ran into his room and sobbed. Coco and Saskia were quiet and then began to cry. Saskia went to her little room and looked around and began to quietly pack. Coco didn't say much at all. He just grimly began packing. Mariangela and Juliette went to their rooms as well, crying quietly, and began their packing as well.

There really was nothing else to do.

We had purchased the house in 1995. Coco was three and a half years old. Saskia was not yet two. They had lived in a house we had rented in Glendale, but were so young they didn't remember it. For Mariangela and Juliette, this was the only home they had ever known.

And now it was time to leave.

That night Marina made a huge meal. The last big meal in the house together. When we were all together, the ten of us, dinner time was like a theatrical production: it started with us all standing and facing the icon of Christ the Pantocrator and quickly running through the Lord's Prayer, and then talking and eating and arguing and joke-telling and discussions and laughter and accusations and gossip. But, this was a sad and quiet meal. The older three girls were gone to college, and it was just the seven of us now, and our time together in this house had come to an end.

We stood and faced the icon. "Our Father," I said. "Hallowed be Thy name. Thy Kingdom come, Thy will be done…" I stopped. I couldn't say anymore. The children continued and finished the prayer without me. Then we ate, mainly in silence, and then cleared the table, and that was the end of it.

The next morning, the children got dressed, locked up their suitcases, put on their backpacks and went off to school. The large, rambling, disorderly house that had been, for most of them, the only home they had ever known, would no longer be theirs.

As we were packing and moving furniture out that morning, the deputies and the locksmith and the investor who had purchased the house all arrived at around the same time. I spoke with the deputies and explained we clearly were moving out, and then the locksmith came and removed all of the locks and put in new ones.

After the deputies left, I went back behind the garage where I had planted three orange trees a decade earlier. I smoked a cigarette. I stood there for a long time, flattened. And then I took a deep breath, and went back into the house and went back to moving everything out.

When each room was cleared out, I went through it. This was our bedroom, mine and Marina's. Where we had slept and talked and made love and argued and laughed together. This was the office where I wrote. This was the upstairs bedroom that Claire and Juliette shared. And so it went with each room until they were all empty. And then we pulled away and we were gone.

As I say, we didn't lose the house on Warwick Road. The house on Warwick Road had lost us.

Two years later, during a homeless period, I was out walking because I couldn't sleep. It was a warm night after a hot day in August. I walked and walked and walked until, almost by accident, I came upon our old street.

The investor had completely renovated the house and sold it to a new family. I walked quietly up the driveway to the house and put my hand on it. The white exterior walls were still warm from the heat of the day.

This house was once mine, I thought. It wasn't anymore. It isn't anymore. It was someone else's house now. They are sleeping in it now.

I patted the house gently.

"You were good to us," I whispered to the house.

I turned and walked away into the night.

Chapter 7: "The Thing of Unclear Purpose and Intent"

By the summer of 2008, we were absolutely broke. During my years away from television, reality television boomed and the sitcom business collapsed and the number of jobs dropped by nearly half. Nobody was going to hire me. There were dozens of guys like me looking for the same job -- mid-40s to early 50s, experienced and expensive, and nobody was going to hire me or any of them.

I desperately searched for other work, but it was not to be found. What publisher is going to hire a guy who claims to know about how to do financial models on magazines (which I did) when he had spent the prior twelve years writing jokes for TV stars?

Our savings and investments gone, and with not much more than a few dollars to our name we couldn't afford cheap hotels anymore, having lost our rental and exhausted the patience and support of family and friends. The tension and anger between Marina and I was explosive. Marina resented that I was not providing for the family the way a man and a husband and a father should. I resented everything else about my life. It was an acrid time.

Marina and I finally separated when she moved to San Francisco on July 4th, 2008. Coco and Saskia were already up with Sasha and Claire for the summer, and it was just me and Marina and Mariangela and Juliette. We trudged up onto the 39 bus that travels from East Pasadena, through Glendale to Hollywood. We got off in Glendale and walked several blocks with their luggage to the Greyhound station in Glendale. I could only imagine what those two little girls were thinking of this situation. A few months earlier they had been living normal little girl lives in upper middle class San Marino, worrying about little girl stuff: you know, homework, boys who bugged them and girls who were mean.

And then one day we moved out of the nice cozy, slightly run-down rental house on a quiet street with a furnace that didn't work because we couldn't even afford it anymore nor a life in thoroughly respectable San Marino. They spent the rest of their school year in a dive hotel in East Pasadena that had hookers outside walking the streets, and a KFC, and a liquor store, and a bad Chinese restaurant and a Korean coffee shop that smelled like menthol cigarettes, and two used car dealerships next door.

Now they were walking, pulling luggage to the Greyhound station to take the ten hour bus trip to stay with their big sisters in San Francisco.

"Why does this keep happening to us?!" Mari screamed to no one in particular one day.

"I don't know, Mari," I said, quietly. "I don't know why anything happens anymore."

We didn't hug, she didn't cry at first, and then she cried and then I hugged her and then she pulled away and then she lay down on the bed in the cheap hotel room and stared at the ceiling.

"Tja!" said Marina. It was her all-purpose sound of unsurprised disgust.
I looked at her in the half-light of the room, and then stepped outside, and walked around to the alley behind the hotel. I sat down against the back wall and began to cry in tremendous heaving sobs. A homeless man walked past at the corner of the street and looked at me. I started to cough and pretend that I was plagued with phlegm. I stood up and spat. He looked away and walked on.

I bought their tickets and the bus pulled up. They got on and I helped them and then hugged both Mariangela and Juliette and then kissed Marina.

"I'll see you in a few weeks or maybe a month, okay?" I said.

"Yeah, right," she said. "I don't have any expectations anymore."

"But I do," I said. "Things'll work out."

I leaned to kiss and she turned slightly away.

"I love you," I said as I stood up. She smiled wanly at me, and I kissed each of the girls again, and then walked slowly off the bus and stood outside and watched as the bus pulled away and then I was alone.

It was just me now for the rest of the summer until I could get a job and rent a place and get everyone back. I would be homeless now, but I wouldn't have to worry about anyone else.

Now, it was just me and Los Angeles. Or maybe me versus Los Angeles, a city I had grown to almost irrationally love.

But Los Angeles isn't a city so much as it is an organism, a massive, living, breathing, metastasizing Thing of Unclear Purpose and Intent. It is shapeless, ferocious, and utterly unto itself. It (and by this I mean the entire 18-million population metropolitan area) stretches out for miles in every direction, not stopping so much as dissipating in certain natural boundaries: the deserts to the north and the east, the Pacific Ocean to the west and Camp Pendleton to the south.

I lived there for twenty years. Or, more properly, was absorbed into it. Absorbed into its relentlessness and ambition and indifference. Absorbed into its smell, its rhythms, and into its bloodstream. I became a part of Los Angeles. And Los Angeles became part of me.

My second daughter, Marisa, who currently lives in Washington, DC, told me once that whenever she smells corn oil, she immediately thinks of Los Angeles. She is transported back to her city -- the smell of Mexican food cooking on grills, the sound of brass instruments playing in someone's backyard party, the eye-squinting sunlight and the hazy air. She feels herself suddenly in a huge Chinese supermarket in Monterey Park, with its dozens of tanks of live fish for sale, and a pigeon flying gracefully across the ceiling while shopper picked knowledgeably through pallets of strange-looking fruits and vegetables, and children stand pleading with worn-out grandmothers for some shiny cheap toy on the rack.

She hears the roar of traffic and the vague whispers of salt air floating in, silently and in secret from the Pacific.

Chapter 8: "Moonlight Sleeping on a Midnight Lake"

After Marina and the younger girls moved to San Francisco, I was homeless.

The first night you are homeless, it has that stinging feeling of a punch in the face.

You know, one of those punches you get in a fight in eighth grade with Rick Lucian. You are circling each other, taking swings, a bunch of other boys egging both of you on, screaming at you both, insulting you both, your heart beating and every neural receptor in your body firing. And then he whips his fist around hard and you don't move fast enough to get out of the way and it hits you square across the cheek and eyebrow.

It stings. It's shocking. It doesn't hurt so much as surprises you. But, of course, you knew it was coming. You shake your head and act like it didn't matter. But it did. He hit you in the face. You feel so stupid. How could you let someone as slow as Rick Lucian hit you in the face? The face! You rage back and swing wildly, hitting him in the arm until finally the woodshop teacher Mr. Hanson sees you and comes out from the school and yells at both of you to stop. The rest of the boys run off and you and Rick are standing there as Mr. Hanson comes running up in that embarrassing way that adults in work clothes do when they run.

"What the hell's going on here you two?" he shouts.

You both look so stupid because there you are all sweaty and worked up and for what? You don't even remember. Rick looks at him, then you, and then runs off. Then you do too. Just like that it's over.

It's like that, the first night on the street: humiliating, painful, and shameful.

Except it doesn't end in a few minutes when you come home and your mother is making soup and she asks you about your day and you lie and say it was fine, just leave me alone.

But your day wasn't fine this time. There's no one there making soup. And you don't want to be left alone. And there isn't a home to go to. Not a room. Not a bed. Only darkness. Well, you think to yourself, so this is what it's like. I'll walk around for a while. It's a nice night. It won't be so bad. Along with all sorts of other lies you tell yourself to convince yourself this isn't really happening. You aren't really homeless.

Except you are. You don't have a place to go.

So you walk around. Then you get tired of walking and you find a park bench to sit on. It's a little past midnight now and evening dew is starting to settle on everything, including the park bench and when you sit down your pants get a little wet.

Over there is a homeless man with his array of belongings in a shopping cart. He has settled in for the night in a corner of the park, everything laid out neatly. He seems to know what he is doing. He seems to have figured out how to handle the night. You study him and his array for a while. That's not me, you say to yourself. I'm better than that.

Except it is me now.

And I'm not better than him.

I am exactly the same as him.

An hour goes by on the bench or maybe only minutes. Your head starts to droop and you fight sleep because you don't want to sleep on the bench because it is so exposed. Someone might come along and beat you and take your backpack or the police might come and arrest you for sleeping in the park. Or maybe a coyote will see you sleeping there and attack. You've seen coyotes out in the city at this time of night, trotting along on some mission. Maybe they only go for garbage, you think, or an old weakened animal. Of course, then again, in the darkness, maybe I look like an old weakened animal.

I just want it to be morning now, you think. I want to have slept in a warm bed under a light comforter I slip off and on all night. I want to wake up at 3 a.m. and look out my window at the trees and hear the sounds of the night and then read for a bit and think and then fall back asleep and wake up three hours later and feel content and hungry for that brown burnt taste of the first coffee and cigarette of the day.

Except this night -- and for all the nights for the foreseeable future -- that won't be your night. Your night will be dark and long, and sleep, when it comes, will be on concrete slabs in hidden corners of buildings.

The sting is gone and now comes the long dull ache of fighting a hard battle against your biggest foe: your life and what has happened to it.

You get up from the bench and walk some more. There it is: a parking garage. It's empty and you walk around it looking for a quiet, dark spot to lie down and sleep. You find it. Under the staircase on the third floor down. The floor is dusty, but the space was dark and warm still from the heat of the day. You lie down, put your head on your backpack so it mimics a pillow, and pull your coat over you so it mimics a blanket, you close your eyes and slowly, almost effortlessly, you fall asleep.

You have defeated the night.

You haven't saved yourself or your family or put yourself back on the road to comfort and peace.

But you have done this one thing.

You have defeated this one night.

Chapter 9: "The Days Are Very Long in Guatemala City"

When you become homeless, you face a number of practical issues. In fact, when you are homeless, all you face are practical issues.

-- Where am I going to sleep tonight?

-- How am I going to clean myself?

-- What supermarket has the best samples today with the most protein in them?

-- How am I going to deal with the rainstorm that is coming tonight when the water starts pouring into my usual spot for sleeping?

-- I have a job interview; I have clean clothes, but how can I make sure I don't smell?

These are the issues you deal with on a daily basis. Relentless, boring, painful issues that relate directly to your body. And that's because homelessness is a relentless, boring and often painful condition.

Your days are very long. The rhythm of work followed by home are gone, and are replaced by long stretches of time with nothing. No company, no conversation, no deadlines, nothing.

Several years earlier, one of my sons played on a mainly Hispanic soccer team in Bell Gardens, a working class Hispanic suburb of Los Angeles. I got to know one of the fathers there quite well. He was from Guatemala City.

"What's Guatemala City like?" I said to him one day.

"The days are very long in Guatemala City," he said.

That was all he was willing to say about his life there. And that probably would be the best description of life as a homeless person. The days are very long when you haven't a home.

It plays out most clearly in ways that surprise you. It's a beautiful autumn afternoon. Normally, I would have spent the day reading the paper and drinking a several pots of coffee while working two or three crossword puzzles. Around 11 a.m., Marina and I would have gotten in the car with one or two or six of the kids and gone to the farmer's market in the parking lot at Pasadena High School, then we would have come home and then I would have come up with an interesting set of reasons for not working in the yard while settling on to the couch to watch college football for several hours, then getting up, having a glass or two of wine as the day turned into night, watched a rented movie, then settled into bed for the evening. Not much of a day, really. Basically filled with desultory tasks, mild pleasures, and comfort. But when I think of those days now, they seem like some kind of lost paradise.

A Saturday for me during my homelessness went like this.

Wake up around 4 a.m., brush myself off and wander around the streets for a while until Starbucks opened. Spend what little money you have left on coffee and hope someone leaves a copy of the Los Angeles Times sitting around so you can work the crossword puzzle. Wait. And wait. At 10 a.m., the Pasadena Central Library opens. Walk up there and go on the computer, and troll the Internet for as long as your time is allotted. It's noon now, or, if you're lucky, early afternoon.

This is now the hard part of the day. You're hungry. Really hungry. It's been about a week since you had a real meal. Time to walk over to the huge Whole Foods on the Arroyo Parkway. That store always has good food samples on a Saturday. Grab a basket or a cart, push it around and pretend to be shopping. (It always helps to put some items in your cart so you look the part.) Let's see, fruits are right here by the door. Try a bunch of orange slices and watermelon chunks. Go over to the bulk section. Ideally, someone has left a plastic bag there unpurchased. The store cannot resell that stuff, so you open the bag and grab a handful of, let's say, chocolate-covered macadamia nuts or some raspberry granola. Go upstairs now because that's where the muffin bits and cheese chunks are. Gorge, but do it subtly. Return your unpurchaseable items to their places in the store, and exit.

It is heading for mid-afternoon now. This is the time you are dreaming of lying on a couch in a warm, sunlit living room, watching college football. I'm walking now, heading over to another public library to use their computers and access the Internet for a while. As the sun heads down, I would head to a coffeehouse in South Pasadena called Kaldi where I could always find someone to talk with. The hours would pass as the various habitués of that place wandered in and out, and I have spent my day in at least some company. Not the company of loved ones, certainly, but at least decent people who didn't ask too many questions about my situation in life.

Night. It is 8 p.m. now and time to return to the Starbucks I started my day at. I find discarded copies of the New York Times, and start working the crossword puzzle. And that is Saturday.

Sunday is the same, and so are Monday and Tuesday and Wednesday and Thursday and Friday. The only variation is public holidays when the libraries are closed and you need to find someplace else to occupy your days.

Every once in a while, however, something stunning happens.

A week before Thanksgiving, 2008, it was another Saturday night. I had not eaten a meal in nearly two weeks, but was satisfied with the samples I'd eaten that day and had saved enough money to buy a Venti Drip at Starbucks. I had lost a lot of weight at this point, and decided to change clothes for the evening. I went to my storage unit, rummaged through my clothes and found a blue turtleneck I hadn't worn in years. I pulled it on, and it fit. I went to the Starbucks, and washed off my armpits in men's room, walked out and ordered my Venti Drip and sat down with the New York Times crossword puzzle from a section of the paper someone had left.

I was working the puzzle when a woman about my age dressed for a coffee date sat down next to me and we started talking.

She was beautiful. Brown hair with streaks of gray, pulled back with a ribbon forming a ponytail. She wore a red sweater, and had tailored slacks and thin, elegant loafers. Her eyes were bright and she had a slender, vaguely athletic frame and was about my age, as far as I could tell.

She smiled at me.

"You look fantastic tonight," I said.

She smiled and almost blushed and thanked me.

"I mean, seriously," I said.

I was full of confidence because what else did I have left? I'd lost everything else. May as well hold on to something I absolutely shouldn't have an ounce of left.

We began to talk, and I was funny and charming and interesting and amusing and everything I would like to think of myself as. My waist was down to the same size as my skinny 17 year-old son, and I had a roguishly handsome and gaunt look, and she seemed completely delighted to be in my company.

After about fifteen minutes, a gray-haired portly man entered, got a coffee and came up to her. He too was wearing glasses and a blue turtleneck.

"Elizabeth?" he said. "Are you Elizabeth?"

"Yes," she said.

He extended his hand. "I'm Jim."

"Ohhh!" she said, looking just a bit disappointed. She turned to me.

"So, who are you?" she said.

"I'm David," I said. "And I'm pretty much one hundred percent certain I'm not your date."

She laughed. Jim did not.

Jim sat down across from us, and Elizabeth kept engaging me in the conversation. Pretty clearly, the wisenheimery, scrawny, vaguely tuberculin-looking version of me seemed much more appealing than the stolidly settled and slightly tense and angry Jim across the table.

"Maybe we should go somewhere else," Jim finally said, tersely.

"Oh, okay," she said.

They got up and left. As she walked out the door, Elizabeth looked back at me and smiled and gave me a slight wave. I waved back.

Trust me, Elizabeth, I thought, you don't want to spend much more time with me. Jim's the guy for you. He has expensive shoes, probably lives in one of those luxury condos up on Union Street. He has a couple of European cars and a reliable dog and forty or fifty thousand dollars in his checking account.

Have coffee with him, Elizabeth. Give the guy a chance. He's probably made some mistakes in his life, which is why he finds himself single in his late 50s, but he's probably a decent person. Have coffee with him tonight, and then next week go see some arty independent movie and then a week later dinner and then a few more dinners and then finally give up and make love with him in his condo that has views of the San Gabriel Mountains and a full gym and a lap pool.

Go up to Big Bear with him and go skiing, and then maybe a long weekend in Santa Barbara. Meet his two grown kids and settle into a quiet decent life with a quiet decent man. The condo will always have heat, the refrigerator will be full, there will be cable television and a good sound system. You could move in there, and use one of the bedrooms for your home office and write.

Don't spend another minute thinking about that wildly funny man who was so charming and had read so much and could talk about anything and was so relentlessly flattering of you. He lives under a stairwell and hasn't eaten a real meal in couple of weeks.

At that was one twenty-minute interlude.

I told Marina about it the next morning during my daily call to her and the girls. She laughed long and hard.

"Well, I can believe it," she said. "You can be very charming."

"It was pretty ridiculous, when you think about it," I said.

"I know! You're homeless!"

We both laughed.

It was tremendously amusing to both of us. I mean, the very idea. The laughter died down, and there was a brief silence on the line.

"I miss you, Marina," I said.

"Ja," she said. "I know. Would you like to talk to the girls?" And then she called them. She didn't want to talk to me anymore, didn't want to think about what the boy she had crossed the ocean for had become. She handed the phone to Mariangela, and didn't say goodbye.

Chapter 10: "The Boy Who Needed a Metro Day Pass and a Drink of Water"

I tried to hide my homelessness, but I didn't fool everyone.

One day, I came out of a Seven Eleven in East Pasadena after buying a Gatorade. I was dressed in my San Marino disguise (dress shirt, dress slack, frequently a tie,) with the satchel on my side. Looked completely respectable. A young man approached me.

"Hey... uh," he said. "Could you get me something to drink, like water?"

To be honest, I had $11.00 in my wallet and I had hoped to have it last me for three more days, when I was expecting a residual check.

"Well," I said, squinting and looking at him. He was maybe 19, and had no shoelaces. He looked weighed down with sadness.

"Don't worry about it," he said. And started to walk away.

"Hold on," I said. "Come with me. I don't have any money on me, but let's get you something to drink."

We walked four blocks over to the Von's Supermarket so I could show him the drinking fountain.

"What's going on with you?" I said.

He told me he was 17 and had run away from home, which was up in Portland, Oregon. He had screwed up and had been caught by his stepfather passed out in the basement from another drinking binge, and they had decided to put him in rehab. He went to rehab, and then slipped again and felt guilty that he had disappointed his mother and stepfather, so he ran away to Los Angeles and was living in a park over in Woodland Hills.

"Okay, I was with you up to the Woodland Hills part," I said. "That part made a certain amount of sense. But how the hell did you end up in Pasadena?"

"I don't really remember," he said. "I woke up this morning in some bushes a few blocks from here, and I've been kinda wandering around trying to figure out how to get over to Woodland Hills."

We got to the drinking fountain and he drank and drank and drank.

"Thanks for showing me that, man," he said.

He was polite and his hands were soft, and he was pale. So he clearly had the look of a person who had barely spent any time on the street. He carried a visible sense of loneliness and sorrow on his young face. He was stooped when he walked. He was, in the truest sense, a lost soul.

"Okay, here's the deal," I said. "I'm going to buy you a Metro Day Pass, and you can use that to take the trains and bus back to Woodland Hills and get your stuff."

"I don't know how to do that," he said.

"It's not that complicated," I said. "Well, it's a little complicated and it's gonna take you about an hour and a half. But you can't wander around here in Pasadena when your stuff's over in Woodland Hills. I mean, come on."

He sighed. "Okay."

"And then when you get your stuff," I said. "The first thing, I want you to get in touch with your parents and tell them you want to come home."

We were walking again, to a train station now. He didn't say anything.

"I mean, they may be disappointed that you slipped," I said. "But they don't want you sleeping in bushes in L.A, and hungry and thirsty and alone. They really don't."

"Yeah, probably you're right," he said.

"Probably right?" I said. "I'm COMPLETELY right! I have kids. I wouldn't want any of them in your situation, and I'd do anything to get them home."

I bought him the ticket and showed him how to get from Pasadena to Woodland Hills by train and bus. And I told him to give me his email address and that I would write him and make sure he made it home to Portland.

He started crying and thanking me and I shook his hand. He looked at me for a long moment. And then he stung me with a question I didn't see coming.

"Are you homeless, too?" he asked me.

"No," I lied. "Why do you ask?"

"It's just that I get that from you," he said. "I kinda get that feeling."

I looked at him for a long time.

"Yeah, well, I am," I said.

"I thought so," he said.

"How did you know?" I asked.

"Doesn't matter," he said. "I can just tell."

Then he walked up the stairs to the train. We emailed each other off and on for several months. He told me he had called his parents that evening and his mother flew down the next day and brought him home and he was in treatment. Then, the correspondence stopped.

Who knows if he made it through treatment and has since moved on to a happy and productive life or if he slipped again into torment and was back on the streets, selling his body for drugs? Who knows if anything he told me was true.

God knows. And he is God's responsibility as well. I bought him a Metro Day Pass. God could take it from there.

Which reminds me, by the way, God. I'm down to $6 now. In case You hadn't noticed. So, here's Your chance. If You wanted to slip me $85,000 right about now, I'd be cool with that. Or $75,000. Your call.

I was once tremendous at prayer. Because I really believed in it. Closed my eyes, sign of the cross, Father Son Holy Spirit amen. Forgive me, Almighty Father, for my many sins. And I beseech You to look kindly on me as a believer that on that final day and hour that you remember me, a believer in Your loving kindness and compassion. This day I ask you today for... Etc.

There was a consistent theme to my requests in that I did not receive what I requested. After several years of this, I decided to take another tack.

I ask you, Almighty Father, that the script I have for sale not be sold. Or that the refinancing I am seeking not close. Or that the job I would really, really enjoy and be great at I not be hired onto. Or that the woman I love remain angry and far away from me.

Apparently God doesn't get sarcasm, because everyone of those requests were granted.

One night, while sleeping in a Public Storage unit I had rented to hold the paltry remainders of my belongings (and which is strictly forbidden under the terms of the contract with Public Storage, so you know,) I woke up and decided I would abandon prayer and just talk to God.

Look, the situation is this, God. I am having major difficulties understanding exactly why all of this has happened to me. I know, I know. I have my health. Thanks, by the way. But what about all that other stuff that makes life, you know, pleasant: employment, housing, regular meals, and my family. I'm not looking to be a millionaire. Just so we're clear on that. (Although, I wouldn't object).

Hello?

Okay. I'll forego all of that for an explanation. Something along the lines of:

"David, the reason all this has happened is because..." You can fill it in from here, God. I mean, I have done some crappy things in my life. No question. You've got me there.

But, as I recall, I repented for them and didn't get struck by a lightning bolt when I had Communion, so… aren't we sort of even on that? The old blank slate deal? Or maybe this is just one of those trials You are putting me through to make me a better person. I'll go with that if that's the explanation.

Besides, I would just point out, in case You hadn't noticed, that there are certain people I could name right now who have been cheating on their wives and have been cruel to their co-workers and dishonest in their dealings and still have got nice houses in Santa Monica and go on vacations to the Amalfi Coast and are driving around in late model German cars. And You know which ones I'm talking about.

I'm not begrudging them their earthly pleasures. I just wouldn't mind a few coming my way right about now. I'd settle for a 1991 Saab Turbo convertible, a three-bedroom apartment, and a dining room table with all eight of my children around it.

Okay, that was a little mean-spirited, and I don't expect You to give me that stuff. Just give me a job. I can take it from there.

Yes, I'm bargaining with you, but I would point out that Abraham bargained with you and this was cited as a favorable trait. Remember that: the whole Sodom and Gomorrah negotiations if he could find one honorable man deal? So, I'm just trying to strike a deal here with you, just like Abraham. See?

By the way – and I'm being serious here – thanks for this storage unit to sleep in tonight. The security guards at Caltech rousted me from my spot under the stairwell and so this is a much better sleeping situation than that, actually. So, thanks!

I heard no stirring from the depths of my soul. No voice calling out to me in the darkness of the Public Storage building saying, 'Be calm, David, for I care for you and am watching over you, for I love you as a father loves his children.'

Nothing. The air conditioning kicked in at the Public Storage unit and it got a little chilly so I pulled a jacket over me as a blanket. Silence in the unit, silence in my soul.

All right. So that's the way it's gonna be. The old silent treatment. Well, let me run something by You: You don't actually exist.

You are just a construct of the human mind, and there is nothing external to the physical universe and all this prayer and belief that I and billions of others have invested in You over the centuries in various forms is all a big steaming pile of crap.

What do you think of that? Huh? Take that, buddy boy.

I don't believe in You!

Oh, all right, I do believe in You.

I just don't know why.

I couldn't honestly tell you why I believe in You and that You love and care for me because the evidence for that is pretty sparse.

But still I do. I cling to it. Maybe I cling to that faith in You out of habit, but I don't think so. I cling to that faith because considering I've got virtually nothing else, faith in You is what's left.

So there.

Just don't do me any favors from here on in, okay?

I'm not giving up on my belief, but I'm not asking You for anything anymore because it's just too disappointing to go on like this. This relationship is just not working for me. I am not going to pray anymore. I'm just going to live my life as best I can and try to figure my way out of this the best I can and as far as our relationship, well, let's put a pin in it for now.

Okay, God?

Nothing.

The air conditioning unit shut off, and I fell asleep.

Chapter 11: "You Look Good, Padre, He Said"

By early August, 2008, it was clear that the firm I had anticipated hiring me from a meager consulting position to full-time was not in the position to do so. That's a mild version of saying I was screwed. I would not be able to afford to feed and house a wife and four children.

Marina and I talked and we agreed to have her stay in San Francisco with the two younger girls and that Coco and Saskia would return to LA and I would find someone in San Marino to take them in so they could continue at San Marino High School. It would be temporary. The firm probably would bring me on full-time by mid-October.

Saskia was easy enough to find a place for. A woman who had helped us in the past offered to take her in "for as long as needed." Shelly was an internist and a single mother herself, and lived in a small house with her daughter, Alana, their three vaguely feral rescue dogs who spent their time mainly in the ripped up backyard, a collection of cats that varied in number because Shelly was a purebred cat breeder as a hobby, and what appeared to be four or five birds, possibly parakeets. I never could tell because it was a large cage right by the dining room table and I don't like birds of any kind and didn't really want to know much about this particular flock.

Shelly took a very motherly approach to Saskia, which she needed. And Saskia ended up spending most of her remaining high school years living nearly full-time with Shelly and Alana and the dogs and the cats and the birds.

Coco was far more problematic. I would find him a place, and the family would agree to take him in, and then after a few weeks they'd want me to find him another place. Not that he was trouble. Far from it. He was an intensely quiet kid who read voluminously. It's just that it was asking a lot of people. Even friends. Over the course of his remaining two years of high school, Coco lived with 14 different families in San Marino.

The San Marino public schools are among the best in California and it was a top priority for me that Coco and Saskia finish high school there so they would have a good start to a college education. That's what I wanted for them. One day in the summer of 2010, I stopped by the high school offices to pick up their registration packets for the year.

The principal was there in the office with the school secretary.

"We tried mailing this to you at your address but it came back," she said. "Do you have a new address?"

"Uh...," I said.

The principal looked at me and then at the secretary.

"Don't worry about it," he said.

"But I need a San Marino address for them to attend here," she said.

He looked at her with a serious look.

"I said don't worry about it," he said to the secretary. Then he looked at me and smiled. "Get your kids registered."

I never intended it to be that way. My thinking was: well, they've been in the San Marino schools since kindergarten. All their friends are here. It's a great high school (and you can look that up) and will provide both of them with the preparation they need for college. Why uproot them and move back to Minneapolis with my 82 year-old widowed father when I may suddenly find work and make things right?

I would meet with both of them most days after school. Because it was San Marino, and because I didn't want to embarrass them, I would meet them at the school or after practices for the various sports teams they were on, dressed in disguise. I would put on office clothes – dress shirt and slacks, polished leather shoes and a tie. I looked like any other San Marino father, home early from the law practice.

It became part of the ruse of my life. I was still an upper middle class father and the kids were still living upper middle class lives. Except we weren't. I was homeless and often hungry, and the kids were living with virtual strangers, sleeping in guest bedrooms, with different mothers making dinner for them. While classmates were driving to school in $50,000 SUVs their parents bought for them when they got their drivers' licenses, Coco and Saskia rode their bikes to school and their father would meet them at the school gate, hungry-looking and sad.

I loved to attend parent parties. It was good to be among adults, but more importantly it was the free food. They were all lovely people and I had no beef with any of them. The mess we were in was my doing. These events did require significant shading of the truth, however. Especially since my main residence was underneath a stairwell on the third floor down of the Caltech parking garage.

"So, Dave, where are you living now?" someone would ask.

"I'm staying over by Caltech," I would say.

"Nice neighborhood," they'd say.

"It's great!" I'd say with a hearty laugh and we'd all laugh heartily in agreement what a great neighborhood it was over by Caltech.

Now, there was your little white lie. I wasn't staying "over by Caltech." I was actually living on campus. Not with the approval of the institution, however, but I appreciated the unintended hospitality, regardless.

And the food at these events: sushi, of course, lots of pasta salads, usually burgers or sausages, and cookies. And cocktails. I would come with my messenger bag that I used to carry toiletries, a change of socks and underwear, and an unread Bible, claiming I had just gotten back from the office and hadn't had time to drop off my bag. I would casually load up my plate, go to a darkened corner of the backyard, stuff the food into the messenger bag, and go back for seconds, thirds or more. And, believe me, nothing tastes better on an empty stomach than three glasses of a $20 bottle of Stag's Leap merlot paired with rotini and salami pasta salad, fourteen chocolate cookies and five plates of sushi. I never saved the sushi. That I ate on the spot.

Coco called me one day to stop by the house he was staying at. He needed some papers signed for school. It was late October and the weather in Southern California had been its usual scorching dry. I hadn't bathed in four days, but I had on a dress shirt and slacks as I walked up to the house. No one was home but Coco.

"What papers do you need signed?" I asked as I entered.

"I don't really have any for you to sign," he said.

"Oh. So what do you need?"

He paused and looked at me for a long time.

"I want you to take a shower," he said.

I didn't say anything for a long moment.

"Really?" I said.

"Yeah, really," he said.

I started to cry.

"I'm sorry, Coco," I said.

He put his hand on my shoulder.

"It's okay," he said. "I understand."

I chuckled.

"Really?" I said. "Well, you got that on me."

I went to the bathroom and while I was in the shower, he grabbed my shirt and underpants and washed them. We watched SportsCenter while the load finished, and he made me a sandwich.

"Well, Viqui will be home soon," he said, referring to the woman of the house.

"I should probably get going," I said.

"You look good, Padre," he said.

"Well, I am a handsome man," I said. And we both laughed as I left.

My children grew up calling me David. It was always amusing to me because I was so clearly the fatherly type (in my mind) that I enjoyed little kids calling me by my first name. But as the agony of these years passed, they began to stop calling me by my first name. The older girls started calling me Daddy, and the boys called me Padre. On some unconscious level they felt a desire to let me know that despite what could be most politely called my reduced circumstances, I had become even more clearly their father. I consider that my finest accomplishment of those years. When we all lived together in a $2 million house on a broad leafy avenue in San Marino with three cars in the driveway and a grand piano and the accouterment of a successful life, I was David.

But now, homeless and hungry, I was Daddy.

One day a year ago, out of the blue, in the early afternoon in the middle of the week, my daughter Claire called me.

"Daddy, I just want you to know that I was thinking about this and I really appreciate all the sacrifices you and Mama made so we could go to school in San Marino," she said.

"Really?" I said.

"Yes," she said. "I know it was very hard for you, and we all really appreciate it. I love you very much, Daddy."

So that's what this was all about. I wasn't just David anymore. I was Daddy.

I was Padre.

Chapter 12: "Are You Ralph Lauren?"

In mid-November, 2008, my mother died.

It wasn't really a surprise. Six years earlier she had suffered a massive heart attack that she survived only through the most strenuous rescue efforts. She had been defibrillated for half an hour before her heart started up again. She was in a coma for nearly a week. And when she emerged from the coma, her short term memory had been fried.

In the six years that followed her heart attack, my father tended to her with a devotion that nearly shamed me. She was able to take care of herself – bathe, cook, clean the house, play cards, do crossword puzzles, and seem like any other 70-something woman. Except she couldn't remember what had just transpired. Her brain functioned, but the part with the memory was gone. Many times my father would come into the kitchen and she would look up and him and say: "Who are you?"

Still, he was unfailingly patient and calm. Never raising his voice, never giving up on living as normal a life as they could. They traveled together, usually by train, visiting us a couple times in L.A. I often thought about him and how patient he was with my mother and how impatient I had been with Marina during the years of her descent into darkness.

Why couldn't I have been to Marina like my father had been to my mother: patient, loving, quiet, calm and devoted?

My brother called me to tell me Mom had died and they would fly me out to Minneapolis for the funeral. The flight was at 1 p.m. out of LAX. One problem: I had eleven cents to my name. I called a couple friends to see if they could give a ride out. No luck.

Fortunately, the LA Metro system of trains operated on the honor system. I could ride a series of trains to within walking distance of the airport and if I were lucky I could avoid the fare police.

I got off the Green Line's nearest LAX stop and started walking. It was about a mile to the airport. I walked through a tunnel and then headed up an embankment to cross over to the terminals. And then the Airport Police stopped me. I was walking in an area not allowed to pedestrians. I was questioned, handcuffed and they rifled through my backpack, taking every item out looking for a bomb. I kept telling them I was just trying to get to the airport to fly out to Minneapolis for my mother's funeral. Sitting on the side of the road, with my hands cuffed behind my back, looking at them picking through my meager collection of clothes, I raged inside. They finished their search.

"Okay," I said. "Thank you." I was polite. It was my little tribute to my mother, who insisted on politeness in all interactions outside the family. "Fucking ass wipe airport cops," I thought to myself as I smiled and went on my way.

The day of the funeral was cold in a Minnesota November way. Which is to say the sky was the color of gray pants and it was spitting snow. It was 12 degrees outside. My father and I got dressed for the funeral. I couldn't even imagine what this day must have been like for him. The woman he had loved since 1953 was going to be buried today. He would be alone now. Not that she was ever easy company. But she was tremendous fun. She was brilliant and argumentative and neurotic and impossible and tender-hearted and high strung and relentlessly compassionate and ridiculous.

Despite her insistence on politeness, she had taught me the pleasure of arguing. And we constantly did. Usually about things you can't possibly argue about. One time, we argued about the direction the Red River of the North flowed. I'm not sure now which side who was on, but I do remember it got pretty heated. It was always like that. There was the argument we got into about how many Serbian Army tanks the US Air Force had destroyed during the aerial assault on Kosovo in 1999. We didn't speak to each other for a week after that one. Or the quantity of cheese on a Papa John's pizza. Or which direction the San Gabriel Mountains were in relation to my house in San Marino. Things like that.

One of the favorite stories all of us had about her was a story my father told about a trip they took to Washington, D.C. many years earlier. They were driving in West Virginia on one of those torturously winding mountain roads my father was exceptional at finding. Early on in the drive, they got behind a logging truck and were stuck behind it unable to pass because it was a two-lane road. My mother was freaking out about the truck. It was going to lose its load and dump all those logs on them and kill them and why can't we pass this darn old truck. Finally, after nearly an hour, my father found and opening and zipped past the truck. Relief. My mother, however, was so stressed out about the life-threatening experience she had just gone through following a fully-loaded loaded logging truck along a mountain road for an hour that she just had to stop and get something to drink. A Coke, a ginger ale, anything. She started pestering my dad to stop and finally he found a small gas station and he pulled over and she ran in and bought a 7 UP. As they came walking back to the car, the logging truck passed them. My father said he just looked at her and they sat quietly in the car for the rest of the trip.

My career as a waiter pretty much ended when she and my dad came to a Good Earth Restaurant in suburban Minneapolis in 1981 and the two of us started a fight over the portion size of a salad she had ordered while I foolishly was their waiter.

She had ordered the Chinese Chicken Salad, and when I delivered it, some concerns were voiced.

"That's it?" she said.

"Yes," I said. "That's the Chinese Chicken Salad."

"Not much chicken," she said.

"There's plenty of chicken," I said.

"There are five pieces. Five pieces of chicken is all I get with this salad?"

"There's more than five pieces!"

"One, two, three, four, five," she counted out.

"On the top!" I said. "Underneath."

"Underneath?"

"You know, mixed into the salad. Come on, Mom. It's a good salad."

"If I just wanted to eat lettuce."

"What? Do you want me to take it back?"

"No," she said, quite put out. "I'll eat it."

"If you want me to take it back, I'll take it back and I'll tell them my mother says there's not enough chicken in the Chinese Chicken Salad!"

My father was quietly staring at his sandwich.

"What do you think, Don?" she said to him.

"Maybe there's more chicken in there."

She dug around a bit, and I glared at her. She found a couple more pieces.

"See?" I said. "More chicken."

"Not that much more," she said.

"Fine," I said. "I'm taking it back."

I went to grab her plate and she held onto it.

"No! I don't want to make a scene."

That, however, had already happened. We had already made a scene. If we hadn't been in a public place it would have gone on longer. The manager came over and smoothed things over. After my shift, he called me into his cramped office and was suggested I consider a career besides waitering because customers didn't come to the Ridgedale Mall Good Earth to listen to me and my mother yell at each other.

We dolefully got into the car and I asked if we could stop and get me a scarf and some gloves because the burial was that day and I didn't have any winter clothes anymore. We went to the Sears at the Ridgedale Mall in suburban Minneapolis. I picked out a University of Minnesota scarf and a pair of cheap gloves. As I was standing in line to pay, a woman in the line next to me was staring at me.

"Can I help you?" I said, vaguely peeved.

She looked around and then whispered conspiratorially to me:

"Are you Ralph Lauren?"

I looked at her for a moment.

"Yes," I said. "Yes, I am."

She gasped but I shushed her.

"Please," I said, looking around so as not to cause a scene because apparently Ralph Lauren was shopping for a scarf at the Ridgedale Mall in suburban Minneapolis on a Tuesday morning.

She nodded knowingly and I nodded back. As my father and I got into the car, we both burst out laughing. Well, I thought to myself, they may not want me as a comedy writer anymore, but I still know a good joke. I mean, I managed to get a laugh out of my father on one of the grimmest days of his life.

Not bad.

Chapter 13: "Oblomov's Dream"

Thinking about it now, I probably should have realized my career in Hollywood was over in 2003 when a Disney executive put his feet in my face.

What had happened was my agent called me up one day and said he had arranged a pitch meeting for me with a development executive at the Disney Channel. They're looking for family comedies, my agent said, and are interested in taking a pitch from you.

I had already written two family comedies that had come achingly close to being produced. Why would the third time prove to be the charm? But, what could it hurt. I didn't prepare anything, however. Normally, when I would go in to pitch, I'd have an entire pilot episode beaten out, a character bible, and a two-season arc ready in case anyone asked. This time, I just figured I would go in and talk about my family. The premise of the show would be my life: a loud, contentious, funny and completely inappropriate family living in a buttoned-down upper middle class community. The father would be an irascible, wise-cracking hot-head and the mother would be an Eastern European woman with a funny foreign accent and loads of unsupportable theories about how the world should be operating if she were only in charge.

Write what you know, as they say.

But that was all I had.

I met the guy. Very pleasant fellow. I started just talking about my family and he started laughing. And laughing. And laughing.

"Oh, my God!" he said. "This is brilliant stuff!"

"Well, it's just my life," I said. "I don't consider it particularly brilliant. In fact, I find in vaguely depressing."

"It's not!" he practically screamed. He vowed to get me a meeting with his boss, the guy in charge of comedy development (or something like that) at the Disney Channel.

A week later I went in. I forget his name now, but he came out to greet me, and he was wearing what was certainly the most beautiful suit I had ever seen in my life. It was a wool, navy blue suit, perfectly cut, and probably cost a couple thousand dollars by the looks of it. He had on a starched white dress shirt, a silvery silk tie… and enormous pink bunny slippers.

Yes, you read that right. The kind of bunny slippers with the face of the bunny on the toes. They were adorable, but they didn't really match the $2,000 suit, I have to be honest.

We went into his office so I could make my pitch.

Now, one thing you should know about pitching to television executives is that they seem to set up their offices in a very particular way. There's the desk by the window so the executive has his back to the window, then two or three high wooden chairs, a coffee table, and a very low couch.

You enter and are offered to sit on the couch.

The executive then comes around from behind his or her desk and sits on one of the high chairs. That way, they are sitting above you, the writer, and you, the writer, are in a supplicant position to them.

See how that works?

So, as instructed, I sat down on the couch, and the executive sat down on one of the high chairs directly across from me, kicked off the bunny slippers and plopped his feet on the coffee table so that they were almost right in my face. I had to lean over to pitch to him. Which I did.

He listened impassively, elbows on the arms of his chair, fingers from both hands touching each other. And he didn't laugh. It was a cricket festival in there of dead air. I finished.

"What do you think?" I asked.

"I think it's very, very good," he said.

"Good, I'm—"

"But, it seems to be missing an element," he said.

"Oh, really?" I said. "What's missing?"

"It's missing an element like, oh, something like a talking dog," he said.

"A what?"

"A talking dog."

"You think the show needs a talking dog?" I asked.

"It doesn't have to be a talking dog, necessarily, but something like that," he said.

"What would be like that?"

He said quietly for a moment and thought. He was really thinking now.

"Really, the best example I can give you is a talking dog. But, you're the writer," he said. "You come up with something."

"But I don't understand what the talking dog means," I said. "What exactly are you looking for with the talking dog?"

"Some kind of magical element," he said, dramatically.

"But this is more like a show about a regular family," I said. "This isn't really a talking dog kind of show."

"Well, I believe you could make it one," he said. "Now, I have another meeting."

He stood up and went behind his desk. I got up and trudged out. As I walked to my car, it was one of the worst feelings I had ever had. It was over.

And then I decided to begin looking for a new career. That seems to have been over before it started.

I started going on Craigslist, Monster.com, Linkedin, etc., sending out resumes. Recently, I did a search on my Yahoo and Gmail email accounts to see how many resumes or job applications I sent out from just that account alone from 2006 onward (I had a different email account before that and that data is all gone). From 2006 until 2011, I sent out 2,541 resumes. That doesn't, of course, include the applications I made directly on company websites or through job search sites. It sounds horrible, but it actually is fairly typical for people in my age group now. We're close enough to retirement that hiring us and investing in us doesn't quite make sense for the employer, but far enough away from retirement that actually retiring doesn't make sense for us.

Plus there was the whole twelve years I spent as a comedy writer, honing skills that are completely useless in a normal office environment: joke writing, story analysis, ability to accommodate the whims of maniacal actors. Not really very transferrable skills, it turns out.

The 19th century Russian novelist Ivan Goncharov wrote one good book: "Oblomov." It concerns an indolent and incredibly lazy Russian nobleman named Oblomov who does nothing and can't make up his mind. In fact, Oblomov doesn't even manage to get out of bed for the first 150 pages or so.

The novel was based on a short story Goncharov had written several years earlier called "Oblomov's Dream." He incorporated the short story into the novel, which, when you think about it, was either a brilliant expansion of a great idea, or incredible laziness on Goncharov's part.

Regardless, the 'Oblomov's Dream' segment of the novel is considered a masterwork of Russian literature. And even in English it is an extraordinary piece of writing. In Oblomov's dream, he imagines a rural Russia of his idealized fantasy. It is a peaceful and contented world, and when you read it, you find yourself wishing you lived in rural 19th century Russia. Oblomov's dream is a beautiful one, but its relationship to the bleak and punishingly difficult life of a 19th century Russian serf is tenuous at best.

I think we all have an Oblomov Dream of one form or another, some last through our whole lives, others are relatively brief flirtations. It is an imagining we put together of a life we nearly could have lived had things worked out.

My first Oblomov Dream based out of a Craigslist job was working for a non-profit media company in Santa Barbara. I answered an ad looking for someone to write a business plan for a "startup media launch." I have written dozens of business plans and love the research and puzzle-solving nature of that kind of project. But I was actually stunned when one day while I was sitting and sunning myself in a bit of despair over my prospects that I got a call from a Santa Barbara number.

It was the company founder, Mark Manning, and joining him on the call was his partner, Natalie Kalustian. Mark explained that he was a professional scuba diver but that the war in Iraq had driven him crazy with anger. So he took a night course on documentary filmmaking at UC-Santa Barbara, and gotten a job as a driver for a private contractor in Iraq. His goal was to go over there and make a movie about that stupid war.

Which he did. In a feat of nearly unspeakable derring-do, Mark moved to Fallujah and went native, so to speak. He was the only Westerner living in Fallujah after the horrific siege there, and he recorded what the war had done to one city in Iraq.

The film, "The Road to Fallujah", was a bit a of film festival hit and Mark got the idea that one of the biggest problems we face today is the poisonous and partisan media environment we live in. Mark wanted to launch a non-profit media company that distributed long and short-form documentary film on the Internet, and to distribute cheap HD video cameras around the world to "citizen journalists."

It seemed like a crazy idea until I saw what happened in Iran on Twitter and Facebook as hundreds of videos popped up about the rioting there.

The company was going to be based in Santa Barbara. I put together a plan that would have the company self-funded with thousands of small donors within 18 months. We just needed a couple large donations ($500,000 or so) to get it up and running. It seemed so perfect. I would move to Santa Barbara, live in a cottage near downtown, the days would always be sunny and I would have a dog and my daughters would go to high school there. In the mornings I would get up early, trot down to the beach, maybe take up surfing (yeah, that's it: I'd be one of those graying 50-something guys out there with a board surfing finally after a lifetime of being nervous about the ocean.) We'd produce dozens and dozens of important, impactful, meaningful films, and the steady drip, drip, drip of our work would gradually change the world, and I'd drink orange juice from a tree in my backyard, and my small house would always smell of coffee and have old movie posters on the wall... and the funding never came in.

The other Oblomov Dream I came up with was from another non-profit launch for an internet-based land conservation company initially funded by Colin Weil, a San Francisco-based engineer and investor who owned 5,000 acres of rainforest in Panama. I did a fund-raising film for him that was shown at a couple house parties. In that dream, I would live in a neighborhood of San Francisco like Noe Valley or Hayes Valley or the Inner Richmond and ride my bike to our offices in the Financial District and I'd wear dressy wool pants and pressed white shirts and have lunches at the Ferry Building and go to the symphony and plays and spend the rest of my life as a Giants fan and a San Franciscan... and the funding never came fully in.

And I remain a Minnesota Twins fan.

Chapter 13: "Back When I Was Older"

In the time I was homeless, I learned a great deal about myself. I learned that I was more resourceful than I had ever imagined, less respectable than I had ever hoped, and more resilient than I had ever dreamed. I also learned something else: there is nothing so beautiful as a bed that is yours in a room that is yours.

This is my little space in the world. Perhaps I share it with someone else or perhaps it is mine alone. But this bed, surrounded by these walls, under these blankets and with my head on that pillow, this is the place. This is Eden, where I go when I am done with my day. For me, I would prefer to share that space with the woman I love, but if she is not there or I am alone, then I am still happy in my room and in my bed.

One of the most important things I learned was about hunger. Of all the psychological states a person can be in – religious ecstasy, joy, erotic desire, despair, intellectual fervor, anger, etc. – I found hunger to be the most complex and profound.

And by hunger, I don't mean, "Man, I missed lunch and I am starving." That's hungry.

Hunger is the state of being that sets in after a few days of little or no food. In the first days without eating, hunger hurts. You feel it and it makes you edgy and nervous and a bit desperate.

Around the third or fourth day, however, something begins to change in you. You begin to move into a calmer state of being. Your anxiety starts to drop. You feel your clothes start to drape off you a bit, which is a nice feeling. There is a sort of bliss that sets in. It is not a completely pleasant bliss, however. It is an ambiguous bliss.

Your ambition for food drops. You stop thinking about it so much, but you aren't happy. Nor are you content. You pass into a stage of not feeling anxiety. It is not a happy state; it is just a state of freedom. You know that there is not going to be a solution to your problem for several days, so you stop worrying about, as Jesus said, "what we shall eat or what we shall drink."

In fact, the Sermon on the Mount actually begins to make a certain amount of sense that it never had to me before. "Consider the lilies of the field. They neither sow nor reap, but I tell you Solomon in all his glory was not arrayed such as these."

In the years leading up to our foreclosure in 2006, the stress and worry of the loss of career and the impending loss of our house had sent me on an eating binge and I had ballooned up to 270 pounds. I had the body of Peter Griffin on "Family Guy."

And then, one sunny morning two years later, I was washing myself once in a Ralph's Supermarket men's room. I hadn't eaten a full meal in 11 days. I took off my shirt and was washing my armpits and I looked at myself. My God, I thought, I have abs!

This is what my body should look like – lean and muscled. All these clothes and food and fat I have piled on myself in the years of living well had hidden my real body. It was a 52 year-old body, but it was muscled and hard and powerful looking. My cheeks were sunken, but my eyes were bright, my arms thin, brown and sinewy.

I am beautiful, I thought.

Here I was now, gaunt and athletic-looking, like the distance runner I had been in high school and college when I ran 12 miles a day. I looked stronger and younger than I had in years. I never weighed myself, but I was wearing Coco's jeans and he weighed 165 pounds. I must have lost about 100 pounds.

Two days after that, I received a residual check for $17.61 from a "Roseanne" episode that had aired in syndication. I took all the money and went to Zankou Chicken, an Armenian chicken restaurant chain in L.A. I ordered the shawarma platter with the special garlic paste, a tabouli salad and pink lemonade. I began to eat it, but stopped. It was too much. My body recoiled, and told me to stop. I bagged it and left and finished it over the next two days.

When you start eating again, then the anxiety about food returns. You begin to worry about your next meal.

When you know there will be no next meal, you stop worrying about it.

When I was four years old, I lived with my parents and brothers in a small two-bedroom upstairs apartment on Fremont Avenue in North Minneapolis, and I had a couple of very odd ideas about the world.

The first was an irrational fear of being kidnapped by gypsies. I cannot figure out for the life of me where I came up with this idea. Our family didn't have a TV so I wouldn't have seen a show about gypsies, nor did we ever go to movies. And there were hardly any gypsies camped out in North Minneapolis that I knew of. Still, I was terrified of the idea being kidnapped by them. They would sneak into my bedroom, grab me, and steal me away and I would never see my mother and father and brothers ever again and I would grow up to be a gypsy and always be sad about my lost former life.

I came home from running errands one Saturday afternoon in early 1987 and found Marina crying. She had just gotten off the phone from talking with her mother and had told her she was pregnant with our third (of what would eventually be eight) child. She said her mother had been furious with her and told she was "acting like a gypsy."

I tried to comfort her by laughing and telling her about my ridiculously irrational fear of being kidnapped by gypsies when I was a kid. Marina didn't smile. She just looked at me and snarled: "Gypsies." Almost like she was spitting it out.

Okay, then, I thought. Maybe we should talk about the weather. Hey, beautiful winter day out there, isn't it?

The other idea I had when I was four was that at one point I had been an adult. I had a pretty vague idea of how this had happened but there was some kind of past life I lived in in which I had been an adult. It had ended under unclear circumstances, and then, unfortunately, I had been born a second time and was now a kid.

Which was a major disappointment.

What's amusing to me to think about now is that in my imagined past life I wasn't a sea captain or a medieval prince or a cowboy in the Old West.

Nope, I was just an adult and I got to do adult things like drive around in cars, go into stores and purchase items, and visit saloons.

I was especially bitter about not being able to go into saloons anymore because I was now stuck being a kid. There were plenty of saloons in my old neighborhood and I was fascinated by them with their darkened windows and the smell of cigarettes and beer that wafted out when someone came out the door and you could hear laughing and Frank Sinatra singing on a juke box. Man, and to think I used to be able to hang out in saloons back when I was older and now I'm stuck being a kid.

My father found this whole business very amusing, but my mother was convinced there was something wrong with me and wanted to have me tested. He's just got a big imagination, my dad said. So my mother scolded me and told me to never talk about being older ever, ever again.

Not so very long ago, I had three cars, a large expensive house with a huge mortgage, a big career, an enormous sad belly, heart palpitations and a tremendous amount of stress and anger.

I don't have any of that anymore.

I was so much older then. I'm younger than that now.

Chapter 14: "What It Is We Loved"

I was talking to a man I know who had suffered his own bout of homelessness. We started talking about the things that meant the most to us when it ended. This was our list:

1. A bed and a bedroom. You walk to a door, you open it, it is your bedroom. You close the door, turn out the lights, slide into your bed, pull the bedding over your body, close your eyes. Maybe you pray, maybe you don't. Maybe you fall asleep right away, maybe you lie there and think for a while. None of that matters. What matters is that this is your room, your bed, this bedding is bedding and not a coat or a sleeping bag or other clothes. This is your little space. Yours.

2. Showers. The feeling of stepping into a shower with hot water? A nearly unmatchable sensuously fulfilling experience.

You get up early in the morning, walk outside in your bare feet, step on something sharp, curse, grab the paper, walk back into the house, start making coffee in your pot, and open the paper up completely on your table, pour yourself a cup of coffee, and start to read. It's morning, my friend. You are at home, reading the paper and drinking coffee.

3. Bare feet and then socks. You get up, walk into the kitchen in your bare feet and the floor is cold. You turn around, go back into your room, put on socks and go back to the kitchen.

4. The smell of food cooking in the kitchen. You open the door and walk into the house and there, a few rooms away, is the smell of food cooking. Maybe it's a chicken roasting in the oven, or a marinara sauce simmering on the stove, or onions and garlic being sauteed in a pan. It doesn't matter. What matters is what it means: some time soon, you will sit down at a table and eat dinner with some of the people you love.

5. Housekeeping. Nobody loves housework. And then I didn't have a house. And then, after a long time, I did again. The pleasure of sweeping a floor, wiping off a counter, putting dishes in the dishwasher... nearly unspeakably joyful. I make my little place clean. It is my place and I have made it clean. I feel comfortable in it now. It isn't a pile of clothes under a stairwell or in the back of a minivan. It is a proper living space and I have cleaned it. I am a decent human being. I can barely think of anything that makes me happier than making my space clean and orderly.

The old saying is that the best things in life are free. I don't know about that. None of these things are free. But they don't cost much. And when you don't have them, they are priceless.

Chapter 15: "The Gun on the Kitchen Counter"

Eventually, I scraped together enough money to find a room to rent in a ramshackle house in a dicey neighborhood in northwest Pasadena. Not enough to reunite with Coco and Saskia, but enough to get off the street.

Rooms to rent are in abundance on Craigslist. There is an endless supply of housing available for a reasonable amount of money and few questions asked. Someone always needs a roommate or a housemate because their latest roommate has inexplicably moved to Portland/is on a semester abroad/entered residential rehab/moved in with their lover/received a short jail sentence.

The room is always temporary, and the commitment to each other is limited.

One place I lived had four other guys in their 20s who appeared to be running some kind of agricultural products distribution operation. Which I didn't mind until one day I came home and there was a gun on the kitchen counter. A pistol.

I came into the living room and they were all staring gape-mouthed at "Family Feud."

"Oh, hey, you guys?" I said.

They looked at me.

"Listen, no big deal really," I said. "But there's a gun on the kitchen counter and could you maybe find a different place for that?"

The really fat guy apologized profusely and went into the kitchen and got the gun and brought into the living room and plopped it down on a table next to the sofa and went back to drinking beer and watching what was apparently a particularly closely contested episode of "Family Feud."

It wasn't really the "different place" I had in mind. But they seemed content with it.

I moved out a couple days later.

In the future, whenever I looked at a place, I always made sure to ask if they had guns in the house. You'd be surprised how many people said yes. Or maybe you'd be depressed.

Not that I object to guns, per se. I just have a policy of not living in a place where the other residents are better armed than I am.

Chapter 16: "Are You Familiar With the Redwood?"

As the months went by in the fall of 2008 and no prospects of stable, sufficient employment emerging, Marina began pressing to return to Germany with our two youngest daughters. The German government provided its citizens with a benevolent safety net. She could move there, live in an apartment her parents owned in Gaggenau, Germany, a quiet little resort town in southwestern Germany. The girls would go to school there and be safe and free from worry about hunger or housing.

She was right. It was over. I wasn't going to be able to provide for us as a family. It was time now to really split up, fully and completely. I hadn't seen Marina and the two younger girls since they had left for San Francisco nearly six months earlier. With the clock now running down on their time in the U.S., I wanted to see them. It was time to go to San Francisco and begin to say goodbye. But how? I no longer had a car, and bus fare and airfare were more than I could afford.

I turned to Craigslist and started looking into Rideshare. It's a simple service. You look for someone who is driving to where you want to go, and contact them and offer to share the ride and pay for part of the cost of gas.

The first Rideshare I arranged on Craigslist was in late December, 2008. It was from Los Angeles to San Francisco. Or something like that. Craigslist Rideshares are an imprecise form of travel. You are hoping to get picked up sort of close to where you are starting from and end up getting dropped of sort of close to your final destination. And you'd like to do it roughly on your schedule.

Flexibility and compromise are essential. You're going to have to go out of your way. And it's not going to happen exactly when you want it.

But for $35 to get from Los Angeles to San Francisco, you don't get to spend too much time complaining. It's a long boring ride and there's really no good way to make it other than by car.

Marina and our two youngest were living in cramped quarters in San Francisco with my with my first and third daughters, Alexandra and Claire. Alexandra worked as a labor and delivery nurse at St. Luke's Hospital in the Mission District of San Francisco. Claire was studying Economics and African Studies at the University of San Francisco.

I had wanted on a number of occasions to come up and visit all of them, but Marina told me not to. She was too angry with me. She had decided she would move back to Germany with the two youngest girls, and she wanted to go as soon as possible. The girls were German citizens but did not have German passports. In order to get them, we needed to present their birth certificates and our marriage license to the German consulate in San Francisco. Once they had those passports, the process of moving there and beginning life in Germany apart from me would begin.

I had delayed bringing the birth certificates up. Marina finally told me that if I wanted to see the girls, I would have to bring up the birth certificates. No other visit would be allowed. First mail them up, and then I will decide if I want to see you, she told me.

Christmas 2008 passed with me alone in Los Angeles. I had sent my younger son, Constantin (Coco) and his sister, Saskia, up to San Francisco for the two-week school break. It rained that day throughout Southern California. One of those cold, piercing rains that come out of the Gulf of Alaska. I spent most of the day at a Starbucks, reading and making phone calls. Finally, I decided the standoff had to end. I would go up to San Francisco and deliver the birth certificates in person, even if that meant I would eventually lose the girls. I couldn't go any longer without seeing them.

I placed an ad on Craigslist in the Rideshare section: "Ride needed to SF. I am a 52 year-old professional male, going up to visit family in San Francisco. Excellent company. I can help with the driving."

I got a few desultory responses, and finally linked up with Marty. Marty was going up to visit his brother in Marin. He lived in Los Feliz and would drop me off in the city. Perfect, I thought. He was leaving on a Saturday morning and returning on a Monday morning. Even more perfect. An entire weekend with six of my eight children and my wife, cramped in a tiny apartment in the Mission District, a week before Orthodox Christmas.

I took the train and bus over to Marty's apartment in Los Feliz, and met him outside his building. Talking to him on the phone, I knew he was a New Yorker. What I didn't realize was how thoroughly New Yorker he was. Marty was standing outside his building waiting for me. He was in his late 60s, a short man with enormous plastic aviator-style glasses, of the type that had been vaguely popular in the early 80s. His were tinted a light yellow. He had a comb-over and large cancerous-looking freckles.

Marty was nervous. He had never done a Rideshare before, but his brother Alex had recommended he give it a try so they could see each other. Marty and Alex rarely saw each other. Alex ran a stationary store in Marin and couldn't get away because the store was so successful it consumed all his time and he wasn't able to travel. Marty, on the other hand, was retired. He had been a salesman, working out of the garment district in downtown LA, mainly hawking ladies better sportswear.

He had moved to Los Angeles in 1966, the year after he got out of the Coast Guard, and had settled in this slightly seedy building in Los Feliz three months after it had opened. He was its senior tenant.

He would have liked to visit Alex in Marin more often, but flying made him far too nervous since 9/11, and there was no direct bus or train route to Marin. Plus, driving to

Marin by himself would mean he would almost certainly get lost. So he thought he'd give Rideshare a try. He explained all this as we walked to his parking place in the underground parking section of his apartment building.

"As you can see," he told me, "it's an outstanding building."

Actually, I couldn't see that. It looked like an utterly generic 1960s Los Angeles apartment building, a completely un-outstanding building.

"I've lived here for more than 40 years," he told me as we walked to his car. "Open your door carefully. I don't want you to scratch the door on the wall of the building."

His car was a 15 year-old Mitsubishi sports car. It smelled like mothballs. Marty cautiously drove out of the underground parking garage, took a careful right turn and headed over to Los Feliz Boulevard and then toward the 5 freeway.

"You're going to have to direct me, David," he said. "I'm not familiar with the directions to San Francisco."

"Well," I said, "it's pretty straightforward. We go down Los Feliz Boulevard until we hit the 5 and then we take the 5 north for about 370 miles. And then we'll figure things out as far as where you can drop me off."

He timidly entered the freeway and was going about 50 miles per hour. Dear God, I thought, this is going to take forever. After nearly two hours, we were outside Gorman, a droopy little town in the middle of the Angeles National Forest, hard by the freeway and Marty announced he had to make a stop to make a phone call with his new "cellular telephone."

He had just gotten one at the insistence of his brother. We got out of the car and I gassed up the car and paid for it, as we had agreed. Marty went inside to use the restroom and came back outside. He was wandering the parking lot lost when I came out.

"I seem to have lost the car," he said.

"Okay, wait a minute," I said. "You got lost walking from the door of the gas station to your car?"

"The air is thin up here," he said. "I'm feeling light-headed. And there's something wrong with this phone. I've tried dialing and calling for days now and it doesn't work."

"How old is it?" I asked.

"Brand new!" he said. "I got it a week ago and it stopped working two days ago."

"Let me see that."

I took it from him, and flipped it open.

"Well, here's your problem, Marty," I said. "The battery's dead."

"The battery? What battery?"

"It's a cell phone. They run on batteries."

"A battery-operated phone? I didn't want a battery-operated phone! What kind of a piece of junk did they sell me?"

"Cell phones are all battery-operated," I said. "When was the last time you charged this?"

"Never!" he said. "I bought it a week ago, used it for a few days, and then it stopped."

"It stopped because the battery died," I said.

"So do I have to get a new phone?"

"No! You just have to plug it into the wall and recharge it."

"So it's worthless."

"Yes, right now it is. You won't be able to use it until you recharge it. Who are you going to call? You can call them on my phone."

"Your phone is working?"

"That's why I offered it to you."

I handed him the phone.

"And where are the numbers?" He said.

I flipped the phone open. "Here."

He stared at the phone for a beat.

"Perhaps you could dial my brother," he said. "This phone is a different model. I…" His voice trailed off. Defeated again by technology.

"I tell you what, Marty," I said. "I will dial your brother for you and any other number you want but on one condition: you have to let me drive."

Marty looked relieved.

"Certainly… provided you don't speed."

"I won't," I said. "I promise."

I dialed his brother, handed him the phone, turned out onto the freeway and pushed the engine up to 85 miles per hour immediately. Marty talked to his brother and told him we were driving through some "extensive mountains" and were on our way.

He finished the call and handed me the phone.

"You're not speeding, are you?" he said.

"No. Absolutely not," I said.

"Because it seems like you're speeding."

"That's an illusion," I said. "It's because we're in the mountains. The air is thinner so it seems like we're going faster than we really are."

"Really? Is that true?"

"Oh, yes," I said, with the gravest of confidence. "It's a well-known concept in modern physics. It's called illusory speed."

"Never heard of that. How do you know about it, David? Are you a scientist of some type?"

"No," I said. "I mean, I try to stay current with modern physics through reading, attending lectures, etc., but I'm not a scientist per se."

"Very impressive," he said. "Such an educated person I have in my car!"

It struck me that I could have continued weaving the tale, but I began to feel badly. Marty wasn't a bad guy, and going much further with the lie would have crossed into making fun of him. I just wanted to drive fast without him worrying.

My tale of my life as an amateur physicist was sufficient to allow him to believe we weren't actually going 83 miles per hour. Nothing more was necessary.

We talked most of the way up, with Marty doing most of the talking. He was from a Jewish family, and grew up in Manhattan. His father was a waiter at a fancy restaurant and wore a tuxedo to work every day. That is how Marty got interested in the garment business. His father was such a good dresser. And then there was his uncle. The one who married Meyer Lansky's daughter.

What a wedding that had been. Better than the marriage. Uncle Sol was not a substantial person. He was handsome, that was for certain, but not substantial. He liked to bet on horses and cheated on Meyer Lansky's daughter with impunity.

"That doesn't seem like a smart idea," I said. "I mean, Meyer Lansky could have had him killed or something like that."

"No," said Marty. "I don't think Meyer Lansky was the type for that kind of thing. Besides she was crazy about him and fought with her father, Uncle Sol, all the time, but eventually they divorced and went their separate ways. Sol died a few years later. Car accident."

"Car accident?" I said.

"That's what the police said. A car accident."

After four and a half hours, we neared the Bay Area. I asked if I could just find a BART station, and go from there. Marty got nervous. He proposed that I drive him all the way to his brother's house in Marin. I sighed long and hard. This was going to add a couple hours to the trip. I wanted to get to the city and see the girls. My brother can drive you to their apartment, Marty offered. Reluctantly, I agreed.

We come now to the matter of Alex, or at least Marty's presentation of him. Alex, according to Marty, was a "real ladies man – very sophisticated." He ran a high-end stationery store in Marin, was an expert on organic food and natural medicine, quite handsome and had "a gorgeous Romanian opera singer" as his current girlfriend. He lived in a luxury apartment that overlooked the bay.

It was late afternoon by the time we got to Marin, and I called Alex and got directions to his building. The building was located in a run-down part of Marin, and was in serious need of upkeep. Alex came down to greet us. He couldn't have looked less like Marty had portrayed him… or even like he was related to Marty. Alex was tall (more than 6'2"), with shaggy blonde gray hair, and in possession of only 40% of his teeth. It seemed unlikely that he would have a gorgeous Romanian opera singer as his girlfriend.

He got in Marty's car and we began the drive back to San Francisco to drop me off at the girls' apartment in the Mission District. Alex was convivial, and wanted me to experience the beauty of the Marin Headlands and drove us up there. I was getting impatient, but it was beautiful. I hadn't been in San Francisco for some time, and there was the city itself, rolling out in front of us, the Golden Gate and the sea.

Finally, I convinced them to head into the city. By the time we arrived at the apartment building on Shotwell Avenue, it was dark.

I hopped out of the car and headed to the doorway. My heart was pounding. I hadn't seen Marina or the little girls for six months. They didn't know I was coming. I grabbed the doorknob to the building gate and turned it. Locked. I was locked out. There I was, maybe thirty feet from my family and I was locked out.

I called the home number. Sasha answered. "Hey, it's David. Um, look, the UPS guy is trying to deliver an envelope that has the birth certificates in it, and he just called me to say that he's locked out at your gate. Could you open up the gate for him?"

A moment later, Mari came running out to open the gate for the "UPS guy" and there I was. Her father. She gasped. We looked at each other, I bent down and hugged her. She giggled, and we walked into the apartment. Mari announced: "Mama, look who's here."

Marina was at the stove, cooking. She turned and looked at me. A look of shock, anger, disappointment and desire crossed her face.

"Well, did you bring them?" she said.

"Yes," I said.

I walked over to her and hugged her. And the six children looked at us, their failed parents and their failed and complicated romance. We stayed in the embrace for a long time. I couldn't break away, but then started to do so. Marina put her hand on my back and pulled me closer for just a bit longer. The room fell silent.

No one spoke.

Finally, Marina spoke, searching for something to break the fragile and emotionally unsettling moment.

"So, did you take the bus?"

"No," I said. "I did Rideshare on Craigslist. I had the funniest ride."

She smiled. "Oh, okay, well, tell me about it."

And then I started to tell the story of me and Marty and his brother Alex. That was the one thing that Marina had always enjoyed about me, despite every other agony in our faltering and doomed marriage. I could still tell a story. I could still make her laugh.

The rest of the weekend blew by. We walked around the adjacent neighborhoods in San Francisco: Bernal Heights, Noe Valley, Mission Dolores. We chit-chatted and gossiped as we always had, and avoided at all cost any discussion of my disastrous career. The business was not launching as quickly as possible, there was little prospect for a stable life for all of us, and she was going to leave with the children for Germany. But that was for another visit. This was too sentimental a weekend for anything as sorrowful as that.

Monday morning, I got up early, kissed all of them goodbye. I'll be back in a week or so, I said. I got on a bus up to Marin, where I met Marty and we began the drive back. It was a melancholic ride but not as sad as I thought because it seemed things may have been resuscitated between Marina and me. The relentless mutual anger wasn't there. It was just a quiet weekend together, like in the old days, when we were happy and in love.

About two hours into the drive Marty woke up.

"Do you mind if I listen to the radio?" he said

"No, go ahead." I said.

He turned on the radio as I drove and began to press his AM presets. Not surprisingly – because we were more than 270 miles from Los Angeles – he got nothing but static.

"That's strange," he said.

"What?" I said.

"None of the stations are working."

"But those are all Los Angeles stations."

He was silent as he pondered the problem.

"They must not get radio service in this part of California."

I paused, and considered my response. Well, I suppose I could have explained the problem he was having with reception... but I stopped myself. Why go into it?

"You're right, Marty," I said. "They must not get radio service in this part of California."

Marty was clearly frustrated, so I decided to change the subject.

"What did you and Alex do?"

"Well, of course, we went out to dinner a couple of times," he said. "And then we went to the Muir Woods. Are you familiar with the Muir Woods?"

"I've heard of it but never been there."

"Well, it's a marvelous spot. Outstanding," he said. "They have redwoods there."

"Redwoods, you say."

"Yes, redwoods. Are you familiar with the redwood, David? Because it's an outstanding tree."

"I've seen redwoods," I said.

"So then you are familiar with how outstanding it is," he said.

"Yes," I said. "Intimately."

I finally decided to raise the question that was really on my mind since I saw Alex.

"Marty, I have to ask you."

"What is it?"

"Your brother Alex."

"What about him?"

"He doesn't really look much like you. I mean, he's got a completely different look."

Marty nodded knowingly for a long beat.

"David, since you asked, I will tell you something because you are a highly perceptive person, with an apparently scientific bent of mind."

"Well, I try," I said.

"Alex is only partially my brother."

"Partially?"

"We share the same mother."

"Ahhh…"

"My father, as you know, was a waiter at a very fancy restaurant in Manhattan. I believe we discussed that the other day."

"Yes, we did. The tuxedo. The celebrity clientele."

"Of course. It was an outstanding restaurant."

He nodded and pondered his next revelation.

"He worked evenings. Six days a week. And, well, as they say, a woman has needs."

His voice trailed off.

It was a truth. I had to give him that. A woman did have needs. And sometimes those were for a stable, quiet marriage to a stable quiet man. A woman sometimes has a need to not live out the lyrics to an Eminem song: we were like what happens when a tornado meets a volcano.

Chapter 17: "A Perfectly Sensible Decision"

"I love smoking," Julie said. "I hope you don't mind."

"I don't," I said, "But let me ask my kids."

I looked into the back seat of the Toyota Four Runner where my two teenagers, Coco and Saskia were sitting. Before I could even utter the question, I had the snarling lip curl look from Saskia.

"Uh..." I said to Julie.

"Okay," she said. "That's cool."

She turned to them. "We'll stop a few extra times so I can smoke outside, okay?"

Coco thanked her. Saskia muttered her own quiet but not convincing thanks.

Julie was just under six feet tall, with blonde hair that came down to her shoulder blades, a pretty and happy face, and a lean, athletic body. She was from Orange County and was on her way back to Berkeley to finish the spring semester of her third year there. She looked like what I had always imagined California girls looked like back when I was kid: tall, long blonde hair, pretty and happy faces and lean, athletic bodies.

We were taking the trip a week after Barack Obama had been inaugurated in late January 2009, marking the first time I had ever voted for a winning Presidential candidate. I tended toward the hopeless left-wing contenders and began my career as a voter in 1976 by working for Eugene McCarthy in a completely pointless third party campaign he waged that season. I have long harbored a hope that I be considered — sometime after my death — for the first alternate to St. Jude as the Patron Saint of Desperate Cases and Lost Causes.

"They seem cool," Julie said about Coco and Saskia, who were in 11th and 10th grade at the time. "What's the story on them?" she asked.

I gave her the short version. They were attending San Marino High School, and we were going up to San Francisco to say goodbye to their mother and two younger sisters, who were moving to Germany.

"Whoa, Germany," she said. "Why are they moving there?"

I told her the longer version. Marina is a German citizen and she was taking the two younger girls, Mariangela and Juliette, to Germany and live on the German welfare system there until I could stabilize my economic situation and bring everyone back home. I didn't comment on the sorrow or heartbreak of this decision, because it was too painfully obvious to me.

Except it didn't seem painful to Julie at all. It sounded completely sensible. One of those decisions that a perfectly sensible couple would come to after a perfectly sensible series of discussion. Unfortunately, neither Marina nor I could ever have been described as capable of perfectly sensible discussions. The decision had been nothing but anguish and sorrow for me. But, in retrospect, I think it was a huge relief for Marina to be leaving, having never really liked America all that much to begin with. She was probably relieved to be leaving me as well.

"Man, this country sucks now," Julie said.

"Well, maybe things'll get better under Obama," I said.

Julie laughed.

"I doubt it," she said.

Saskia laughed at Julie's laugh. Saskia likes cynical people who say cynical things.

"You agree with me?" she said, looking at Saskia in the mirror.

"My mom says nothing is going to change," Saskia said.

"Your mother has a very bleak view of the future," I said. "She never thinks things are ever going to get better."

"Well, maybe she's right, David," said Coco.

"Man, I'm riding with a bunch of young cynics," I said. "I'm in my fifties and I think things are going to get better, and you guys are all young and think things aren't. What the hell?"

Julie had a theory. She'd had this discussion with her father many times. He was in his late sixties now, had grown up in Southern California, gone to UCLA, run a successful business, retired, remarried, had a baby and spent most of his days surfing.

"This country topped out in about 1987, as far as I can tell," said Julie. Which would show an amazing amount of perception on her part because 1987 was one year before she was born.

"Since then it's been pretty much downhill. I mean, look at me. I'm in my third year at Berkeley, and I'm gonna transfer to Mills College to finish up because I can't get my English degree in four years at Berkeley because I can't get all the classes I need."

"I've heard that's a problem," I said.

"It's a huge problem now in California," she said. "It'll take me two more years to finish at Berkeley and tuition is really expensive, so it's actually cheaper for me to go to a private college and finish in one year than it is to go to Berkeley, even though I prefer Berkeley because it has one of the best English departments in the country. But whatever. Their loss, not mine."

That was true. We had moved to California in 1991, and one of the selling points I had argued to Marina was the UC system was a great university system and it was really cheap for California residents. It was one of the biggest reasons that California such a great place to live.

The relentless degradation of public life and public institutions in recent years had really taken their toll on my optimism, but I was still sticking with it: California was the best place, America was the best country. I really believed what the Italian essayist Luigi Barzini wrote back in the 70s, that in the end, America would come down on your side, the side of the angels.

It was a hard view to hold on to. I had lived in San Marino, one of the wealthiest suburbs of Los Angeles, and, as a result, I had gotten to know a number of very rich people. And I discovered something surprising: they were some of the angriest people I'd ever known. As far as many of them were concerned, the government wasn't taxing them to provide for the public good; the government was stealing from them to redistribute their money to people who weren't as smart or successful or hard working as them. Most of these guys were my age and had grown up in Southern California, and they resented the changes that had swept across the region in the ensuing fifty years. To them, the region had gotten too big, had too many immigrants, too much crime and too much trouble.

It wasn't the tantalizing diverse cosmopolitan region of my imagining. It was a good place that had simply gone to hell.

Julie didn't really strike me as one of those layabouts stealing money from my tax-paying friends in San Marino. She wanted to go to a great public university with cheap tuition, study English, become a teacher, get married, buy a house and enjoy her life and go surfing with her dad every day after she was done teaching. She didn't want to leave college with an oppressive load of debt that would constrict her life decisions for the next ten years, force her to leave California for a job, and live somewhere in exile until she was middle-aged and had saved enough and her family was stable enough that they could maybe afford to move to within twenty miles of the beach.

To be honest, she seemed to have a better grip on the reality of life in California nowadays than I did.

But, according to her, she could see it coming. And so could Coco and Saskia. They could see it coming with their own lives. Both of them could hardly wait to leave California. We said goodbye to Julie at Ashby BART station and rode the train over to the Mission District to meet up with the rest of our family.

The next day, I got dressed up in a pair of dress pants that no longer fit because I hadn't been eating much and had lost so much weight. I figured if I was going to be a supplicant to the German government, I should at least look like a respectable person.

Marina and I went to the German Consulate in San Francisco, where I presented them a notarized letter indicating that I could not afford to support my two youngest daughters and that I was granting custody to my wife, Marina, and permission to take them to Germany. There they would -- being German citizens -- receive sufficient state support to provide for rent, food, education, and health insurance. Things I could only partially and sporadically provide them.

The young woman at the German Consulate looked at me when I handed her the letter. "I know you are very sad to do this, but perhaps this can help," she said in her perfect German-accented English. "It's a good thing they are German nationals." Her sympathy touched me.

I nodded and smiled half a smile.

There was a long silence and then Marina spoke.

"Okay, then," she said. "I'll book the flights."

Chapter 18: "What She Could Not Say"

"Who are you getting a Rideshare with?" Marina asked.

"A Romanian industrial designer who had been in San Francisco visiting his girlfriend," I said.

"Ach, Romanians," Marina said. "Watch out for him. They're all thieves."

Coco and Saskia laughed. They enjoyed Marina's petty stereotypes that frequently turned out to be true.

A moment later Nicolae pulled up. Coco and Saskia cried as they hugged Marina goodbye and then their two younger sisters. We got in Nicolae's car, and by then we were all sobbing.

"Forty dollars," Nicolae said, charmlessly. I handed him the money and we pulled away. Coco and Saskia looked back at their mother and sisters and waved until we turned the corner and were gone.

A week later, I returned and accompanied Marina, Mariangela and Juliette to the San Francisco Airport. I hugged the girls very hard, not wanting to let them go.

"I love you," I said to Marina, but she didn't say anything.

"Please," I said. "Just say it."

"I can't," she said. "Not now."

They passed through the security gates, and the girls, twelve and ten, looked back at me. Then they waved and were gone.

I didn't know when I would see them again.

Chapter 19: "Now What? When There Is No What, Only Now"

I came home on a long, anonymous ride with someone I do not remember now. Coco and Saskia were safely ensconced in relatively stable living situations, but I was homeless again. As I got off the Gold Line at the Lake Avenue Station in downtown Pasadena and walked up the stairs from the station in the center of the freeway and walked toward Colorado Boulevard, the aire smelled like snow. It had rained the day before in Los Angeles and the San Gabriel Mountains, which rise above Pasadena, had a coating of snow on their highest elevations.

Sometimes the air in Los Angeles is so sweet with the smell of blooming flowers you can almost taste it. Usually in the winter, just as the mountain laurel trees are blooming and a big, col storm has swept through and scrubbed the dirt from the sky and the streets and snow settles in San Gabriel Mountains. This is the best time to be in Los Angeles. Everything feels clean.

"Now what?" I thought to myself as I walked along Lake Avenue, with no place to spend the night quite yet. It was a pretty night; the air was sweet and snowy.

I didn't have an answer.

There was no "what" now. I would have to think of something. I'm homeless. I've lost everything I ever owned. And now I've lost my wife and my family. That's a bit of a big thought. Things'll get better, I said to myself. I just know it.

Actually, I didn't know it.

I'll just have to come up with something.

What was the one thing I was really great at? What is my strength? Well, clearly it was nothing that provided an income.

But it was this: my greatest strength is an improvisational sense for life. I can figure things out. I had done it before.

Back in the 1970s, my high school -- along with just about every other high school in America, I bet, -- put on a production of a pedantic play called "The Night Thoreau Spent in Jail."

It was about an incident in the 1850s in which the American Transcendentalist, Henry David Thoreau, refused to pay a poll tax which had been levied to pay for the Mexican-American war. (On a side note, the idea of actually financing a war with existing tax revenues is something we ought to revisit, but that's another story). So he was jailed for one night and, oh, boy, that was something that idealistic 16 year-olds and their 20-something theater teachers could relate to in 1972.

I worked on the stage crew for our school's production and I remember thinking the play was pretty lame, but that one girl who was on the crew with me named Jill looked really good in that blue turtleneck and jeans and penny loafers and probably it would be great if I actually talked to her and I wonder if she would go out with me to a movie or something and hah, probably not, she probably likes John Thorvilson although he does have a girlfriend... oh, crap! I'm supposed to be pulling up the curtain right now!

Anyway, I never actually spoke with that Jill girl, although I did run into her about twenty years later and you know what? She still looked great in a turtleneck and jeans.

So let that be a lesson to you: talk to the Jill girl.

This is, in fact, the main lesson I took from "The Night Thoreau Spent In Jail."

Eight years later, I myself spent a night in jail. I wasn't protesting a war or engaged in criminality, but a woman was involved. I haven't had much of a career as a criminal.

Although if being a jerk were a crime, I think I probably could have spent a fair portion of the late 90s and early 00s fully incarcerated.

In 1980, I was working as a journalist. A newspaperman, in fact. I was the Managing Editor of the International Falls, MN, Daily Journal. It was a five-day-a-week afternoon paper. On my first day on the job, the publisher, Dave, took me to the back of the building to a loading dock.

"You see that truck there?" he said to me.

"Yeah?" I said.

"Your job is to make sure that they are full of newspapers every day by 1 p.m.," he said "If you can't do that, you're fired."

That was my romantic life as a newspaperman. I made sure the paper got put together every day. I didn't really hone my skills as a reporter or writer because, well, I just didn't have the time. My job was confined to making sure that day's edition got through the production cycle and on to the presses and in time to fill the trucks by 1 p.m.

It wasn't a job I was particularly suited to because it involved a careful eye for detail.

One of the other downsides of this job was that at the time I had a girlfriend who lived seven hours away in southwestern Wisconsin.

So, to summarize, I had a job I wasn't particularly good at, but I did have a girlfriend I never saw.

Who could ask for anything more out of life?

Anyway, one weekend in early April, I decided to go down to visit this girlfriend. I left International Falls at 1 p.m., just as the trucks were leaving the loading dock. I was driving my car, a 1967 Volkswagen Station Wagon. It was not a great car.

Once you leave International Falls, there's really nothing but pine forest for a couple hours. Not that there's anything wrong with pine forest for two hours. But if, say, for example, your engine seizes up about one hour into this section of the trip, the wonders of a two hour drive through a vast pine forest immediately loses its appeal.

I pulled the car over and walked for a bit and found a gas station/roadhouse/grocery store/post office. I asked the guy there what his recommendation would be. He suggested a towing company in Virginia, MN, about 45 minutes away.

I called and arranged the tow. It was $50. Which, in 1980 David Raether dollars, was an astronomical sum. Especially since I left International Falls with $100. This was back in the day when I didn't have a credit card or much money. Kind of like my situation in 2012.

Virginia is known as "The Queen City of the Range." The Queen being Elizabeth I, the supposed Virgin Queen of England back in the 1500s, and the Range being the Mesabi Range, a range of low iron-filled mountains in north central Minnesota. Virginia is an iron-mining town, along with several other towns in that area filled with orange dust from the iron just below the surface, including Hibbing (hometown of Bob Dylan and Kevin McHale), Eveleth, Mountain Iron, etc.

The mines here are vast open pit mines. They produced the raw materials that formed the steel that powered the American economic engine from the 1920s to the 1970s. If you had an American car during the 1960s, the steel came from iron mines carved out of the Mesabi Range.

This area is known as the Iron Range. Or, in Minnesota, simply, "The Range." If you tell someone in Minnesota, "I'm from the Range" it implies a certain toughness of character, a certain earthiness and hardheaded working class badassness that is to be admired, esteemed, really.

Take two outstanding Minnesota writers, for example.

Bob Dylan? He's from The Range.

F. Scott Fitzgerald? He's not from The Range.

Both are great, great writers. But now let's say you were in a bit of a jam and needed some help. You wouldn't ask F. Scott Fitzgerald. You'd ask Bob Dylan. Why? Because he's from The Range. See how that works?

Pretty simple, really.

So there I was in Virginia, down to $50. I called my girlfriend and told her I wouldn't make it and explained why. She seemed disappointed, but not devastated. And it turned out later she was already seeing somebody else and I had just freed up her weekend. So that was a good thing for her.

Well, what do you do when you're 23 years old, footloose and fancy-free in Virginia, MN, and have $50 burning a hole in your pocket?

I went drinking.

And there were plenty of saloons to drink in in Virginia. Around 10 p.m., I realized I was down to about $40 (drinks were cheap in those days), and didn't want to spend another penny in Virginia. A motel room would have cost me about $19. Hmmm... Do I really want to spend $19 on a motel room in Virginia?

Nope.

I walked over to the Virginia city jail, and introduced myself to the officer at the desk.

"Hi," I said. "I was traveling from International Falls down to see a friend in Wisconsin and my car died about 45 minutes north of here and I spent all my money on the tow into town and I can't afford a motel room."

"Yeah," the officer said.

"So what I was wondering is if I could spend the night here at the jail?" I asked.

"Sure," he said. "We've got plenty of cells available right now."

He pointed out that should "trouble erupt" (and this was always possible in Virginia), and they needed the cells for arrestees, I would have to leave.

No problem, I said.

And he registered me in the jail log. I was listed as "David Raether, boarder."

He showed me the cell and told me to keep the door open because he didn't want to have to come back and unlock me.

And so I spent the night in jail.

Two things I learned:

One: Jail cells are not designed for your sleeping comfort.

Two: I didn't have a cathartic moment of transcendental vision.

The next morning, I got up and called my friend Tom in International Falls and asked if he would come down and get me. He said yes. I went over to a bar that I had established a beachhead the prior night.

Bars opened early in the morning in Virginia in those days to accommodate the drinking needs of miners getting off the 11 p.m. to 7 a.m. shift in the mines. While I was nursing a morning beer, I got to talking to an old guy there who was, like me, a big fan of Sam LoPresti.

Sam LoPresti was a native of the Range, and in 1941 was the goalie for the Chicago Blackhawks, one of the few Americans in the NHL at the time. He set an NHL record that year for most saves by a goalie in a single game in a game with the Boston Bruins, who happened to have Frankie Brimsek in the nets for them at the time. Brimsek was also from The Range. LoPresti faced 83 shots in that game, and let in two, and lost the game.

"Man," I said to the old guy, "I would love to meet Sam LoPresti and congratulate him on that game he had against the Bruins in 1941 where he made 61 saves."

"Oh, he made a lot more saves than 61," the old guy said.

Now, it should be pointed out that if an NHL goalie makes 40 saves in a game nowadays, it is considered a remarkable performance.

"Nah," I said. "It was 61."

"Well, let's go ask him," he said. "C'mon. He owns the bar across the street."

And so we did. We crossed the street to a bar called Sam and Bucks, which Sam LoPresti owned with his partner, Angelo Buccanero. We entered the bar, and there was Sam LoPresti, a strong, bald-headed man in his early 60s.

"Hey, Sam," the old guy said. "This kid here says you only made 61 saves in that game against the Bruins in 1941!"

Sam LoPresti laughed.

"No," he said. "It was 81."

"81?" I said. "You made 81 saves in that game against the Bruins in 1941."

"Yup," he said. "81 saves."

And then he laughed.

"Almost 40 years ago now," he said.

I settled in to a stool on the bar, and we started to talk about hockey and then about life on The Range. It's a good life I got going here, he said. Yup. Things have pretty much worked out good for me.

My friend showed up and I got up to leave.

"Well, it was a big honor to meet you, Mr. LoPresti," I said.

He shook my hand.

"Hey, thanks for knowing about me," he said. "It's a big honor to have a young guy like you to come in outta nowhere and tell me I was a hell of player."

I smiled.

"Because I was," he said. "I was a hell of a player."

He died in 1984, but I think of him from time to time and the night I spent in jail in Virginia, MN, Queen City of the Range.

The point is this: once you realize you're screwed and there's nothing you can do about, just go with it. Improvise. Let the trail you have landed upon open up before you. It might lead to more sorrow. But it might just lead you to Sam and Buck's, and you might meet Sam LoPresti. Or someone like that. Someone you never expected to ever meet. Someone who might change your life.

And another thing: talk to the Jill girl. She might like you, and that might change your life. You just never know.

Chapter 20: "The Guy Who Knew About Chickens"

Over the next couple of years, I frequently traveled between Los Angeles and San Francisco to visit my oldest daughters, who were living in the Mission District of the city during that time. Sometimes I went on my own, sometimes with either Coco or Saskia or both. We were all lost souls, bouncing and improvising our ways through America and our lives. The conversations I had with the people I met on these Rideshares changed my life. They helped me to heal and inspired me to start again.

****

There is something deeply untamed about Los Angeles, almost feral. It doesn't operate like other cities. It is profoundly bewildering to visitors, particularly visitors from the East Coast. Los Angeles doesn't seem to have a center. It has dozens of centers. It isn't laid out on a grid. It is laid out on a maze. The centers of wealth are clear and obvious. The centers of power are not. It is an ugly city with tidy slums.

It is also the most densely populated metropolitan area in the United States, according to the Census Bureau. More than 7,000 people per square mile. More densely populated than New York City.

This always surprises people when they hear it. How is that possible? The reason is fairly simple: New York City stops. It hits the Hudson and basically, that's it. Sure, there's New Jersey, but once you cross the Hudson, things thin out pretty dramatically.

Things don't thin out in L.A. It is city for miles. Many people flying into LA for the first time at night are struck by how long they see the lights of the city. The jet flies for an hour over nothing but city as it comes in from the east.

And yet in all of that urban density and sprawl, there remains within the city a wild and uncontrollable heart. Griffith Park, for instance, which is only a couple miles from downtown LA, is more than 4,000 acres of almost pure wilderness right in the middle of the city. It is filled with cougars, bear, deer, and oddballs living off the grid.

Don't believe me? The Los Angeles Times reported on Aug. 14, 2012, that a cougar is wandering unmolested around the park. The park is only a few miles from downtown Los Angeles. So while you're sitting there among throngs slamming down cocktails at L.A. Live after a Lakers game, just know that a few miles away, up in those wooded hills, there's a cougar lying in wait. Go ahead. Make a wrong turn into his territory.

And then there are the urban farmers. Urban farming is, of course, illegal in Los Angeles. Which means, of course, that it is a regular activity. Thousands of people keep chickens in their backyards. We ran into one of them on a ride up to visit Sasha and Claire in early autumn, 2009. There were five of us in the car: me, Coco and Saskia and the driver, a Jamaican woman who was going to visit her boyfriend in San Francisco. And this guy who knew a lot about chickens.

The Guy Who Knew About Chickens was about 27 years old, and lived in the Echo Park neighborhood of Los Angeles. One of the rules of Los Angeles neighborhoods is if your neighborhood has the word "Park" in it, it's not so hot a neighborhood. The chicken guy had lived in Echo Park all his life, he said. He lived on what he sounded like a particularly unfashionable street that had a lot of animal life: pit bulls, feral cats, and his chickens.

He was a big believer in chickens. And he liked them -- for their eggs, for their personality, and for eating. Although he loved chickens, he had no problem slaughtering one of his every once in a while, especially when they got older and stopped producing eggs at a reliable rate.

"Older chickens are mainly good for soup," he said. "I wouldn't really eat them, you know, in the roasted format."

He said every chicken had a distinctive personality. Some were bossy, some demure, some neurotic, some laid back and some sneaky. The sneaky ones were the ones you had to watch out for. They were always figuring out some way into your garden, where they would eat your vegetables. The bastards.

"Eat the sneaky ones early," was his advice. "You'll spare yourself a lot of trouble."

This, I told Coco after the ride, is valuable life advice you can apply to just about any situation, especially in Los Angeles. Eat the sneaky ones early.

Chapter 21: "Not Every Day Is a Gift"

People who engage in Rideshare are, almost by necessity, a more open-minded bunch, less dogmatic about life and its prospects, largely reasonable. It's hard to be doctrinaire about things when you take a complete stranger in your car for six hours.

And many of the drivers I've ridden with are women.

When I tell people this, generally they are shocked. But Ridesharing is different than hitchhiking. You answer the ad on Craigslist, they get your phone number and email address, they can see who you are by looking you up on Facebook, and they talk to you on the phone to get a sense of who you are.

The main attribute you both are looking for is this: Is this person gonna be cool about the ride? For me, I'm just trying to get to San Francisco or LA. I'm not looking to get into a big political or religious discussion, I'm not looking for a lifelong friend, and I usually don't even get a last name. In fact, one of the reasons I haven't used last names is because I don't know them anymore, if I ever knew them at all. It's Paul, it's Vicky, it's Erica, it's Juan Carlos. That's all you get. That's all you really need.

It's a long boring ride, gas is expensive, and nobody really likes doing it alone. Are you going to be cool about it?

Of course you can fly, but at $170 at the cheapest round trip, that gets expensive. And you have to go through all the guilty-until-proven-innocent indignities of air travel nowadays. Or you could take the train. Well, actually, you can't. There is no direct train between Los

Angeles and San Francisco. There are trains that go up the coast, which are fine if you're retired and don't mind spending a day or so making the trip.

Or, there's Greyhound. Which generally takes about eleven hours.

And then there's Rideshare. If you're with a decent driver and they can pick you up reasonably close to where you live and drop you off reasonably close to where you're going, you're looking at five and a half or maybe six hours city to city. And usually the company isn't bad. Sometimes, it's actually kind of nice.

Karen was driving a rental car. We met at the Budget Rental Car office on Arroyo Parkway in Pasadena when it opened on a Saturday morning. She was driving up to the Bay Area in the rental ahead of her husband, who was driving up with all of the gear she needed for a multi-media presentation she was making the next day.

"What's the presentation about?" I asked.

"Surviving cancer," she said.

Karen, now forty-two, had been diagnosed with breast cancer during her junior year at Stanford, dropped out to go through treatment, which included a mastectomy. She tried to return to Stanford, but found herself not so interested in Stanford anymore. She returned to Los Angeles, took a year off and spent a lot of time walking around her hometown of Santa Monica. She eventually finished her undergraduate degree at UCLA, and embarked on a career.

Five years later, cancer was detected in her remaining breast. A mastectomy was suggested as an option and she took it. She wanted it all cut out of her, she said. Every molecule of the cancer.

I have to be honest, I fought the urge to look at her chest. I mean, what was left?

And then she sort of called me on it.

"I've got nothing up here now," she said.

"Sorry," I said. "I was, you know... wondering."

"Yeah, well, now you know," she said.

"Again," I said. "I'm sorry."

"That's okay," she said.

When I met her, she'd been cancer free for fourteen years. She had married a few years earlier, and lived in a small house on a hill in the Highland Park neighborhood of Los Angeles. She showed me pictures of the house -- a little bungalow of the type so common on the east side of LA. It was one of those houses built in the 1930s with the low sloping roofs, big porches, and small rooms. The kind of house that is easy to keep cool even in the tremendous summer heat we get on the east side of Los Angeles and the San Gabriel Valley.

It was a modest house, the way most houses were built to be in the 1920s and 30s in Los Angeles, when it was still a sleepy Western outpost of America, a place you went to retire or get away from the winter, or hide out from the family that always seemed to know best what you should be doing with your life in Minnesota or Michigan or Ohio.

These houses are never elegant or refined or eye-catching. They seem to be like one of those people who moves slowly, talks slowly, breathes easily and live to be 113, and don't really have much to say for themselves.

She said when she saw the house she wanted it immediately because it made her think of the old Crosby Stills and Nash song, "Our House." As soon as they bought it, she did what the song preached: she bought two cats, and she kept them in the yard, life used to be so hard, but everything is easy 'cause of you. Karen had been on as fast a track as you can be in: the right high school, getting into Stanford, everything would move forward in a big way. And then she got breast cancer at nineteen. And everything slowed down.

She gives lectures to cancer survivor groups now, and was driving up to talk to a group in Berkeley.

She was unsentimental about the disease and its impact on her life. She had twice had a brush with death. But it didn't make her religious or lustful for life or panicked. And what she told me has stayed with me since that ride.

"Not every day is a gift," she said. "Some days are just a hassle, no matter how much you have survived."

Chapter 22: "Wait a Minute, Is Your Dad Mexican?"

I was standing at the North Hollywood Red Line station, next to the guy who sells tamales, just as I had promised Tony. I was returning to San Francisco for Christmas, 2009, after a one day return trip to bring Coco back for a soccer game. On that particular Christmas break I went back and forth between Los Angeles and San Francisco six times to accommodate the kids' Christmas break sports schedules and a family visit to the City. One way up it was all three of us, then back with Coco a few days later for a soccer tournament, then back up myself and then back down with Saskia for a water polo tournament, then back up with both of them and then when break was over back with all three of them. All with Rideshare. This was a solo journey back up to the City.

I had told Tony I have grey hair and that I would be wearing a blue sweater and green sunglasses. I'm a fifty-four-year-old professional, I'd said. I always made it a point to use the word professional because if you tell a prospective Rideshare driver that you're a fifty-four-year-old professional, you sound like a reliable and safe rider for the six-hour drive. Although, technically, a professional is probably somebody who has an advanced degree in one of the professions, like medicine or law or accounting, and, to be honest, I was a professional only in the sense that occasionally I am paid to do something.

My phone rang. It was Tony.

"Hey, bro, the guy I'm riding with, Maurice, is looking for you. He's a big black dude in a gray sweatshirt."

I turned around to look, and there was Maurice. He was black and had a gray sweatshirt, but he wasn't particularly big. He had a pleasant, unlined, and happy face. In his early 30s at most.

"Are you David?" he said.

"Yup," I said.

He smiled.

"Tony said you're a big black dude," I said.

"Oh, man, I hate when he calls me that," he said, with a tone that suggested the weariness of someone who just had a familiar prank pulled on him. Again.

Tony was a short Mexican-American guy. He and Maurice had the sort of relationship that seemed to feel like it was entering its fourth decade together, even though neither of them appeared to be more than thirty-two years old.

On this ride, the music would be rap. A broad selection of the major rap artists. "Look, man," said Maurice, "I promise we won't listen to rap the whole way."

First of all, I didn't mind if we did. Second, we listened to rap the whole way up.

As we were driving through Gilroy, Tony started getting upset about the smell of garlic. Gilroy is, of course, the self-proclaimed garlic capital of the world, and the overpowering smell of the huge fields surrounding the town really don't put anyone in the mood to debate this claim. It's actually fairly pleasant, in an overpoweringly pungent sort of way.

Tony, however, hates garlic. Just the thought of it upsets him. He started ranting against garlic: the smell of it was disgusting, it was like a bad version of onions; no, it was worse than that – garlic smelled like the socks of a guy who hadn't changed them in a few weeks. It was a rant Maurice had no doubt heard a hundred times. So to get Tony's mind off the smell of garlic, Maurice started talking about cars.

"What's your dream car, Dave?" he asked me.

"A bicycle."

"Really?" said Maurice. I could tell this was an astounding thought to him. "What kind of bicycle? One of them Lance Armstrong bikes that weighs six ounces and cost fifty thousand dollars?"

"Nope," I said. "I want a newer version of the Bianchi Milano I have now."

"What kind of bike is that?"

"It's black and looks kinda retro and costs about six hundred bucks."

Tony and Maurice both looked back at me. There was silence in the car for a moment, and then Maurice looked back at the road.

"Man, you are a funny white dude," he said.

"I want a Maserati," he said. "What about you, Tony?"

"I don't care what kinda car I have," said Tony. "Just so long as it works. But check this out. My dad is dreaming of getting a Silverado pickup. That's all he can talk about."

"Wait a minute," said Maurice, studying Tony for a moment as if he'd never looked at him closely. "Is your dad Mexican?"

And then we all three of us laughed hard and for a long time. Why? Because most times people aren't what you expect them to be, but other times they are exactly what you think they might be.

Chapter 23: "When I Fall In Love As Sung By Nat King Cole"

You can hear it in your head right now, can't you? Almost see it. Nat King Cole, in a sleek gray suit, standing by a piano, singing "When I Fall In Love." And you can't help but sing along, especially when you get to this point in the song:

And the moment I can feel that

you feel that way too

is when I fall in love with you—

Saskia, my fourth daughter was 17 years old at the time, and we were riding back home to Los Angeles in April 2011, after a visit to San Francisco to see my oldest daughter, Alexandra (Sasha), who was visiting from New York. Now we were riding with Rebecca and Jessie in Rebecca's ten year-old Prius. It was a 2001, the first year the Prius was sold in the US, and it still looked like a generic Japanese subcompact. Uh-oh, I thought.

This is going to be one of those knees-in-my-chest-for-six-hours in this midget car. Fortunately, Rebecca was so short (the top of the trunk came up the middle of her chest) and kept the seat so far forward while she drove, I could stretch out comfortably. Probably one of the few times a six-foot tall man could honestly say he stretched out comfortably in the back of a 2001 Toyota Prius.

Rebecca was about 4'9", with thick, muscular and inelegant legs. She lived in San Diego and was on her fourth year attending her fifth community college. She said she was studying artificial intelligence.

"Or something like that, "she said. I don't really know what I'm studying. I just like taking classes and learning stuff."

Jessie was finishing up a chemistry major at UC-Berkeley and was going home to Poway, California, a pleasant suburb of San Diego. They had had known each other since high school, but it wasn't until a holiday party at a friend's house just after Christmas, that, for reasons no one can ever explain really, a spark lit between them.

Jessie was a foot taller and about 100 pounds heavier than Rebecca. Jessie wore a shapeless black billowy skirt that came to just about the knee, purple tights that were a bit too large, thick brown sensible sandals and a dark red sleeveless top. She intended to finish her degree during the first semester of the following school year at Berkeley, and then head to grad school and become a researcher. She seemed the more serious of the two women, but she giggled at just about everything Rebecca said. She acted like Rebecca was just the cutest thing on the planet, and I imagined that she made Rebecca feel so happy that when Rebecca looked at Jessie she saw that beautiful black hair and bright intelligent eyes and loved how she was so smart and could talk about anything.

We had been in the car for ten minutes when I whispered to Saskia, "Are they a couple?" Saskia looked at me, shook her head and mouthed "Obviously."

I was pretty sure that, fifty years after Nat King Cole crooned the words, the moment that Rebecca could feel that Jessie felt that way too is when they fell in love.

After it became clear to them that Saskia and I were cool about it, they began to talk sweetly and low to each other, and sometimes caressed each other's leg from time to time. At one point, Rebecca let out a long, contented sigh after Jessie ran her hand along Rebecca's leg and leaned over and gave her a kiss on the ear.

They were so in love, it just made me happy to be with them. I imagined the night it happened for them, when they fell in love. It would have been a cool, breezy San Diego winter night, and they were out walking together after that holiday party. Suddenly, they stopped, looked each other in the eye, and one of them leaned in closer. From an open window of a nearby house, maybe they heard the sound of Nat King Cole singing a ballad by Victor Young and arranged by Nelson Riddle.

In a restless world like this is,

love is ended before it's begun.

And too many moonlight kisses

seem to cool in the warmth of sun.

It seemed to Saskia and me as we talked about them later, when Rebecca and Jessie gave their hearts, it was completely. It was, as I said to Saskia, "an old-fashioned romance of the best kind, the kind they write songs about."

Chapter 24: "Pranjay Loves Los Angeles"

I was meeting Pranjay at the Dublin BART station by six and riding with Pranjay in his Nissan Quest minivan back to L.A. He was a few inches shy of six feet tall, and seemed to be a few pounds short of 100 pounds. There was nothing to him.

Pranjay was working on a fellowship in reconstructive dentistry at UCLA and was driving back to school after visiting family in Dublin, CA. He was a quiet person, and didn't seem in the mood to talk. He seemed at first like one of those guys who doesn't have many spare thoughts in his head outside of finishing his education, then marrying the right woman, then buying a proper house and then living a proper life with a neat yard and proper children. And then engaging in a proper retirement and then a quiet and uncommented upon death. He seemed like, a person so far beyond dull it would be difficult to think of a word for.

"Do you mind if I play my iPod?" he asked.

"No problems," I said. And closed my eyes and leaned my head against the window and figured I would fall asleep. And then I woke up. Pranjay had the most eclectic iPod I've ever run across: Indian pop, Guns N Roses, Russian pop, Loretta Lynn, Brazilian jazz, Jimi Hendrix and Johnny Cash. And he liked to sing along. And he had a lovely and unafraid singing voice.

He particularly liked "I Walk the Line" and asked if I would mind if he sang along. With some hesitation, given my previous experiences with driver/singers, I said no, I didn't mind.

So he did. It looked like so much fun, I joined in. And then he played it again and we reprised our trio with Johnny Cash again. We sang our way through his iPod. There were a number of Indian pop songs I had never heard that he sang at the top of his lungs for me. I enjoyed them quite a bit

As we got closer to the LA Basin, we were quiet again, and I asked him what he thought of his adopted city.

"Oh, I love Los Angeles," he said.

"Really?" I asked. "What do you love about it?"

"Well, it's clean, it's pretty and it works."

Now there were three words I had never associated with Los Angeles. I generally thought of it as dirty, ugly and disorganized, but intensely interesting.

"Seriously?" I asked. "You really think LA is clean and pretty and that it works?"

"Oh, absolutely!" he said. "It's a great city. Everyone should come here and see it!"

Pranjay had surprised me again.

We got to Van Nuys in six hours. He was headed to Westwood so he dropped me off at the Sepulveda Orange Line Station at noon. It was hot in Los Angeles, but the station was nearly empty. I transferred to the Red Line at North Hollywood, went down to Union Station, and then took the 79 bus home to South Pasadena. I went into my apartment. It was cool. I went upstairs, laid down to take a summer nap. I hummed to myself. I keep a close guard on this heart of mine. Because you're mine, I walk the line.

I fell asleep, and woke when the sun had already set.

Chapter 25: "Twompson Sets Us Straight on the Human Digestive System"

I found a Rideshare ad looking for a rider to Los Angeles. I called Paul and we agreed to the price and the pickup location and time. I was about to hang up when Paul stopped me.

"Hold on," he said. "One more thing. Are you a smoker?"

"No," I said. I had recently quit smoking, and was feeling pretty good about it.

"Because I'm allergic to cigarette smoke," he said.

This turned out to be the first in a long series of assertions by Paul that I didn't believe. We met at the Downtown Berkeley BART Station where I got in the backseat of a rented Dodge Caliber with a young woman who was in the middle of a modest nervous breakdown.

Paul, it seemed, was not planning on going to Santa Barbara, which she had hoped he would consider. She was a student at UCSB and needed to get there by five p.m. for a symposium. She had agreed to ride with Paul, hoping to convince him to go to Los Angeles by way of Santa Barbara.

But that wasn't going to happen. I was going to Pasadena, and so was the guy in the front seat, Morgan. There was no way we could be convinced to go all the way over to Santa Barbara just so she could get to her symposium on time. Which was actually okay because she had another Craigslist Rideshare lined up anyway with some guy over in San Francisco who was going to Santa Barbara.

We dropped her off after a block as her panic set in and she sprinted back to the BART station to go into San Francisco to hopefully meet the guy going to Santa Barbara and... well, to be honest, I was tired of thinking about her and her transportation problems, and anyway, Paul was about to pick up the last passenger.

After driving around for a few minutes, Paul found him. Oh, crap, I thought.

First of all, he was dressed up in what could best be described as a caricature of the young white rapper. San Francisco Giants cap on sideways, Giants jersey, pants pulled down to mid-ass, stupid gold bling that, of course, featured an enormous dollar bill symbol. (Hadn't that Sir Mix-A-Lot or somebody like that definitively done the giant dollar bill symbol back in the 1990s? Weren't we done with that yet?)

Feh, I thought. I gotta spend the next six hours in the back seat with THIS guy?

"Hi, I'm Twompson," he said as he sat down and adjusted himself into his seatbelt nervously. "And it's Twompson, not Thompson."

Feh with a headache, I thought.

Paul wrinkled his nose. He drove a block and suddenly said, "Excuse me, but I believe I smell smoke of some kind."

"Not me," I said. "I do NOT smoke."

Twompson fessed up. "Look, I'm sorry," he said. "I was staying with my sister, and she's an enormous pothead." My heart was soaring with hope. Maybe Paul would bounce Twompson for smoking!

"And did you smoke?" asked Paul.

Please, please confess, I thought. Get this guy out of here.

"Me? No. I don't do drugs," Twompson said, his face open and baffled and hurt.

"Well, okay," Paul said.

Stuck with Twompson. For six hours.

Paul was both the fastest and most inept driver I've ever ridden with. But he did illustrate P. J. O'Rourke's theory on the best kind of car. O'Rourke, who co-founded the

National Lampoon, and later wrote a series of funny books of journalism and advice, and has had a nice career as an automotive writer, said that the best kind of car is a rental car.

It's 376 miles from the Downtown Berkeley BART Station to the Lake Avenue Gold Line Station, where he dropped me and Morgan off in Pasadena. He made the trip in 5:16.

Most of the time he was driving about ninety miles an hour, but he had the unnerving habit of swerving every once in a while. A rented Dodge Caliber is probably a fine car for darting around a city but not really designed for high speed Formula One style driving on an Interstate.

Paul also had some of the most crackpot ideas I've ever heard of. The first he offered when we entered the Central Valley on the 5.

"You see all these clouds?" Paul said. "They're not real."

"They're not what?" said Morgan, the guy in the front seat. Morgan was in his late 20s, maybe early 30s. He was from a small town outside Birmingham, England, and had earned a Ph.D. in microbiology from UCLA and was doing postdoctoral work at Caltech on the flagella of microorganisms. Paul had chosen the wrong person to offer his theory that the clouds were the work of the government.

Morgan had two things going for him that made him a skeptic: he was a highly educated scientist and he was English, a nation of people, in my experience, who are dubious of just about everything Americans propose.

"Do you mean they're seeded?" Morgan said.

"No, I mean they're not real," Paul said. "The government makes them."

"The government makes them?" Morgan repeated. He wanted to make sure he had just heard what he had heard.

"Yes," said Paul. "Those clouds are made by the government."

Morgan was silent for a while. It was one of those uncomfortable moments where you realize you're going to be stuck inside a car for the next four hours or so with a Complete Nutjob. I really didn't know what to say. But Morgan came to the rescue.

"Well, then the government has done a fine job," he said.

Paul was stuck. He was sitting on a dynamite conspiracy story and we weren't biting. Time to move on to something bigger, he decided.

"The government does a lot of things. Did you know, for instance, that tsunamis are created by the government?" Paul said.

"What?" I asked.

"Oh, yeah," he said. "They create these tsunamis because it's good for the construction business."

"That sounds highly dubious," said Morgan. "I've worked with government scientists, and I can tell you that they are no smarter than non-government scientists, and believe me: none of us are capable of creating tsunamis or ending droughts."

There was silence in the car.

"Oh, really?" said Paul.

"Yes, really," said Morgan.

"I don't know about that."

"Well, I do," said Morgan, and then he stared out at the blank landscape of the Central Valley.

Mercifully, Twompson was listening to rap on his headset so Paul couldn't engage him in this conversation for support. I had the feeling he could have talked Twompson into anything.

"What do you think, David?" Paul asked me.

"I gotta be honest, Paul," I said. "I think that's crazy talk about the tsunamis and the clouds."

"Okay, then," said Paul, in that tone of voice a person has when he realizes nobody believes him about the giant monster right behind them who is about to eat them and then suddenly does. He dropped the conspiracy theories to focus on skittering across lanes at 95 miles per hour and terrifying me in the back seat.

Several hours later, as we were coming through the Santa Susana Mountains Paul couldn't resist anymore and started up again. He gave us his theory of vegetarianism.

"The reason I'm a vegetarian is because the human digestive system is most like that of the deer's," he said suddenly and for no particular reason. I don't recall anyone mentioning vegetarianism, but Paul liked non-sequiturs. Morgan didn't seem to really want to argue.

"I'm a vegetarian," said Morgan. "But not because of deer. I just don't care for the whole business of slaughter."

"Well, the deer and the human share a similar intestinal structure," Paul said. "And deer eat a diet of berries and other vegetational fiber. So, if it's good enough for deers, that's good enough for me."

Whatever, I thought. I don't care what you eat or why. Just please, please, please stay on the highway.

Twompson, however, had pulled out his ear buds a few minutes earlier, had listened to Paul's vegetarian theory and finally spoke.

For the next ten minutes, Twompson gave all of us a mini-lecture on the evolution of the human digestive system. It was a tour-de-force, completely brilliant demolition of the digestive system justification for vegetarianism – the elongation of the human intestine, the development of our teeth, the change in diet that occurred when we began to live in organized communities and began farming.

"Now, if you want to go vegetarian for moral reasons, that's fine," Twompson concluded. "But there is no scientific basis for arguing that the human species is by nature herbivore."

There was silence in the car for a few moments. Then I looked up to Morgan, the Ph.D. in microbiology and researcher at Caltech.

"Is he right?" I asked.

"Yes," said Morgan. "Basically, and, in fact, in every detail, Twompson is right."

I had completely misjudged Twompson. He wasn't just a poseur. He was a person who read books and was curious and intellectually ambitious and apparently brilliantly self-taught.

In a half hour, we arrived in Pasadena. And while I was happy to be back in such a short period of time, I regretted I hadn't spoken to Twompson more. I might have learned something.

Or maybe I, in fact, had.

Chapter 26: The Ten Commandments of Rideshare"

I had a Rideshare once with an engineer. He was about 26 and was going from Oakland to San Diego. There were five of us in the car, and he was charmless. But he had an interesting theory on Craigslist.

With the depression we're in – and this is a depression not a recession – there's a lot of excess capacity in the U.S. economy," he said. "What Craigslist does is provide a venue for this excess capacity to get put into use."

His point was illustrated by the car. He could drive from Oakland to San Diego by himself and have four empty seats in the car. And this would be excess capacity. So why not fill it with people who have a need for an inexpensive and only slightly uncomfortable ride along that route? It made perfect sense and I utterly endorsed it. Everyone should use Rideshare. I've never had a problem. Well, I've had some problems, but mainly they're irritating companions in the car. But I never felt unsafe.

That being said, should you decide to provide a Rideshare, or join in one, here are ten commandments I have picked up. All on one ride.

Thomas had a fifteen-passenger Ford van, and was heading to Santa Rosa on business. He hoped to get a few riders to share the cost of gas and was flexible about where he could drop us off.

Seemed ideal. I told him I was hoping to get to the East Bay, but dropping me off at any BART station in San Francisco would be fine. Worked for him. We agreed to meet at Union Station in downtown Los Angeles the next morning.

He would be driving in from Riverside and was going to pick up another rider at Union Station and a third at USC.

"So don't be late," he said. "I'll be there at nine a.m. sharp."

I'm a bit of a fussbudget when it comes to punctuality, so this sounded good to me. Nine o'clock rolled around and no Thomas. I called him. "I'm close," he said.

"I got a little lost but I'm on the 60 right now and should be in downtown LA in about fifteen minutes."

Well, I guess in comparison to being in Albuquerque, he was close to downtown LA, but if he was still on the 60, he wasn't really close to L.A. The 60 freeway runs from somewhere in the Inland Empire to somewhere near the edge of downtown LA. Not exactly to downtown LA, but just on the perimeter. Which, if you are familiar with the scope of downtown LA, is equivalent to being on the outer edges of the solar system. "My GPS says I'll be there in fifteen minutes," he said.

Forty minutes later he showed up.

The drive from downtown LA to San Francisco usually takes about six hours. Sometimes you're lucky and you get a guy who drives really fast and you can do it in five and a half hours, and sometimes you're unlucky with the traffic and too many stops and it takes six and a half or – worst case – seven hours.

Thomas took eight-and-a-half hours to get from Union Station to the outskirts of the city of San Francisco. Along the way, he began to drive me completely mad. He seemed to have figured out a way to do just about everything wrong with this Rideshare.

So, as a guide to future drivers and riders, here are David Raether's Ten Commandments of Rideshare.

1. *Eat breakfast before picking up your rides.* Don't stop at the world's busiest McDonald's next to USC and order a complicated breakfast and eat it slowly and carefully while sitting at a table inside.

We kinda want to get going here. We all realize that carefully chewing your food leads to good digestion, and that is an important part of overall health. But, dude, you're eating a McDonald's breakfast, which, as far as I can tell, could never be construed as an important part of overall health. JUST FINISH EATING, for God's sakes! Or finish eating in the van. WE WANT TO GET GOING!!

2. *I live here. If I tell you to go a particular route and disregard the complicated route the GPS is telling you, trust me.* So, for instance, you don't have to get on the freeway to drive from Union Station to USC. You can take side streets. Sure, it's not what the GPS says, but trust me. I live here. I've done this before. You live in Riverside. Maybe the freeway is the way to go anywhere in Riverside, but I know what the freeway is like here in downtown LA at this time of day, and trust me, side streets are better.

3. *We're not in this for companionship.* We're just trying to get somewhere. As fascinating and heartbreaking as your divorce may have been to you, it's really not as keenly interesting to us.

In fact, after about fifteen minutes of your complaining about your ex, I started to feel that she was eligible for sainthood for her ten years of putting up with you and your yammering about the hand creams you sold and how your new shoes fit so well because you had made a careful study of your foot, and the Montgomery Ward's store in your hometown in rural Illinois and how it's closed now but was such a busy enterprise back in your youth. Ten years she listened to this?! Holy crap, I couldn't take ten hours with you.

And it would have come close to ten hours, but I asked to get out at the Millbrae BART station, a long way away from the East Bay, because I simply could not spend another minute with you. And so did the other rider, a quiet man in his forties who wore two flannel shirts and said, "Whatever, man" to whatever you were talking about. "Oh, my God," he said as we rode up the BART escalator together. "That guy was unbelievable!"

"I know," I said. "I felt like shooting myself in the head the whole way up."

4. *You are not a better singer than Marvin Gaye.* Don't even try. I don't care if you think "a black man has gotta sing." Actually, sometimes a black man doesn't gotta sing.

In fact, sometimes a black man shouldn't sing. Sometimes, we can all just silently sit and listen to the glory of Marvin Gaye's voice. Unaccompanied.

5. *If I'm dozing off, don't wake me up to continue the discussion.* That's all I'm saying. Don't poke me as I doze off to tell me more about the changes you're planning for the seat covers of the other van you bought last week.

6. *Is there any way possible you could be louder when using a straw on your drink?* I believe the answer is no.

7. *I know what the speed limit is. How come we're the only ones obeying it?* And don't tell me it's because you're black and the CHP loves to pull over black drivers. I've ridden with black drivers, many of whom have gone way, way faster than you and were never pulled over. In fact, there go two cars driven by black guys right now. They're probably going 80, and probably will get to San Francisco and start having fun a million hours before I get there. My nerves are shot and my stomach hurts from fighting the urge to put my foot on the accelerator.

8. *If you asked for only $20 figuring you were going to get five or six riders and then only got three, don't ask us for extra money.* And don't smile and say it's a tip and hey, sorry, but a couple people didn't show up who said they were going to show up and this drive that you were hoping to make money on you're now losing money on. This all falls into the category of Not My Problem. Ask for $40 up front. I'll pay it. Don't ask me for more

money when we're stopped AGAIN, this time in San Jose and you're spending too much time cleaning your windows.

9. *I'm sure the skin creams you are going to sell at this flea market/sales convention/house party are fantastic. I don't need any.* No kidding. I really don't.

10. *It shouldn't take 8.5 hours to drive from USC to the Millbrae BART Station.* It really, really, REALLY shouldn't.

Chapter 27 "Looking For a Woman to Hang Out With"

It was a clear and blustery day in San Francisco, one of those beautiful early November days in the City when there is no fog and the air is cool and there is a swirling wind and everything seems like it is in a sharp focus.

It was the first Saturday afternoon of November 2009. My daughter, Claire, had taken Coco and Saskia out thrift store shopping, but here I was, slumped on an old couch in their apartment, watching a soccer match.

Not just any soccer match, though. This was the Superclasico, the twice-annual, superheated match from Buenos Aires between the two great rivals of that city: River Plate and Boca Juniors. It was on Fox Soccer Channel. The Superclasico is one of my favorite sporting events to watch, especially when it is played at the creaky La Bombonera, the home stadium of my favored team, Boca Juniors.

A few years ago, the London newspaper the Daily Telegraph put out a list of the ten sporting experiences you must have before you die. On the top of the list: attending the Superclasico at La Bombonera.

And, in fact, even before I read that list, one of my life dreams was to go to Buenos Aires someday just to see this match. A friend of mine did it once. He flew down from Los Angeles to Buenos Aires on a Thursday, walked around the city on Friday, and went to the match at La Bombonera on Saturday. On Sunday morning, flew back to LA, and said he never felt the same about life after that. Everything about life suddenly seemed too short and passing and not quite enough. He didn't go to work for two days. Just stayed home with his wife.

Nine months later, he and his wife had another baby. It was a girl and they named her Sofia, which is the Greek word for wisdom. He isn't Greek.

This was our third trip up to San Francisco that fall for Coco, Saskia and me. Marina and the little girls had been in Germany for ten months, and we had been separated for 15 months. The job situation was still muddled, and I seemed no closer to getting them back than I was when they had left the previous winter. While I had managed to rent a place for myself, employment with the company where I provided market research was punctuated by bouts of optimism and despair about the fate of the company.

This was going to work!

This was going to be a disaster!

Unfortunately, that roller coaster was not what Marina was willing to accept anymore. The deal was simple: I had to have a long-term employment contract with a stable company providing health insurance and she would return. Nothing short of that. The problem was in 2009, that kind of job was not easy to come by.

Don't worry, I kept telling myself, things will work out. That's what I always told myself, even in the worst of it. It was a slender reed to hold on to, my mantra: things are gonna work out. I had no evidence this was ever going to be true. Still, it was sometimes the only thing I had going for myself. Things are gonna work out and we'll all be back together. Just like in the old days.

What else could I tell myself? It was over?

I just couldn't tell myself that.

As odd as it might sound, I didn't have the courage to give up.

"The girls are getting used to it here," Marina had told me a week earlier. "I'm making a life for myself here, you know, lessons, concerts; it's not ideal, but I'm making a life here, David."

A thought creeped in.

Maybe the move to Germany wasn't just about our financial situation. Maybe Marina had actually left me. It wasn't just unemployment and housing. It was deeper than that. She was done with me and the marriage.

I ran that thought through my head. It was the first time I remember actually thinking it. She was happy without me. Didn't want me anymore. Sure, if I suddenly got a job and everything, she might come back. Or she might not. I wasn't part of the equation of her life anymore. I mean, she hadn't actually said 'I love you' to me since 1998. But she seemed to still enjoy me on some level. It was still a marriage and I was still in love with her. Right?

We talked all the time, but only because I called. She never called to check on me. I always ended every phone call with "I love you" and she would respond, 'Okay' or 'Ja.' And that would be it.

Wow, there's a thought. It's over. The big David and Marina adventure is done.

I turned away from the soccer match and looked out the window. It was sunny and sharp outside. Sunny in San Francisco! What was I doing inside?

Unlike Los Angeles, where the status quo is always sunny, always bright and chaotic and frantic, San Francisco is completely different. It is often gloomy, usually overcast, but in a funny way, it felt cozy.

It never, ever, feels cozy in Los Angeles. L.A. isn't a cozy place. It is an exciting place, dangerous, dazzling, dirty, interesting, murderous and funny. But it is never cozy.

Maybe I'll take a walk, I thought. I could watch a replay of this game later. I don't mind watching soccer games even when I know the result. I can watch good games several times over, in fact. They are like chapters in a very long and complicated novel. Most are even worth rereading.

I put on a sweater -- a sweater! -- and a jacket, zipped it up and stepped outside. I would be walking around in a t-shirt in L.A. at this time of the year. But here I needed a sweater and a jacket on a sunny day.

Sasha and Claire lived in the Mission District, and I didn't really care for it all that much. It was all right in its way, but I knew what I wanted. I would walk west up 24th Street to the Noe Valley neighborhood. A family neighborhood. Settled. Mothers with strollers. Pleasant bars and coffeehouses. A nice cozy neighborhood.

Noe Valley seemed like a place where you could land and spend fifty years happily until you died in your sleep and all the neighbors would come to your funeral and tell stories about your life and laugh and then go home and have some soup, watch the news and go to bed in their warm cozy bedrooms, which seemed in abundance in Noe Valley, as far as I could tell. Probably it isn't that way, but this was how I imagined Noe Valley to be were I to live there.

I settled at a table in a coffeehouse and sipped a coffee. At the table next to me was a couple, both of whom appeared to be about my age, gray-haired and dressed in sweaters and slacks. The man was saying something and the woman was laughing and then agreeing and then the man would say something else and she would laugh a bit more and slap him gently on the arm and bend her head forward as she laughed.

It was conspiratorial talk, the kind that couples have.

I watched them for a while and then the woman slowly slid her hand across the small table and put her hand on the back of his hand. They looked at each other and he leaned into her and kissed her lightly on the lips and then looked at her and she smiled. And then he said something and she laughed again.

That was it.

That was what I was missing so much.

The presence of a woman.

A woman my age.

Man, I was lonely, but not just general loneliness or the alienation all of us feel even in a crowded room.

This was a very specific loneliness. I was lonely for a woman. Somebody to walk around the streets with. Someone to sit in a coffeehouse with and run stuff by. Someone to sit at a table with and read a section of the paper while she reads a book. Not sex. Just company. The company of a woman, and a woman my age.

What I had plenty of was male conversation. I could go to Kaldi, a coffeehouse in South Pasadena I frequented, and find a bunch of guys to talk to. But that wasn't what I wanted. I wanted a woman to talk to because women talk about things in different ways.

What I missed was sitting with a woman and gossiping and talking about clothes and people we liked or were disgusted with, as I imagined that couple in the coffeehouse was doing. A good conspiratorial conversation that couples have because sometimes when you are a couple, it is the two of you versus the world and the happiness of being a couple sometimes is in defeating the world by simply being happy together.

I walked back down the hill to the apartment and watched the end of the game. It was your typical madly passionate Argentine game, and after it was over I was excited by it and was thinking it would be great to explain what excited me about it to a woman. A smart one who didn't necessarily care about sports but would listen anyway and smile and laugh about it when you talked, the way I would smile and laugh when she talked about what she was interested in that I didn't care about.

Nah, forget it.

Just forget about it, David, I told myself.

Things'll work out.

Marina will be back soon enough and then you can talk to her again. I made a coffee and sat at the table by myself and drank it.

But what if Marina is gone for a really long time?

What if she never comes back?

She had a self-possessed and distant tone in her voice now when we talked. She was making plans for her life there. The kind of plans you make when you're settling into a place for a long time.

Nah, she'll come back.

I thought about the game, and then I thought about that couple in the coffee shop again, and then about my friends and their daughter Sofia.

You know, it wouldn't be the worst thing in the world to get to know a woman up here, someone just to hang out with when I came up with the kids.

Coco, Saskia, and I returned to L.A. on Sunday night on a Rideshare. I don't remember the ride, but Coco reminded me that the driver was the dullest guy we met on the Rideshares we did together. He said that guy talked a lot about insurance or finance or something like that and I completely drew a blank. Didn't remember him in the least. He said that he and Saskia sat in the back seat and rolled their eyes for five hours, and couldn't believe I was able to talk to a person that dull for that long. I don't remember a word of it.

On Monday I was working on yet another research project when I decided I would do what I'd seen dozens of men do on library computers—and had been so disdainful of — I would post something in the personals ads — men seeking women — on Craigslist.

We were going up to San Francisco in three weeks for the long Thanksgiving weekend. I would run an ad, looking for a woman. I typed a headline.

*"**Visiting from Los Angeles, looking for a woman to hang out with.**"*

Then the ad.

"I'm a former television writer up from LA and will be in San Francisco for the Thanksgiving weekend. I'm looking for a woman my age (early fifties) to hang out with -- coffee or a museum. That sort of thing."

And really, no kidding, that was all I wanted.

At least that's what I told myself.

Chapter 28: "San Francisco Apartment Building Burns to the Ground; Galavanting Father Blamed"

Okay, I thought as I sat at the computer at the San Marino Public Library. I had just sent off four more resumes, and I noticed that I had received an unusually large number of emails. A day earlier I had posted the ad on Craigslist looking for "a woman to hang out with."

There were dozens of responses. I was excited. And then I began to read them. Feh. Clearly, they were hookers or phishers. I ended up getting about 50 responses, but only five were legitimate.

I read through each of them, and one struck me immediately.

The email address was readytodateagain. She identified herself as a woman named Annie, and she said she had responded because she was a writer, too. We started a correspondence by email over the next couple of weeks. It turned out she was a real writer. An essayist and critic with a Ph.D. Sheesh! A regular smarty pants. And I found her on Craigslist! Who knew? Probably some bookwormish woman, though, who smells like a library or something like that.

After a sufficient number of emails in which we became assured the other wasn't some kind of freak, we became Facebook friends.

Once I got on to Facebook, and saw her photos, my immediate reaction was: "Uh-oh. I'm in trouble here." She was exceptionally pretty in a quiet way with soft eyes and curly red hair that rounded her narrow intelligent face in a beguiling way.

There was something familiar about her as well. It seemed like I knew her or had met her or seen her around or something like that. There was something about her I recognized. I didn't figure it out until many months later when I was going through some old scripts I had written. In 2002 I had sold a romantic comedy sitcom pilot to what was then Fox Family.

It was called "Frankie Loves the Girl" and was about two people who meet on the night of high school graduation and then don't see each other again until their 20th reunion, when much has changed. The female lead was a character named Clarice. Her character description: 'Clarice is a tall redhead with an intelligent face." Clarice moves to Berkeley after graduation. Writers often create characters of their fantasies.

As I looked at Annie's photos on Facebook, there was Clarice staring back at me, a character I had invented eight years earlier.

I really was in trouble now.

While I was on her page, she went to my Facebook page and immediately messaged me:

"Wait a minute. You're MARRIED?"

"Separated," I wrote back. "For about a year and a half. She lives in Europe."

"Oh," she wrote. "I'm separated too."

Whew! I thought. Dodged a bullet on that one.

This woman seems fantastic. But I also was worried that she thought I wanted something more than I was interested in because in one of her first emails to me she mentioned that she was looking to make new friends, perhaps a friend with benefits. But then I dismissed that second part. Nobody actually says something like that. And if they do, they don't actually mean it.

She gave me the link to her website that had all of her essays and other writings, and told me she was getting her first book published. The website contained excerpts from the upcoming book, book reviews and criticism she had written, essays, etc. I found one from the San Francisco Chronicle about motherhood.

I started reading it, and it was about raising her two sons with her partner... okay, hold on, hold on. Her partner was a woman!

This woman is a lesbian!

This is perfect! This is exactly the type of woman I am looking for: a lesbian. She's smart, she's well educated, she's a professional with a great job, she's a published writer of considerable intellect... And best of absolutely all: she's a lesbian. Nothing could happen!

"Dear Craig Newark," I started to write in my head, "Thank you after all these years for delivering to me on your website the perfect woman."

I wrote to her after reading the Chronicle essay: "Hey, I read your essay in the Chronicle about motherhood."

"Yes," she wrote back. "Complicated story there. I'll explain when we meet."

This just proves my whole original theory on the "friends with benefits" line: nobody really means that when they say it. She was a lesbian. I could certainly be a friend but what possible benefits could I provide a lesbian other than a few laughs from a professional joke writer?

We agreed to meet the day after Thanksgiving. Sasha was in Ecuador for two months working in a mobile surgical unit traveling around the Ecuadorian countryside performing surgeries. So it would just be Claire, Coco, Saskia and me for Thanksgiving. We went up early on Wednesday, and arrived in mid-afternoon.

It was sunny and pleasant and cool in the Mission District when we arrived at the apartment. Claire met us joyfully, and we walked six blocks over to the nearest Trader Joe's and bought the fixings for a Thanksgiving dinner.

Annie was with family at Asilomar, a state park and resort near Monterey, CA. And we were texting each other. She told me the resort had been designed by Julia Morgan. I wrote back and asked if Julia was a guy. She was offended and ranted about how could I possibly think that a woman couldn't be an architect. I explained that I thought Julia might be an unusual first name like another architect I knew of named Cass Gilbert. For years, I explained, I thought Cass Gilbert was a woman, but only recently I had learned that Cass Gilbert was a man.

"Who is Cass Gilbert?" she wrote.

"He designed the Minnesota State Capitol," I answered.

"Okay, you have way too much information in your head," she responded.

Which she was right about. I do have way too much information in my head. But it is a large head, with exceptional storage capacity.

We continued texting about what we were doing on this Thanksgiving. I told her about making the turkey, about the happy times I was having with my kids.

Then I got a text from her that read: "I wonder about your kiss."

I froze. Oh, my God. What have I gotten myself into?

"My kiss?" I wrote back.

"I meant your kids. Sorry."

Huge exhale. Another bullet dodged.

It would be the first Thanksgiving in which I was handling the preparations. I read online on how to roast a turkey, how to make mashed potatoes and how to make cranberry sauce from scratch.

I might point out at this juncture that cranberry sauce made from scratch from real cranberries in one of those little plastic bags is remarkably delicious. Next Thanksgiving you have to host yourself, make it. Just follow the instructions on the little plastic bag. Believe me, you will not regret that decision.

If I had one piece of advice to give out for the rest of my life it would be this: make your own cranberry sauce.

Anyway, things went off without a hitch, and the next morning while I was waiting for Annie to call to arrange for a time and place to meet, I started making a soup out of the turkey. Hmmm... I need celery. I decided to run across the street to get some celery at the Delaria's Supermarket on 24th and Van Ness. I came home and my phone was blinking.

Oh, crap! I missed her call! I am such an idiot! She must think I'm some kind of jerk not answering her call. Stupid, stupid, stupid.

I checked the voicemail, and there was her voice: sweet, soprano, self-assured and pretty. "Well, I suppose it's time to just do this. I am going on a quick walk down by the Bay and then I figure we can meet in the early afternoon around 2 p.m. I'll meet you at the North Berkeley BART station." And then she left her numbers.

I called them both back and she answered and I apologized profusely for missing her call and explained about the turkey and the dinner the day before and how I was making a soup out of the turkey carcass and have you ever made a soup out of turkey carcass and how, well, you really should have celery and I didn't have any –

"You got the details about where and when to meet?" she interrupted.

"Oh, yes," I said. "Sorry for going on and on about the turkey soup thing."

She laughed.

"No problem," she said.

"Well, it's a big deal for me because I've never made a turkey soup before. Or a even turkey until yesterday and it went great. I mean, the mashed potatoes weren't anything special. I kinda screwed them up, but the turkey was really good and ... hey how was your Thanksgiving?"

"I'll tell you all about it when we meet at the North Berkeley BART at 2 p.m.," she said.

"Right," I said. "I'm talking too much. I'm sorry."

"No, that's fine. It's just that I'm on a walk right now."

"Okay. Okay. See you soon."

I hung up. My heart was racing. She actually *sounded* beautiful.

I mean, what happens if I go over there and she actually is beautiful and I really like her and this whole 'woman to hang out with' thing becomes the fraud that it is?

No, wait. She's a lesbian.

I'm okay.

Calm down, David. Just relax. Be cool.

Finish making the soup, shower, get dressed, and go over there. It's gonna be fine.

You've never been to Berkeley. There's all those smart people over there. Probably some museums or something like that. Fancy conversations in coffeehouses. Me with a beautiful lesbian having fancy conversations with fancy, smart people in fashionable Berkeley coffeehouses.

'Dear Craig Newmark, I just really want to thank you once more for...'

Let me look at her photo again.

I went online and looked at her photo on her website.

My stomach got a full of butterflies.

Oh, man. This woman is beautiful. She's just drop dead beautiful. What have I done? Of all the idiotic schemes I've gotten myself into, this is right up there at the top of the heap, up there with becoming a New Zealander.

Claire came into the kitchen. She and Coco and Saskia were going shopping on Valencia Street. Did I want to join them?

"No, that's okay," I said, trying to act blasé. "I'm going over to Berkeley."

"Berkeley?" she said. "That's cool. What are you gonna do in Berkeley?"

"Oh, uh, I've got this friend who lives over there, so… uh, we're gonna meet in Berkeley and hang out."

"Sounds fun!"

"Should be," I said. "I've never been to Berkeley."

Whew! Dodged another bullet of having to explain that I was meeting an unattached woman my age for coffee and walking around.

I don't know why I was so nervous about that. I had lots of women friends, women I would talk to for hours at a time, completely unencumbered by any desire or complication.

What was I so nervous about with Annie? I mean, we're just looking to be friends. With benefits, in her case, but, uh, clearly, uh, that was not was I was looking for. I mean, come on. Get serious. "Friends with benefits." May I introduce you to the tooth fairy as well?

Because that sort of thing only exists in the movies.

They left and I got dressed. Heads up here: this paragraph will be the girlie part of the story in which I describe what I wore. My theory going into this was to look casual but dressy at the same time for the non-date. Because that's what it was: a non-date.

It took me about a week of careful thrift store shopping, but here is what I put together: jeans ($3.99 from Goodwill of Pasadena), a pressed dress white shirt ($1.99 from the Pasadena Salvation Army), silvery dress socks ($2.99 Ross), a cream-colored blazer ($6.50 from Out of the Closet Thrift Store in South Pasadena) and black loafers ($7.50, from Out of the Closet Thrift Store in Pasadena). Total cost including sales tax: $26.01.

I walked over to the BART 24th St. Mission Station, paid my fare and starting riding to the North Berkeley BART to meet Annie. I found a copy of the San Francisco Chronicle sitting on a seat and read an article on whales or something and then tried to work their easy crossword puzzles and couldn't. My mind was racing by the time we arrived at the MacArthur Station in Oakland.

Okay MacArthur... then let's see that BART map.

Ashby, Downtown Berkeley, North Berkeley. North Berkeley. That's where we're meeting.

Oh wait, was it Downtown Berkeley? Did she say Downtown Berkeley? Man, I need to listen to what people say. I'm such a fucking idiot!

She had such nice voice. Kind of really nice soprano voice. She's probably a really cool kind of a Carole King kind of a woman.

No, it was North Berkeley. I remember that because it had three syllables. Downtown Berkeley has four syllables. Downtown Berkeley. Four syllables. North Berkeley. Three syllables. Yeah, definitely it was North Berkeley. I would have remembered a four syllable station name.

Okay. Okay. Calm down.

Oh, man, this cream-colored jacket is a complete disaster.. I look like some loser B movie producer hanging out at Caffe Roma in Beverly Hills.

What was I thinking? This is a disaster. No, wait. Hmmm... No, it's a good jacket.

The socks are good. Shirt is good. I liked ironing it. Man, I used to iron my shirts all the time. That was good.

You're gonna be fine. I mean you can make anyone laugh. If she hates me, I can at least make her laugh.

Holy shit she was so beautiful in that one photo leaning on the chair. Really good writer, too. Man, she's gonna hate me. I write jokes. I write shit.

'Oh, you're an essayist and critic? That's interesting, Annie. I write shit myself. It's a little different kind of writing from what you're doing, what with me being in the whole shit-writing field.'

Come on, David. Nothing wrong with writing jokes. It's an honorable profession.

I mean, look at me. I look like I just stepped out of a ten year old Mercedes I'm behind on payments for because I overpaid for a house in Santa Monica.

Maybe we'll go to a museum. That would be good. I would love that. Look at some paintings. Yeah... I could talk about paintings. Paintings are good to talk about because anything you say sounds smart.

Okay what happens if you want to kiss her? You don't! We've been through this. No kissing her even you really want to.

What if she kisses you?! Oh my God! No, that's not gonna happen. There is no way a woman that beautiful is going to kiss you. Besides, she's a lesbian. You're in the clear.

Good. Good.

Maybe I should think about soccer.

Soccer...

Soccer...

Nothing!

She had a really nice voice. I mean she sounded a little nervous. But that's normal. Out for a walk. That's healthy. She sounds healthy. Very healthy person. That's good.

Now, this whole kissing thing, David... you're not gonna kiss her. Okay?

And she's not gonna kiss you because of the whole shit-writing thing. I mean, she's an essayist and critic and you, conversely, are in the shit writing field.

Definitely, kissing is NOT gonna happen. Which is a big relief.

Thanksgiving was good. We really cooked everything. And then we'll have a soup...

WAIT!!! I DIDN'T TURN OFF THE STOVE!!!

Yup. I had forgotten to turn off the stove.

So, this was God's punishment on me for going to Berkeley for coffee with a woman and trying to pretend it's not a date: the apartment building the girls live in is going to burn to the ground. The turkey soup pot is going to melt, a fire will break out, and then the entire block the girls live on is going to go up in flames.

I can just see the report on the news tonight. They'll be interviewing the San Francisco fire chief and he'll say: "Apparently, the fire started in this apartment building here on Shotwell when the father of one of the residents went on a date with a woman in Berkeley and left the stove on. During this holiday period, folks, be sure to remember as a fire safety precaution to never go on a date with a woman in Berkeley. It can only lead to tragedy."

The news reporter will shake his head in disgust and then flip back to the studio and the two anchors will shake their heads in disgust over my date. "What was he thinking, out galavanting like that?" one of them will say to the other. "Obviously, he wasn't thinking," the other anchor will answer.

What a disaster. What was I thinking?

I tried calling Claire but we were underground now on BART and I had no reception. Oh, this is just great, I thought. I'm gonna come up out of the subway and the first thing I'm gonna do is make a phone call on my cellphone. Yeah, she's gonna love that. This is turning out just brilliantly. First, I'm going to burn down an entire block of 1910-era apartment buildings in San Francisco, and then I'm going to be Mr. Los Angeles Asshole Guy by making a phone call as soon as I meet her.

The train pulled into North Berkeley and I ran up the stairs trying to get reception and came outside and there sat Annie. I gasped. She stood up and smiled and walked toward me. She was wearing jeans and a blue sweater and comfortable white cross-training shoes. She was really beautiful. Of the drop dead variety.

"Hi," I said.

"You made it," she said.

She hugged me.

Okay, that I did not see coming. What was that all about? I did not see a hug coming. What the hell? Is something going on here between us that I don't know about? Or maybe this is one of these Berkeley things they do: hug people you just met.

We broke away.

"Look," I said, "I don't want to seem like some L.A. asshole, but I have to make a phone call. You know, I was making a turkey soup from the turkey I made yesterday and I forgot to turn the stove off and I have to call my daughter to get home and –"

"Go ahead," Annie said, with a smile. "Make the call. I wouldn't worry about the soup. You had the heat on low, right?"

"Simmer," I said.

"I wouldn't worry, but go ahead and call."

Whew! Dodged bullets three and four. I wasn't going to burn down several square blocks of the City of San Francisco and she didn't seem to think I was an L.A. asshole.

We walked up several blocks to the Peet's Coffee and Tea in North Berkeley. I was so happy and excited to be with her I couldn't stop talking. She was sitting there smiling and listening to me the whole time, and finally she brought up a stunner of a subject.

"I want you to know that I am looking for a man," she said.

Now here's one of the moments in my life where there could have been a fourteen car pile up right outside the window into a parade of naked woman, clown cars, and Pope Leo VII, and I wouldn't have noticed. Wouldn't even have looked out the window. I stared right at her.

"Oh. So, uh... You're not a lesbian anymore?" I asked.

"Well, I never really considered myself a lesbian so much as a woman who fell in love with a woman," she said.

"Call me picky, but I believe that is the definition of a lesbian," I said.

She laughed.

"Well... I consider it a difference," she said. Annie explained that she had been straight all her life and had a number of serious love affairs with men through her late 20s, but then, just as she was about to turn 30, she fell in love with a woman co-worker. They had been in a domestic partnership for 21 years, and she had borne two sons through alternative insemination and her partner had adopted them.

And then, as happens sadly with many marriages, it ended. And now, a year and a half later, she was out there, and wanted to meet a man and get involved.

Well, this certainly thickens the soup, I thought to myself.

This isn't a woman I am going to be able to be pals with. I find her too attractive, too compelling. As she told me her story, I sat there and tried to calculate how, exactly, I would be able to not fall in love with her. Because the longer I looked at her and her soft blue eyes and sweet smile and listened to the voice and the substantial mind and heart behind it, not falling in love with her seemed just about impossible.

Falling in love in your fifties after a long marriage and with a large family isn't rocket science; it's much more complicated than that.

I had dodged a bunch of bullets on the way to meeting her and not screwing it up.

Falling in love with Annie, however, was one bullet I was just not going to dodge.

Chapter 29: "Like In the Movies"

There's a Serbian expression Marina told me once: "Kak na filmu."

It means: "like in the movies."

What it refers to, somewhat derisively, is that moment, at the end of a movie when suddenly and miraculously everything turns out exactly right. In other words, something like that would ONLY happen in the movies. Never in real life.

I didn't kiss Annie that night of our first meeting.

Well, okay, I did.

But it was a terrible kiss. You could ask her.

It was 8 p.m. and we were in her car at the North Berkeley BART, where she was dropping me off to go back to Claire's apartment in the City. We had been together for six hours, walking all over Berkeley, drinking coffee, driving to restaurants, then walking some more. You will not be surprised to hear that I was doing most of the talking.

I hadn't even touched her, except for a couple of times when she was on the outside of the sidewalk and I was on the inside.

"Excuse me," I'd say. "But I need to do this."

And I would take her by the shoulders and gently pull her in front of me and then to my side so that I was walking on the outside and she was on the inside of the sidewalk.

She found this a vaguely objectionable pre-feminist act of ludicrous chivalry. It wasn't really that. Well, it sort of was that. But mainly it was to get my late mother's voice out of my head. I can still hear her saying this to me:

"The man should always walk on the outside of the sidewalk so if in case a car jumps the curb, it slams into you and kills you and you don't have to spend the rest of your life feeling guilty that the person you were with was killed and not you."

Got that?

So you can imagine the stress I was under walking along a street in Berkeley with this thoroughly modern, strong, independent and self-possessed woman and she's on the OUTSIDE OF THE SIDEWALK!! Some car is going to come along and jump the curb and slam into her and then I'll spend the rest of my life wracked with guilt. Why didn't I take the brunt of the out-of-control Toyota Prius careening down Cedar Avenue in North Berkeley? Why? Why? Why? What kind of horrible person am I?

So, naturally: "Excuse me, Annie, but I need to do this."

And then I'd lightly take hold her shoulders and gently sweep her past me to the inside of the sidewalk.

And then this from her: "What am I? Some kind of delicate flower you have to protect?"

No, I'd start to say, and then I'd try to explain about my mother and Annie gave me this look of: 'What the hell is wrong with you? It's the 21st century now. We're all grownups here.'

Trust me, Annie, there's plenty wrong with me that goes way, way beyond my neurosis about what side of the sidewalk you should be walking on and what side of the sidewalk I should be walking on.

What is particularly ironic about all of this is that at one point we were crossing a street on our way to the North Berkeley Peet's and I was expounding on something in an animated way (which would be the normal way I speak about everything) and a car actually almost ran into me. And Annie grabbed me and saved me from being hit by the car. In a very odd way, my mother, once again, was right, because the car would hit have her had she not been on the inside of the street.

Be that as it may, that was the only time I actually had physical contact with Annie the whole time. And that required an enormous effort on my part. What I really wanted to do was slide my arm around her waist and pull her close to me while we were walking. Or reach my hand over and take hers in mine while we were sitting in Fat Apples restaurant and then lean over and kiss her on the lips.

That's what I wanted to do. Oh, okay, I wanted to do a lot more than that. But I couldn't muster even a hand-holding moment in a restaurant. It was just pure terror the whole time, so I overcame that by talking virtually non-stop for six hours.

So there we were sitting in her car at the North Berkeley BART and it was time to go. We exchanged pleasantries about how nice it was to meet the other person, and she said she was exhausted from being with me and I had a lot of energy, to put it mildly, and then I said well I should probably get going and then I leaned over to kiss her and she leaned in to kiss me and I banged into her upper lip and nose and kissed her for what was approximately one picosecond and then said good night and got out of the car and skipped off to enter the BART station.

I got to Claire's apartment and entered and she and Coco and Saskia were sitting on the couch watching TV.

"How was Berkeley?" Claire asked.

"Berkeley?" I said. "Oh, right, Berkeley. Berkeley's great. It's great. It's, uh, you know, over there and... you know, has stuff. In it. Which, you know, a lot of cities do."

The three of them stared at me.

"What are you guys watching?" I asked.

"'Arrested Development'," Coco said. "Greatest show on television."

"I love this show," I said, completely relieved that there would be no extensive line of questioning coming up about my activities for the day.

The next morning, Coco and I were watching "It's Always Sunny in Philadelphia" when I got an email from Annie.

"Great meeting you yesterday. I'm going to see 'The Blind Side'. I would love it if you could join me."

Okay, this was what I was dreading more than the first date: the second date.

I needed to think about this one.

I looked at Coco.

"Hey, Coco, I have to step out for a minute to answer an email," I said.

"Who'd you get an email from?" he asked.

"From... work," I said.

"You don't have a job," he said.

"I have sort of a job," I said. "I'm consulting to those soccer guys."

"Why are they emailing you on the Saturday after Thanksgiving?"

"Because it's obviously important and I need to respond to it!"

I left in a huff and walked around the streets of the Mission District for ten minutes, fretting about how to respond. Okay, she's talking about a matinee, which means the movie would end about 3 p.m. and then there'd be lunch or something and then she'd suggest we go over to her house for a glass of wine and God knows what would happen next. Well, actually God DOES know what would happen next.

I couldn't do it.

I responded: "Annie, I would love to but I'm spending time with the kids and we're watching 'It's Always Sunny in Philadelphia', which is a great show, by the way. You should watch it. I'll call you later."

Just take that horse out back and shoot it because that was really, really lame.

But it was the best I could come up with. Sorry.

We saw each other four more times over the next month as we returned to San Francisco frequently for the holidays. And every single time, I resolutely avoided touching her or even giving her a kiss. Early in the Christmas break, we went and saw "Up In the Air" with George Clooney. We were sitting in a movie theater in downtown San Francisco and every time she leaned into me, I would lean away.

Finally, we agreed to meet on Dec. 30, 2009, to go to an art gallery on Geary Street. There was an exhibit of photos of the Mission District from the 1940s she wanted to see. I wasn't much for the exhibit, myself, and afterwards, Annie suggested we go out to Ocean Beach.

We caught the 33 bus that goes interminably along Geary until we finally arrived at Ocean Beach. It was a typically cold, cloudy and blustery winter day in San Francisco. We walked along the beach for a bit, but it was too cold to enjoy and she suggested we go into the Beach Chalet restaurant for a drink.

We were sitting at the bar, and she was talking about the novel she was writing and the seven main characters and I started talking about "Middlemarch" by George Eliot, which has a wide array of characters but focuses just on two main characters. She then launched into an animated speech about the novel and what she had gone through to get this far with it and how much she was struggling with certain aspects of the story and I sat and watched her eyes and was struck with how pretty she was and how much I really wanted to kiss her.

And so I did.

"Excuse me," I said. I took her drink and set it on the bar and then I pulled her to me and I kissed her on the mouth, long and hard. She pulled me close as well and we kissed again. We broke away and the bartender was standing across from us. He was maybe 25 years old, and staring at us, a little stunned. Here were two 50-somethings making out at his bar. He didn't seem to know whether to tell us to cut it out or to just keep going.

"Sorry about that," I said to the bartender. "I really wanted to kiss her. I've been wanting to kiss her for a while, and so…"

He stared for a beat.

"No," he said. "I was just wondering if you wanted another drink or something."

"We're good," I said.

"Very good," said Annie, and then she giggled.

I felt a massive weight lifting off me. My shoulders dropped and I suddenly felt lighter than I had in years. It was nice to feel desire and have it returned to me.

Annie told me later that had I not kissed her that day, she was going to write me off. She wondered what was wrong with me. I was fun and interesting and interested in her, and yet I wouldn't touch her, not so much as hug her. She had decided that this would be the last time she would see me, and as we were riding out on the 33 bus and I was jabbering away about this and that, she had been smiling and looking at me and thinking, 'What is this guy's problem? Why won't he kiss me? If he calls me tomorrow, I'll tell him I'm busy. That's it.'

The afternoon was ending. We walked out arm in arm from the restaurant like college students in love. We got on the bus and she threw her legs over me and we kissed and cuddled and looked utterly ridiculous to others, but I felt very happy and cool.

The two of us acting like this on the bus reminded me of a similar incident on a bus when I was 16 years old. I had been to a record store in downtown Minneapolis and bought a Muddy Waters album and was riding home on the bus and a blonde Italian girl named Nancy was sitting in the back of the bus with her boyfriend, this Irish loser boy named Frank. They had both dropped out of school and I felt so superior to them until I saw them back there making out.

I sat near them and Nancy saw me. I had actually thought Frank was alright for a long time because he had taken up smoking when he was twelve like many of my friends, but had always cautioned me against it. But then when he was around 14 or so, he decided to bully me around one afternoon – I never figured out why – and after that I decided he was a loser, even though he could do this cool thing with his eyelids where he folded them up. It kinda made everyone nauseated when he did it, but that was the extent of what I saw Frank contributing to the world: occasional bullying and the eyelid folding trick.

"Oh, hey, Raether." Nancy said. Frank nodded and smiled a happy smile and then went back to kissing Nancy's neck.

"Hey, Nancy," I said. "How are you doing?"

"I'm fucking great. I'm so glad to be outta school. I'm getting my GED and then I'm moving to Chicago with Frank and work in my cousin's restaurant. Screw this fuckin' Minneapolis bullshit."

"That's cool," I said.

I didn't know really what else to say. Although I had always admired Nancy's ability to curse. I mean, she could swear better than most guys I knew.

Then she and Frank started making out again. I looked down.

I had never even kissed a girl and here was Nancy and her boyfriend Frank making out like crazy and they probably were gonna have sex that night on the couch in her parents' basement, and they had plans and they were leaving stupid North Minneapolis and were gonna do stuff like work in restaurants and have lots of sex and read the Chicago papers.

Who was really the loser here? Me. The guy who was taking piano lessons and going to Sunday School and mowing the lawn at his parents' house and had never even kissed a girl.

Oh, yeah, I thought, as I looked around the bus with Annie having slung her legs over mine and cuddling up to me. Check this out. I'm making out with my girlfriend on the 33 bus and we got it going on, unlike all you losers who are working today and going home to your apartments to make soup. We're Nancy and Frank now and we're way cooler than any of you.

I thought about them as the bus rode on and we were so happy, Annie and I. As the 33 bus headed east over the hills, fog rolled into the City, and the sun went down, and lights started coming on in the houses and stores. And we went to her house and watched a screwball comedy from the 1930s and then she took me by my hand and walked me into her bedroom and we made love and fell asleep as the fog moved across San Francisco Bay and slipped down onto Berkeley and everything was silent like the moon.

FADE OUT

END OF FILM

Hold on, hold on.

That's kak na filmu

We didn't go to her place and have sex like Frank and Nancy and then move to Chicago and start a new life there. Our present lives were inescapable. And they always would be. That's the difference between falling in love at 16 and falling in love at 53.

You can't just move to Chicago together and get a job in your cousin's restaurant and screw this fuckin' town. You've already made a life of your own, and you can't just shed it and neither can she. It is part of who you are and part of what she is and it is all of what both of you are falling in love with at 53.

Annie's son was coming home that night, so that ruled out her place for the evening. And I wasn't really ready to tell my kids that I had a girlfriend or that I had fallen in love with her because I hadn't even said it to her yet. I wasn't even ready to tell myself that.

So the evening would end with me getting off the bus and kissing her one more time and taking another bus home while she continued on and caught BART to the North Berkeley station and went home alone.

Not like in the movies.

Like in your real life.

Chapter 30: "The Perfect Three Act Comedy"

I had been calling Annie regularly, content in talking to her, completely and utterly unaware of the agony she was going through with me.

In March, about a month after I had last seen her, she sent me an email in which she told me she had fallen in love with me but realized I was not available and so no longer wished to contact me. The email pissed me off. This isn't something you do in an email! You call the person, and tell them on the phone. Or you do it in person. You don't dump somebody by email.

Do you? I mean, am I right here?

I decided to ignore it. It seemed like the kind of overreaction to things that Marina often had and if I just pretended she hadn't written that, it would go away. Yeah, that's it. That's the ticket. Just keep calling her. She'll forget this whole "it's over" thing.

I kept calling her, engaging her in happy conversation. It was a relief, really, to talk to her. Coco and Saskia were struggling mightily with the end of our marriage, and I was weighed down with horrible sense of failure at the ending of it. A half hour with Annie on the phone once or twice a week was a little vacation.

I hadn't seen her, but I decided to surprise her. Her book was launching on May 1, and she was having a party to celebrate it. I decided to go up to Berkeley to surprise her by showing up unannounced at the party.

I arranged a Rideshare with a painter in downtown L.A. who was bringing one of his paintings up to a buyer in San Francisco and driving back the next day. I could do this! I could leave the two of them for one night. He was leaving at 1 pm. Was going to drop me off at the Mission and 24th St BART station and I was going to go to Berkeley and then take a cab to the book party.

I was going to change into my suit and pink tie in the men's room at Cafe Venice in the Mission (I know the guy there.)

Friday afternoon I was going to tell Saskia and Coco I was going up to San Francisco. I was nervous. It would be the first time I would admit to them that I was interested in seeing a woman other than just as a friend.

Saskia came home from school first.

"Remember, tomorrow's the Pasadena Farmer's Market," she said and had a rare smile. That was our fun group activity on Saturday mornings. Saskia and I would bike over to the Pasadena Farmer's Market and buy fruits and vegetables together. And then we'd go home and cook dinner and then at night watch a movie and then discuss the movie.

No problem, I thought. Plenty of time to go to the market with Saskia, come home, shower, pack, and take the train downtown to meet my ride.

"What movie should we watch tomorrow night?" She asked me.

Well, there it was. The posed question that twisted the plot. Every Saturday Saskia (and sometimes Coco) and I would watch a great American movie and then discuss it. I felt it was my duty to make sure they had seen the basic oeuvre of American film. So we had watched "American Graffiti," "Chinatown," "Fargo", etc. And then we would discuss them. They were the kind of movies that were evocative of particular times and places in American life.

She wanted to watch "Reds" again.

Made sense. Great movie. And she was taking the American History AP test in a few weeks. She liked to hear me talk about that period in American history. The final flowering of the Progressive Movement. The transition of the US into a global, imperialistic power (according to me.)

Talking about "Reds" would give me a chance to let loose my diatribe against Woodrow Wilson and how the introduction of American military power into Europe created the conditions that directly led to the rise of the Nazi Party. I could talk about the Russian Revolution and its impact on the American Left. (As a side note, as a nearly lifelong left winger, I've never been much for Woodrow Wilson. For one, he was openly racist. And in pretty shockingly blunt ways. For another, he should have quit after his stroke, but, no, he let his wife run the country. Not that she couldn't do that, but I don't recall anyone voting for her. And that's just the start of my beefs with Woodrow Wilson. Oh, I could go on and on about Woodrow Wilson. And believe me, I have. Ask Marisa. On the other hand, don't ask Marisa. She'll just roll her eyes and say something like: "Oh, man, can he go on and on about Woodrow Wilson.")

There was my choice: a night with Annie celebrating her book. A night that would have surely led to me saying the words she so longed to hear and I so longed to say.

Or a night with my daughter who was struggling mightily with the separation of her parents.

"Well, uh, Saskia..."

Time froze.

Then: "If you want to watch 'Reds' again, then let's."

"Great," she said.

"We could watch it tonight," I said.

"No," she said. "I want to study tonight."

And so we watched it on Saturday night. Not on Friday night. I did not go up to Annie's book launch party.

I was so conflicted about what to do. I had fallen in love with her, but couldn't say it. Just simply couldn't say it. Even to myself.

Okay, that's a lie. I did say it once. I confess that now.

I was lying in my bed one night in the house in East Pasadena I had rented and that Coco and Saskia and I shared.

I was so happy to have a home. I was so happy to be with Coco and Saskia. I was so happy when they rode their bikes back from school and came through the door and said, 'Hey, Padre.' I was so happy to make them dinner and talk late into the night with them.

And there I was, one night in early February, lying in my bed and thinking about Annie, and her eyes and her shoulders and the sound of her voice and it was very late and Coco and Saskia were sleeping and the house was quiet and the noise from the streets and the freeway nearby were just loud enough to mask a loud whisper.

"I love you, Annie," I said that night.

Then I sat up with a start, got out of my bed, and slipped out of my room and walked down the short hallway and opened the doors to both of their bedrooms to see if they were sleeping. Yes, they were. I looked at my two children and watched them sleep, as I had done when all of them were younger. On many nights in the houses we lived in when we were all together, I would awaken at two or three in the morning and I would silently move through the house and look into each bedroom and look at each of my children sleeping and sometimes I would lean down and kiss them and then would step back silently out of the room and make the sign of the cross to the room and slip back into my bed and fall back asleep.

On this night, I crawled back into my bed and couldn't sleep because all I could think of was Annie and her eyes and her shoulders and and the sound of her voice, but I went silent and I didn't say "Annie, I love you" out loud again until several months later when I said it to her and it was too late because she had fallen in love with someone else.

In mid-February, 2010, Coco, Saskia and I went up to San Francisco (on a Rideshare, of course). Claire was leaving for a year in Africa at the end of the month and it was a long weekend. I figured I could get away for a few hours to see Annie. Saskia was also interested in applying to UC-Berkeley, so the two of us would visit the campus together on Saturday. Annie was excited and told me her younger son was in a crew regatta on Lake Merced in San Francisco that morning, and would I like to come over to watch his team race? Sure, I said, but Saskia and I are planning on going over to UC-Berkeley at 2, so would we have time to get back for that?

Yes, she said. Plenty of time. Both of his races will be done by 9 a.m.

It sounded great to me. I'd never seen a crew regatta, and I'm always up for any sport. I figured I could go over to Lake Merced, which is in the southwest corner of the City, watch the race, come back to the apartment in the Mission District, pick up Saskia and the two of us could go over to see the campus.

Annie's former partner was going to be at the event, so she asked me to not really touch her while I was there out of respect for the situation. I had met Annie's former partner several weeks earlier and we have a nice relationship to this day. I often run into her while I am out bicycling around Berkeley and she is out walking and we always stop and chat.

I went on Google to get mass transit directions. To be honest, I wasn't quite sure what part of Lake Merced the regatta was on, so I figured, well, it looks kinda close to San Francisco State University. I'll take BART and the Muni over to there and then walk to the lake. What a disaster. I got to San Francisco State University, and started walking, and Lake Merced wasn't really anywhere within a reasonable walking distance of the college. I found the lake finally and went south around it. About an hour later, I arrived at the site of the regatta. Annie's son had just finished his race as I came walking up. She looked so very happy to see me and I apologized profusely for being more than an hour late. But, I figured, there would be other races and we could watch them before I had to get back to the apartment in the Mission to take Saskia to tour UC-Berkeley.

"Well, let's leave," Annie said.

"Oh," I said, a bit confused. Hmmmm... she seems in a big hurry to get out of here. And I guess that'll mean I'll miss the other races. Well, she must have some kind of appointment back in Berkeley. We kissed when we got to her car and then headed back toward the City.

"The girls' apartment is on Shotwell in the Mission District," I said. "You can just drop me off there."

"Oh," she said, sounding a bit confused herself. "You want to go back to their apartment right now?"

"Sure," I said.

We drove back and she pulled up in front of the building, I leaned in and gave her a kiss, and hopped out.

"I'll be back up in a couple weeks," I said.

And she drove off.

Well, that was an odd morning, I thought. I went all the way over to Lake Merced, walked for an hour and a half, and then Annie was in a big rush to get out of there. Huh. Nice to see her, though. She looked really pretty this morning. But a bit of a bust of an experience. I should have studied the map closer so I could have gotten better transit directions because I noticed several buses drive right past the boathouse. Oh, well.

That's my version of the story.

Here's what happened to Annie that morning.

Annie was excited because it was Valentine's Day and I was in San Francisco. She had arranged to take her son's freshmen crew over at 5:30 in the morning to Lake Merced Valentine's Day Regatta. We would watch the races together, and then she would leave early with me and her former partner will bring the crew team home so Annie and I could go to my house where we can make love for several hours on Valentine's Day. It would be Valentine's Day lovemaking.

Then I showed up late and missed the first race, and arrived just in time to see her son's crew completely fail in their second race and they were devastated. But she figured we could leave quickly and go back to her house in Berkeley. Then I asked to be dropped off at my daughters' apartment in San Francisco.

Now she was devastated. What is going on here? Doesn't he want to be with me? Annie thought. She went home alone and felt awful and cried for an hour. And that night she went to bed alone. Why am I wasting my time on this man? she thought to herself. He isn't available to me.

See? Two versions of the same story. And I had no clue.

We saw each other once more before the end of the month in the middle of the week. I came up to the City for a job interview, then went over to Berkeley to meet her for dinner. It would be the last time I would see Claire for at least a year, so I spent the night at Sasha and Claire's apartment. I was leaving for L.A. in the afternoon, so I said my goodbyes to Claire early in the morning, and then went over to Berkeley to meet Annie for breakfast.

I reminded her that I didn't think I would be able to make it up to see her until June, when Coco and Saskia were going off to Germany to spend the summer with their mother. I sat with her in her car in the North Berkeley BART station and kissed her.

Go ahead, David, say it out loud now! Now is the time!

Just say it: "I love you, Annie."

And yet I couldn't.

It was what I could not say.

Not at that moment.

Why not? I asked myself a thousand times later. Marina had stopped saying "I love you" to me ten years earlier. If Marina refused to say it to me, why could I not allow myself to say "I love you" to someone else?

What was wrong with me in that moment? Maybe after all this sorrow and loneliness, I was afraid of being happy. Maybe that was it. I do not know.

What I do know is that I did not see Annie again for more than a year.

Three months after our last meeting, I dropped Coco and Saskia off at LAX for their flight to Germany, and I had the summer to myself. I settled into a chair in a coffeehouse and called Annie and asked if I could come up to see her the next weekend.

"I don't think that's possible," she said.

"Oh, why not?" I asked.

"Because," she said, "I'm seeing someone now."

I took the words in for a moment, and then asked her if I could call her right back. I ran into the men's room and vomited. Actually vomited.

How was this possible? But I was in love with her. How had I completely missed this one?

I called back.

"Sorry about that," I said. "I didn't feel well there for a second."

"Oh," she said.

"What do you mean, you're seeing someone?" I asked.

"I mean, I thought it was over between us," she said. "I wrote you that email, and you just ignored it and I was destroyed. I cried for days and finally I decided to move on, and I've met someone."

I asked to be excused again, and went back to the men's room and vomited again.

I called her back and she explained that when I didn't seem to want her the way she wanted me, she had decided to find someone else. And she had. A very nice and quiet man.

"What does he do?" I asked.

"What does he do?" she asked back, completely confused.

"For a living?" I said.

"He's an engineer," she said. "What does that matter?"

"I don't know," I said. "I'm just really upset. And I don't know what to say."

She said she was falling in love with him now, and it was over between us.

And that was beginning of the longest summer of my life. I was now really alone. The kids were gone, and the woman I had fallen in love with but had been unable to say that to had met someone else. I suppose I have been more miserable when I was homeless and starving, but emotionally that summer was nearly unbearable.

We talked often that summer and finally, one day, while I was walking on a hot afternoon and talking to Annie, she was really pushing me about what had happened between us.

And then it came out. What should have come out six months earlier in the North Berkeley BART parking lot when I said goodbye to her for the last time: "I love you."

But it was said poorly. I'll admit it. It was blurted out, and the exact words were: "Alright, fine, I love you."

"Well, it's a start," she said. "But you're going to have to work on the tone."

"I know," I said. Then I said it softly: "I love you, Annie."

There was silence on the line.

"So now what happens?" I said.

"Nothing," she said. "I've made a commitment to this man, and I just want to see where that goes."

"What does that mean?" I asked.

"It means I want to see where it goes with him," she said.

"So, what? I tell you I love you and we just send each other Christmas cards and that's it?"

"David," she said. "Nothing changes."

And it didn't. In late August, Saskia returned and that was the beginning of our last year together, me and Los Angeles.

Annie and I gradually cut things off, and we stopped communicating altogether in early November.

I never stopped thinking about her, however, and never quite was able to shake the feeling that I was in love with her. But life was moving on. She was disappearing from my life.

And then one night in January, I was out for a walk in Pasadena. It was one of those lovely January evenings in Southern California where it is just cool enough to wear a sweater and the air is fresh from the snow in the mountains.

I felt happy. Content, almost. Yes, I was alone, but it wasn't so bad now. Saskia was still in L.A., things were looking up. It was a good night to be alive.

My phone rang, and I looked at the caller ID. Annie was calling. Hmmm, I thought. I wonder what she wants?

I answered.

"Hello?" I said.

"David?" she said.

There was her sweet soprano voice again.

"Wow, Annie?" I said.

I was breathless and my heart was racing. "What makes you call?"

"Well…" she paused. Then she said it: "I want to come to see you."

We talked for an hour and she wanted us to give it another try. She had ended things with the engineer. She said he was a kind and decent man, but she couldn't stop thinking about me.

"The poor guy didn't have a chance," she said.

Really? I thought. But that just seemed ridiculous. He had a real job. He owned a house. He was kind and decent. I'm the guy who shouldn't have a chance!

She told me she was still in love with me, but to this day I still find that hard to believe. How do those things happen? Where does love come from and why does it go? Or stay?

Annie is a precise and orderly person, disciplined about everything. I am imprecise about everything, improvisational, chaotic. When I think about us in musical terms, Annie is Bach in a Sunday afternoon concert hall, and I'm Coltrane late at night in a crowded, smoky room. Both are great, but in different ways and for different reasons.

She wanted to see if there still was something, possibly, between us. We agreed to have her come down for a visit in early March. Just to check it out. She was in love with me.

"I love you, Annie," I said.

"And I love you, David," she said.

When we finished talking, I was breathing hard. I bent over and put both of my hands on my knees and gulped for air, as if I had just finished a sprint after a 12 mile run.

So there you have it: the perfect three-act romantic comedy. Boy meets girl. Boy loses girl. Boy wins girl back.

Ta-da!

The end.

Right?

I mean, after all this longing and loneliness and disappointment, boy wins girl back. There would be no possible way we could screw this up a second time. Right?

Please tell me I'm right. Please agree with me.

You're shaking your heads 'no', aren't you? You're sighing and looking down, aren't you? We're gonna screw this up, you're thinking. It's going to get complicated and confusing and sad all over again, isn't it?

Stop agreeing with me! Tell me it's all gonna go great from here on out.

You're shaking your heads 'no' again. Please don't. Please tell me it all works out.

This won't be a perfect three-act romantic comedy, will it? Because Annie loves Coltrane but maybe not the crowded, smoky room of my life. And I love Bach, but maybe not the Sunday concert hall of hers.

And thereby, perhaps, will hang the tale.

Chapter 31: "The Truman Capote Look-Alike Contest"

In late August, 2010, Saskia was flying home from her summer in Germany for her final year of high school. The day before, Marina had called my lifelong friend Eric and vented and told him that Saskia was extremely angry about coming back to L.A. and hated me.

So as I went out to LAX I was very nervous. We met and I hugged her for a long time. I held her for, well, it seemed ten minutes, but it wasn't. She was a bit stiff. She said she closed the window on the plane as they flew into Los Angeles.

"I didn't want to see it," she said. Then sighed. "Well, only one more year."

"Or less," I said. "Maybe we'll move before then."

We stepped out and caught the shuttle to the Green Line station to begin the nearly ninety minute journey home to Pasadena by trains. We got on the Green Line, and it began to hit her.

The city, I mean. Los Angeles.

The swarms of people, sweaty, tense and ridiculous, crowding onto the Green Line. The dozens of little Mexican kids. The black hustlers walking up and down the aisle selling snacks and individual cigarettes. The ranchero music on the iPods. The smell of corn oil. And the talking.

She began to smile. I began to talk, as well. This is what she missed about Los Angeles: its feral and unsentimental energy.

I started my conspiratorial commentary on our fellow passengers that she enjoys so much. Saskia calls it "the winner of the Truman Capote look-alike competition", an homage to that scene in "Annie Hall" where Woody Allen and Diane Keaton sit on a bench in Central Park and Woody Allen provides a stream of comments on the passing array of humanity. One of the people who walks by is dressed like Truman Capote (and, in fact, in the film, it actually was Truman Capote playing himself). Woody Allen says: "And then there's this guy: the winner of the Truman Capote look-alike contest."

It amuses Saskia to no end when I do this and there was plenty of material on the trains: the transvestite with the pretty pink top, the fat Armenian kid, balding already, and his fat Armenian girlfriend, arguing with each other.

And that one guy. The talker.

"When I didn't have any money I would walk every day from East L.A. to Wilshire and Western. It's 23.5 miles and I went through 20 pairs of shoes in two months..." and on and on. The classic Los Angeles Bullshitter. And me, poking holes in every piece of his utterly implausible tale. If he didn't have any money, I pointed out to her, how did he afford 20 pairs of shoes? And if he walked 23.5 miles everyday, why was he still 60 pounds overweight?

Saskia began laughing, laughing so hard she was crying.

We arrived at Union Station, came up out of the subway and onto the platform for the Gold Line to Pasadena. The heat finally hit her -- that late August Los Angeles heat, hard and dry as hay. We got on the train and as we headed toward Chinatown station, she put her left arm around my neck and leaned her head against my right shoulder. Flawed as it is, Los Angeles was still home. Flawed as I am, I was still her father.

"I missed you, Daddy," she said.

"I missed you, Saskia," I said.

She started to cry. I put my arm over her shoulder and she moved in close. And that was the beginning of our last year together.

Chapter 32: "St. Joseph Watches Over a Woodshop in Lincoln Heights"

Perched on bluffs straddling the Los Angeles River just east of downtown, Lincoln Heights, one of the oldest neighborhoods in Los Angeles, boasts a slew of well-preserved Victorian mansions.

This description makes it sound as if Lincoln Heights would be among the most desirable neighborhoods in Los Angeles. And, maybe, someday in the future, given the relentlessly changing nature of Los Angeles, it will become, again, one of the most desirable neighborhoods in Los Angeles.

A pretty compelling argument could be made, however, that it has been, for some time, one of the least desirable neighborhoods in Los Angeles. It is now a working class immigrant neighborhood, mainly Latino, with a large number of recent Asian immigrants mainly from Southeast China and Vietnam. Gangs have bedeviled Lincoln Heights in recent years, and the garbage-strewn Los Angeles River with its massive graffiti "installations" on its cement banks, magnify the dreariness that is now Lincoln Heights.

Still, it has its charms. And, in my experience, these are best discovered on bicycle.

I was looking for a dresser for my bedroom in the place I had just rented in South Pasadena in 2011. I had found what appeared to be a remarkable bargain. The Craigslist ad mentioned a five piece "Italian" set: two dressers, two nightstands and a large mirror. I called and spoke to the seller's daughter who told me they wanted $180 for the set.

"You really should come and take a look at it, because I don't know if you'll like it or not," she said.

She gave the impression that she had run the ad to prove to her father that this particular collection of pieces belonged in the dump and couldn't be sold for even this low price. Please, she seemed to be telling me, come over and tell my father he should just throw these pieces of junk away and stop trying to selling them.

"Where do you live?" I asked. She gave me an address in Lincoln Heights.

"Great," I said. I hopped on the Gold Line and got off at the Lincoln Heights/Cypress Park station. The Gold Line starts in a highly suburbanized area of east Pasadena that is known as Hastings Ranch. It heads west through the center of Pasadena, then southwest to gentrified South Pasadena and then farther south and east to Highland Park.

Highland Park has been an Hispanic neighborhood for several decades now, but currently is weathering an invasion of hipsters. The same invasion that turned dumpy, ethnic Eagle Rock into a neighborhood of comic book stores, tattoo parlors and ironic bars is now heading into Highland Park. It remains to be seen if Highland Park will survive in its current form, although there is no reason that this entire section of Los Angeles, including Lincoln Heights, shouldn't one day be the sedate, gentrified middle class region of the city it once was.

However, there is a long-standing rule of thumb in Southern California that if you live in a neighborhood or city with the work "Park" in the name, it's likely to be a bad place to live. Therefore, Highland Park may be immune to hipsterization and the inevitable ensuing gentrification simply because of its name.

I got off the train at the Lincoln Heights/Cypress Park station—there's that word Park, again—and rolled my bicycle down the long ramp heading east on Avenue 26. It was about a fifteen-block ride through the heart of Lincoln Heights, which is the heart of East Los Angeles, and East Los Angeles, a pretty compelling argument could be made, is the true beating heart of this difficulty city. Not Hollywood or the lush and quiet streets of the

Westside. East Los Angeles is rugged, hard-working, lively, and full of tiny grocery stores, children playing and women pushing strollers, and tattooed guys riding around in low-riders.

I pulled up on my bicycle and pushed the iron gate away from the driveway and greeted the seller, a pleasant, neatly-combed man in his late 60s, wearing a City of Los Angeles sweatshirt. He had an over-decorated yard – knick-knacks of every sort, bird baths, ornate flower pots with struggling plants, and, since this was the Eastside, the nearly ubiquitous statuette of Our Lady of Guadeloupe.

He saw me and laughed.

"You rode here on your bicycle?" he asked.

"Yup," I said.

He laughed again.

"We don't see too many guys who look like you riding a bicycle in this neighborhood," he said, making no effort to contain his amusement. Which would be true: not a lot of fifty-four year-old white guys with gray hair and dress shirts are riding their fashionable Italian city bicycles around Lincoln Heights these days.

"That, I believe," I said.

I didn't want the set. It was dented, with some unexplained gashes, and made of some sort of furniture-y product that contained wood fragments, plastics and various types of glues and a mahogany veneer that looked more like a photograph of a mahogany veneer.

"No thanks," I said. "I really need a dresser, but this probably won't work for me. Do you have anything else?"

"Well, I have this other dresser in the garage," he said.

We walked over to the garage, and there, covered in a fine layer of dust, was a remarkable piece of oak furniture. It was nearly eight feet long, about four feet tall and two feet deep. It was solid oak. Handmade, I could tell. It was way too big for my apartment and there was no way could I get it upstairs into my room. It was ludicrously large for all of the rooms.

But I had to have it.

We bargained a bit and settled on a price of $125. His daughter showed up and clucked about me not buying the Italian set and seemed relieved I had purchased the other piece instead. She was carrying her year-old daughter, who she introduced as Genesis, who had pretty gold stud earrings and bright brown eyes.

"One more thing," I said. "I don't have a truck to move it."

He laughed. Not only didn't I have a truck. I was some kind of crazy white guy who didn't even have a car!

"I'll bring it over in my truck when my son gets home," he said.

"I'd appreciate it."

I rode back to the Gold Line, getting briefly lost on the way back. But I didn't mind because there was one more surprise in store for me. After a wrong turn, I found a jewel of a workshop where a man, his brother and a son made furniture out of oak and mahogany: ornate table chairs, immense bed frames, and handsome sideboards. I would have bought all of it had I the money or the space. The place was stacked to the ceilings with works in progress. There was no showroom. You walked in, and made your way past work benches and saws and there were the samples, stacked up here and there.

I noticed a large, thick table with elegantly shaped legs, rounded edges, ready for staining.

"What a beautiful table," I said. "Who are you making it for?"

They smiled and shrugged.

"I don't know," said the brother. "Some guy." Then they both laughed.

"Maybe you know him?" the brother asked. "He has hair like you."

I laughed.

"Not many guys who look like me come into your shop, do they?" I said.

"No," he said. And then they both laughed even more.

I got a card and vowed to call them to when I was one day a little less impoverished. I would order a dining room table with room enough for all of my children, should we ever all be together again. It would be made of sturdy oak, with simple but curving legs and strong chairs, good for leaning back and sharing stories.

On my way out, I spotted a large icon of St. Joseph, the stepfather of Jesus, hanging on the wall. St. Joseph is a common image in wood shops because he was a carpenter, as was his adopted son. Joseph and Jesus worked in wood, probably making tables, beds and chairs in Palestine. And now his image watched over these woodworkers as they made tables, beds and chairs in Lincoln Heights, once, one of the loveliest neighborhoods of Los Angeles.

Chapter 33: "The Ants"

King Size pillow-top mattress. Silk! Matching box spring. $200. Better than anything you'll find at IKEA!

Topping anything I'd find at IKEA seemed like a pretty low bar, but I did want a king-sized mattress. I wasn't really quite sure what a pillow-top mattress was, although it sure sounded appealing, especially after having spent a fair amount of time in recent years sleeping under staircases in public parking garages, on the floor of my storage facility unit, or in the back seat of a 1997 Chrysler minivan.

In the winter of 2011, things were going well. I was back with Annie and I had put together enough money to rent a two bedroom apartment in anticipation of the return of my younger daughters. I had helped launch a company called Storyboard Graphic Novels and it seemed as if things were going to go very well for a very long time. I needed furniture, however.

You know what else, I thought, maybe I need a pillow-top mattress, too. Whatever that is.

I called, and Jonathan, the mattress owner, gave me the pitch.

"Plus, it's two-sided, one for fall and winter and the other side for spring and summer," he said, finishing up.

"How, exactly, does that work?" I asked.

A brief silence.

"I don't really know," he said. "I've only had the mattress for a few months so I mostly used the fall-winter side and I only switched to the spring-summer like a week ago. But it works."

I didn't say anything.

"Sort of," he said. "I think."

"Why are you selling it?" I asked.

This is the single most important question in any Craigslist negotiation. There's one thing you know for sure about any item listed for sale on Craigslist: the owner doesn't want it anymore, regardless of what it is. Why they don't want it is what's important. Lately, the main reason for getting rid of furniture on Craigslist seems to be "downsizing." The old, 'We're moving to a smaller place and we don't have room for X in the new place.' I bought a nightstand from an upper middle-class Chinese-American couple in an elegant Spanish-style house in San Marino. They were selling everything. And seemed eager to move it fast. There was a sort of sad quality about the selling.

"Where are you moving to?" I asked the woman.

"We don't know yet," she said.

For a couple in a huge hurry to move, not knowing where you were going didn't seem like very good planning. Later, I checked on a foreclosure website and sure enough, the house had been scheduled for auction. It made me a bit sad.

On the other hand, $50 for a nightstand is still $50 for a nightstand.

Besides, I had lost a house to foreclosure. In fact, the house I lost was just around the corner from this one. I knew that ocean-deep sense of anxiety, and an extra $25 from me for their nightstand wasn't going to change the fact that they had lost a five-bedroom, four bath, completely renovated house on a fashionable street in a highly-regarded town.

I was one of the ants coming in and picking over the scene after the fact. I didn't really resent people doing it to me when we were selling our stuff. They were looking for a bargain. And I had had stuff to get rid of that had once seemed so essential. I had been in their situation: what I needed wasn't nightstands or exercise equipment of dressers or ottomans. I just needed cash. Everything else that had once filled these rooms and made me so happy now had to go.

The battle was over, and this couple, much like myself a few years earlier, had lost. The ants were coming to pick over and clean the carcasses of a middle class life.

I was now one of the ants.

Jonathan answered my question about why he was selling his mattress.

"The thing of it is," he said. "I'm moving to Taiwan in a week."

"You're moving to Taiwan?" I asked. "Do you have family over there?"

"Nope," he said. "I'm actually not even Chinese."

"Do you have a job over there or something?" I asked.

"Nope," he said.

"So you're just moving to Taiwan because...?" I asked.

"Well, I've got this friend, Derek," he said, "and he has family over there and I can't find work here so we're gonna go over there and see if we can get something going over there."

"So you're an American guy who is moving to Taiwan because you can't find work here?"

"Yup."

"That's a bit of a twist on the old American immigrant saga," I said.

"I guess," he said.

"You're living the American *emigrant* saga," I said, chuckling at how clever I was. Look at me, turning it around, making a pungent observation with wordplay.

He didn't say anything for a moment.

"So, the thing of it is, my brother told me, 'Get all of your shit outta my place before you're gone, dude."

In my mind, the price on the mattress had just plummeted.

"Well," I said, "How's $30?"

Silence.

"Hmmm," he said, pondering how much he hated me for hammering him down on the price and then about his brother getting tense about him leaving all his shit in the place and how much it sucked to leave America because it couldn't provide him with work and how lame that American emigrant line was of mine.

"$75?" he said.

"$60 and we're done," I answered. "Oh, and you have to bring it to my place."

"Sure," he said, probably a bit relieved and a bit resigned. One less thing for his brother to hassle him about. One less thing he knew his brother wouldn't throw into the dumpster at the back of their building just to make a point about how he had made it and Jonathan was moving to Taiwan because he couldn't get anything going here. He could turn to his brother and say, 'Hey, I sold the mattress. So gimme your truck and I'll get that and the rest of my shit outta here too. And then I'm gone and I'm not getting you anything from China, dude.'

And there I was, suddenly, in possession of a king-sized pillow-top dual-sided silk mattress for $60. Now all I needed was a bed frame, a couple of nightstands, some lamps, a dresser or two, and a set of curtains and I would have an actual bedroom of my own for the first time in three years.

Chapter 34: "My City"

In June, 2011, Saskia graduated from San Marino High School. We had spent a year together. A week after she graduated, it was time to take her out to LAX for her flight to Germany to visit Marina for the summer. At the end of the summer, she would fly from Germany to Minneapolis with her older brother, Cristian, and start college at Gustavus Adolphus College in St. Peter, MN.

St. Peter is pretty little town of about 11,000 souls set in rolling green hills about an hour southwest of Minneapolis. The residents are mainly of Swedish and German heritage, and it sits hard by the Minnesota River, a pleasant river that flows northeast to join the Mississippi just south of St. Paul.

She was all packed. We got a ride over to the Gold Line Station in South Pasadena. I was quaking inside. This was it. The last of my children was leaving Los Angeles. Mariangela and Juliette would return to the U.S. eventually, I hoped, but I would be living elsewhere by then, in the Bay Area. At San Marino High School, they have pavers that commemorate each class, listing every graduate's name, the championship sports teams from that year, and the name of the musical. There are six Raethers in the cement in the central courtyard at San Marino High School: Alexandra (2002), Marisa (2004), Claire (2005), Cristian (2008), Constantin (2010), and now Saskia (2011). This was it. There would be no pavers with Mariangela (2014) or Juliette (2016). They would graduate from high school somewhere else.

The train arrived and we boarded and it headed southwesterly toward Union Station. As we passed through Highland Park, I pointed out the large hand-painted icon of Our Lady of Guadalupe on the garage door, with the words "Hector y familia" hand lettered next to it. We had passed it dozens and dozens of times.

We were both so sad and both so silent, and then I spoke.

"Well, they won't have anything like that in St. Peter," I said. I couldn't think of anything else to say because my heart was breaking.

"No, they won't," said Saskia.

"Yeah, there's no place anywhere quite like Los Angeles." I was struggling. Cliché piled on cliché. "You'll see. Growing up here has had a big impact on your life. You'll never forget it."

Saskia was silent and then I looked at her as she watched the jumbly, disordered mess of the east side of Los Angeles roll by as we journeyed to downtown.

She began to cry.

"My city," she said, quietly.

I pulled her close to me and began to cry as well. She had entered its bloodstream, and now Los Angeles was not just the place where her life had gone so disappointingly wrong. It become a part of her and she a part of it. And she could say, honestly and purely, of this complicated and difficult place: "My city."

In the ensuing months, I prepared for my move north to San Francisco. I was alone in Los Angeles now, but this time it was different. There wasn't a school year to look forward. No one was coming home at the end of the summer, no more school sporting events, or parent parties, or working in the concession stand at football games.

That time in my life was over. I had a few years left with the younger girls when they return from Germany, I hoped, but the big mad rush of a large, loud family barreling its way through a proper, wealthy town was over. I had an old friend urging me to move up to help him launch his website. It would mean leaving Los Angeles, of course, but it would be a real job and I would be closer to Annie.

No more of these long drives through central California with strangers, no more intense weekends with her that seemed to always stumble. I would live in Berkeley and we could see each other like normal people do: dinners during the week sometimes, meeting for coffee and riding around on bicycles like people who are dating do.

A few months later, in the fall, I moved up to Berkeley. On a Rideshare, of course. I didn't really need to go by Rideshare, but this would be my last one as well. Rideshare had saved my life. The rides took me to parts of my disconnected family, and brought me to Annie, and then back home.

We packed up into the truck and headed out north on the 5 freeway toward the Santa Clarita Valley. As we hit the top of the hill, I looked back at Los Angeles as the car drove and watched until the lights of the city disappeared behind the Newhall Pass.

I was leaving her now, and would live the rest of my life, happily and in exile from my city, the City of Our Lady, Queen of the Angels.

Chapter 35: "Thanks, But I'm Going to Pass on the Orgy"

The ad on Craigslist sounded perfect: "One bedroom in a five bedroom house. Easy walk to BART and the Berkeley Bowl. You can get to downtown SF in 35 minutes from here. View of the Bay. Mellow roommates."

To be honest, I was really up for some mellow roommates, because in the thirty years since I had met Marina, married, formed a family, lost it and lived on my own, sometimes in pretty dicey circumstances, a house with five mellow roommates sounded awfully appealing. When I was married and the eight children were all still at home, I would only cite one or maybe two of the ten of us whom I would call "mellow."

I had moved up to the Bay Area to pursue work in "content management." That's a new category of job that has emerged with the increasing complexity of websites. They need people who can write and edit and figure what should go on these websites, etc. Is it basically the old desk editor job in newspapers? Yes, it is. Except this isn't really journalism. It's, uh, well, come to think of it, Content Manager is a pretty accurate title.

The Bay Area comes in four basic parts: The City (San Francisco, and please capitalize the 'C'), the East Bay, the Peninsula, and the South Bay.

First of all, forget the City. Too expensive and one of the worst public school systems in America. If the girls were going to come home, I couldn't live in the City. Which led to the Peninsula (which includes the cities in Silicon Valley). Nah. I have been to Palo Alto many times, and while it is a lovely city, there is a certain insufferable specialness to the people there. We're rich! We're smart! We went to Stanford! Yay to all that, as far as I'm concerned. No objection. Just it starts to grate on a person after the first twenty seconds or so.

Okay, the South Bay.

No. The Bay Area's version of Orange County, without the ludicrous, over-the-top fun. Irvine without Newport Beach. Just tract housing, stolid schools, acceptable motor vehicles, concert venues and amusement parks, shopping malls, and immigrants from Asia working as engineers.

That left the East Bay. Oakland would be okay if it didn't have as much crime as Detroit and worse schools than San Francisco. Well, that led me to Berkeley. Which, fortuitously, is where Annie lives.

I settled there and took an almost instantaneous dislike to it. It wasn't the fact that the libraries are closed for Malcolm X's birthday, or that Columbus Day is called "Indigenous Peoples Day". It wasn't the grimy idlers on Telegraph Avenue selling patchouli oil and friendship bracelets. Or the beggars on Shattuck with their pit bulls and guitars. Or the signs that read "Nuclear Free Zone" when you enter city limits. I'm in favor of all that stuff: I don't mind patchouli oil. Friendship bracelets are nice. Who doesn't admire Malcolm X or think that indigenous peoples deserve some recognition? I like dogs, and am a big advocate of more guitars and fewer nuclear bombs.

It's just, well, enough. I get the point. Berkeley is an island of left wing-ism in a sea of liberalism. It isn't diverse. Everybody is pretty much on the same page here: And listening to Berkeley people tell me how 'diverse' their city is really got on my nerves. It's about 60% white, about 10% African American, another 10% Latino, and the rest mainly Asian. In other words, pretty much like any other American city.

You want "diverse"? Check out Glendale, CA, which was once one of the whitest of places in Southern California. Drive around the southern half of Glendale now and I challenge you to find signage in English. It will be in Farsi, or Armenian, or Spanish, or Russian. *That's* diverse. To me, at least. Diverse is no majority population, but plenty of aggrieved people living next to each – and not especially happy about it either -- only due to a series of mistakes committed by cousins and other family members fleeing some sort of political or economic or social disaster in their various homelands. Welcome to Glendale.

When we lived in Glendale in the 1990s, the school system had children speaking 37 different languages. Many of which did not use the Latin alphabet.

Berkeley, however, does have its charms. And gradually they began to grow on me. It is a city of low-slung bungalows and appropriate footwear and earnestness. It is a place where people grow artichokes in their front yard and say "thank you" to the bus driver when they exit the bus.

Chief of Berkeley's charms is that it may be the single largest collection of oddballs and oddball causes in the United States. Initially, this may come across as leftist politics. But, no, you eventually realize, it's just contrariness, a passionate, unironic commitment to eccentricity.

Often you'll see it on BART. One time I met a guy on BART with a queen sized mattress. "A mattress?" I said. "Really?"

"I'm moving," he said, flatly, as if this was the most obvious thing in the world a person would do -- move their furniture on a subway.

Another time I met a man in pajamas riding from the Downtown Berkeley BART station to his apartment one stop away near the Ashby BART station. He was sipping a cup of Peet's Coffee. He explained he had awakened and realized he really wanted a Peet's coffee and didn't really want to bother to get dressed, so he got on BART at the Ashby Station, rode up to the Downtown Berkeley station, walked over to the Peet's and got his large coffee, and was returning home.

"It's really good coffee," he said. As he sat there, on the train, in his pajamas and winter coat, sipping away. He made a good point. Peet's does make good coffee.

In 2010, a series of protests rippled across the UC-Berkeley campus as students rose up to protest the opening of… a Panda Express restaurant. Because, as we all know, a fast food Chinese chain restaurant is, of course, uh… It's… hmmm… Can't really come up with the words for how utterly wrong and what a complete and utterly horrifying violation of human decency it would be to have a Panda Express in town. This went on for months, until finally the Panda Express people gave up and moved on. In its place? The Berkeley Student Food Collective, which sells "local, seasonal, humane, and organic foods at prices that everyone can afford." Okay. I guess that was worth it. On second thought, no. I've been to the Berkeley Student Food Collective, and I would have preferred a Panda Express.

And then there's the whole glorious Free Speech Movement of the 1960s. A lodestar moment in American political history, really. Who can forget Mario Savio's speech on the steps of the university's administration building, Sproul Hall: *"There's a time when the operation of the machine becomes so odious, makes you so sick at heart, that you can't take part! You can't even passively take part! And you've got to put your bodies upon the gears and upon the wheels...upon the levers, upon all the apparatus, and you've got to make it stop! And you've got to indicate to the people who run it, to the people who own it, that unless you're free, the machine will be prevented from working at all!"*

Thrilling political rhetoric. Soaring and powerful. The issue in question? What kind of student organizations would be allowed to set up tables in front of Sproul Hall and seek members. Their other big "accomplishment" was People's Park, an undeveloped and shabby plot of land near the campus that is primarily noted for its enduring filth.

So here I was in Berkeley now. I had speculative employment with a web startup down in Silicon Valley, and my life was starting over. I needed a place to stay and these guys were looking for a mellow roommate.

I got an email back from Minda, who was subletting the room, that she would be showing the place at 7 p.m. I suppose I should have been a little leery right away. I mean, whoever heard of the name Minda? Was it short for something?

"No, my name is Minda," she said.

Okay, then. Apparently, your parents couldn't come up with a full first name. I'm cool with that. Mellow, in fact.

I got there early, and there were already three other people there for the showing: Claire, a pretty 25 year-old French woman who was working on a graduate degree in neuroscience at UC-Berkeley; Michael, a 28 year-old nervous guy who worked in finance in the City and seemed a bit overwhelmed about his decision to move to the Bay Area; and Sebastian, a 26 year-old from Kiel, Germany, who was working on his Ph.D. in physics at Berkeley.

We were all a bit desperate. Claire had just broken up with her boyfriend and moved out of their apartment in the City. She seemed a bit fragile from the experience, and was just looking for a place that was clean and decent and close enough to the university so she could walk and not spend a half hour on BART thinking about her broken heart. She had a neat and orderly quality, earnest and sweet. She told me she was from a village in the French Alps, and missed home and her mother and father. One cross word and it felt as if she might break into tears.

Michael had a crew-cut and short pants and carefully trimmed fingernails. He was originally from Pennsylvania, and had studied finance at Penn. He had worked in finance in New York City for a few years, and lived in Brooklyn. He said he had been the only un-hipster white guy in his neighborhood of Brooklyn and grew to hate New York. He decided to move west and try life in San Francisco. If his goal was to find an un-hipstery place to live, San Francisco may have been a bad choice. I'm thinking Wichita, Kansas, or Birmingham, Alabama, might have been better choices for him if his goal was an unhipster city.

"What do you do?" I asked him.

"I work in anti-money-laundering," he said warily.

"What's that?" I asked.

"It's complicated," he said. And left it at that. And definitely gave the impression that he would prefer no more questions. From any of us.

A decidedly un-mellow moment of silence followed.

Michael looked like an FBI agent, to be honest. He was staying with friends in San Francisco and was in despair of ever finding a place to live in the City. Google, Facebook, Apple and other booming tech firms in Silicon Valley were hiring thousands of young engineers, virtually none of whom wanted to live in tract housing down there just yet. They were filling up San Francisco and the firms were accommodating this desire by offering special bus services from San Francisco to their offices. He responded to one ad on Craigslist seeking a two-month sublet, and there were 27 people there, all seeking the same thing.

"I have been living in hotels and would prefer a less expensive alternative," Sebastian said, in a precise manner. He was nearly 7 feet tall, and had enormous feet and a goofy smile. He had just arrived in Berkeley a week earlier to work at the Livermore Laboratory and finish his Ph.D. He seemed to have everything mapped out for the next five decades of his life. I almost expected him to begin discussing his retirement plan, but he didn't.

And then there was me – a white-haired, 55 year-old comedy writer with a vaguely unsettling middle-aged background that reeked of failure.

Minda was moving to the Mission District to live with her boyfriend on a two month trial basis. She said that if it worked out, the room would be available for longer than two months. But if not, then she would be back in early January. She and Kevin, one of the other roommates, worked at an institute in Berkeley that specialized in artificial intelligence research.

"And not just for computers," Kevin explained. Our belief is that artificial intelligence has capacities to change the nature of human existence, he said, and told us they were working on life extension projects, including, even, human immortality. I looked at him and chuckled when he said this. He didn't. He was completely serious.

Kevin was short and handsome and had a stubble beard and blonde tints in his hair. He said he had three girlfriends. I believed it.

I'm not big on human immortality. My mother's mother lived to be two weeks shy of her 100th birthday. Somewhere along in her 80s, she decided to see if she could hit 100. It was a big goal of hers. Which was amusing to me because she was one of the great hypochondriacs of all time.

She was forever telling people she was going to die of her certainly fatal heart condition. I was visiting her once when I was 12 years old. We were eating breakfast together in her kitchen and I was studying a small painting she had above the kitchen table of the sea. It always struck me as odd that she had a painting of the sea in her house because she had lived in the Wisconsin all her life and had been to the ocean once. In the late 40s. She and my grandfather were in New York City as part of a meeting for the Rural Electrification Association and they went down to Battery Park, looked out at the Statue of Liberty, and then went back to their hotel in Midtown.

"The ocean," she told me, disdainfully. "I wasn't that impressed to be honest."

Yet, there it was. A seascape above her kitchen table.

"Do you like that painting, David?" she asked me.

"Yes, I do, Grandma," I said. "I like it very much."

"You can have it when I'm gone!" she said. And then burst into tears.

"What's wrong, Grandma?" I asked. "Where are you going?"

"I'm not well," she said through her sobs. "I don't know if I will make it until Christmas! I have to lie down."

She went and laid down and rested that morning.

And then got up later that morning and lived another 30 years.

When she was 99 years old and just two weeks away from her 100th birthday, she was hospitalized in poor health. She really was not going to make it until Christmas this time. She was floating in and out of consciousness for several days in the hospital. One day, she woke up with a start and looked at the nurse.

"What day is it?" she asked.

"November 4," said the nurse.

"That's enough," said my grandmother.

She closed her eyes, slipped back into unconsciousness and died the next day, ten days shy of her 100th birthday.

I am pretty sure at a certain point I'll think to myself the same thing: That's enough. But best wishes on that, Kevin. If you figure it out, I'm pretty sure I'll pass. No thanks. A century of life is gonna be more than enough for me. I mainly want to find out how the stories of my childrens' lives play out and to see the US play in a World Cup Final. That pretty much covers it, as far as I can tell.

I might be persuaded otherwise, but I figure if 2056 rolls around and I'm still around, 2057 can start without me.

Two of the other roommates, James and Ken, ran a company that sold an herb from Southeast Asia that they marketed on the internet.

"It's completely legal," Ken said, "so don't worry."

Minda asked Ken to explain what life would be life at the house for the new roommate.

"Well, it's pretty mellow here," Ken said. See? Minda wasn't kidding about the whole 'mellow' thing.

Concentrate really hard on staying mellow, I thought to myself. *This seems like a great place to live for a while. Stay mellow. Be mellow. Mellow. Mellow.*

"James and I run this company out of the house, so we're pretty much always here. Kevin works during the day and travels lot. My girlfriend, Emily, and I share the master bedroom. We like to have parties every few weeks and they generally last until 4 a.m. We keep fairly odd hours, are into polyamory, tend to stay up and talk a lot and that's about it."

Hold on. You're into polyamory?

"Could you repeat that last part?" Claire said, a bit shaken.

"Yeah," said Ken. "We have parties, we often stay up late, we're into polyamory, and we talk to each other a lot."

"Okay," said Claire, a little shaky. She definitely wasn't in a tiny little Catholic village in the French Alps with her mother and father anymore.

Another roommate, Emily, came in, friendly as could be. She had brassy red hair she came by naturally, and was a bit portly and a happy person. "How is everyone?" she said, smiling broadly.

"We're tense," I said. "We're all trying to act polite but we all really want to get Minda's room."

Emily laughed.

"Well, I've got a great cure for tension," she said. "But it involves lots of sweating and you won't be wearing that sweater!"

Everyone laughed nervously.

A few minutes later, we all left as the roommates decided to discuss who would make the best roommate.

I walked to catch a bus.

"Please, God," I said to myself. "I'm desperate and need a place to stay. Don't have them pick me. The last thing I need is to live in a house that hosts orgies. I have enough trouble sleeping as it is. I don't need an orgy going on downstairs."

A day later, Minda called me to tell me they had chosen me as the roommate. Once again, God gives me the opposite of what I asked for!

"Really?" I said.

"Yes," she said. "It was because you laughed when Ken mentioned we like to use nitrous oxide at our parties. We agreed that you were cool."

Well, I guess I could take this as a compliment. A group of orgyists thought I was cool because I laughed at the idea of them using nitrous oxide at one of their "parties".

"You know, Minda," I said. "I really liked you guys and the view of the Golden Gate Bridge is awesome and everyone seems so interesting, but the thing of it is, I have already found another place to live."

"Oh, no!" she said. "We were really looking forward to having you as a roommate. We are having a party on Saturday to welcome you."

"I'm sorry," I said. "I'm sure you'll find someone cool to move in there."

"Well, you can still come to the party," she said.

"Thanks," I said, "But I don't have a clean bath robe right now."

Chapter 36: "Begging Is Not Allowed at the Denny's on San Pablo Avenue"

It was 3 a.m. and the house was cold and I had been awake for an hour and a half. I tried reading a book on socialism in South America that I found on the bookshelf, but even that couldn't put me to sleep.

What I wanted now was an all-night joint that served oatmeal and coffee and had comfortable booths and sleepy waitresses and a table where I could do the New York Times Sunday Magazine crossword puzzle. I've been doing these long enough now that I find them to be scalable mountains. They're not that hard, generally very clever, and solvable if you are willing to devote some time to them.

And some time to devote to a crossword puzzle is definitely what I had on my hands right now.

I checked on my smartphone to see if there were any all-night Edward Hopper-type places in Berkeley.

There weren't. Which, I would argue, is a significant failing of this city. Significant.

The closest place I could find was a Denny's in El Cerrito, way up San Pablo Avenue. Google directions indicated it would be a 35 minute ride. I sighed. Well, why not? I'm not going to get back to sleep at this point.

I bundled up, took $5 in cash and left my wallet at home because, well, it's not that great a neighborhood up there and $5 would cover coffee, a bowl of oatmeal and a tip.

The night was frosty. It was 38 degrees out. And a breezy ride on a bicycle in 38 degrees while suffering from insomnia wasn't as much fun as I thought it was going to be.

I arrived at the Denny's, which is a quite large one, and had only three tables occupied. I grabbed a booth close to the door, settled in with my coffee and puzzle and oatmeal and felt better. But not much. Actually, I was feeling sorry for myself. Lonely, sleepless, vaguely sad about everything. And let me say this, if you ever find yourself in this mental state, the Denny's in El Cerrito, CA, isn't exactly HappyFunland.

And then he entered, a homeless guy. But one of the most desperate-looking I had ever seen. He wore only a filthy sweatshirt, torn filthy jeans, old basketball shoes without laces. His clothes hung on him and he looked near starvation. And cold. But he waited politely at the host stand to be seated.

"Just one in the party," he said.

The waitress took him to a booth across from me. He sat down and studied the menu. The waitress returned with his water. He ordered two entrees, a couple of side orders (hash browns and home fries), some oatmeal, a large orange juice and coffee. She took his order and went to the kitchen. He blew into his hands to warm them, and she returned.

"Excuse me, sir," she said, meekly. "How will you be paying for this?"

"With my debit card," he said. And reached into his wallet, pulled it out with a flourish and handed it to her with the gravest of confidence. She left and he looked over at me and smiled.

"I am starving!" he told me. "I could eat three breakfasts." Which is, in fact, what he ordered.

The waitress returned.

"I'm really sorry, but your card was declined," she said.

"What?!" he said. "But I know there's money on there!"

"Maybe you should call them," she said, and gave him his card back. She walked away, and the man slumped in the booth. He looked utterly desperate, and put his head in his hands, and sat quietly moaning for a moment or two, and then looked up at me.

"Hey, man," he said to me. "Could you buy me breakfast?"

"Sorry, I can't," I said. Which was true.

He got up and went to the other two occupied tables in the restaurant and begged from them and got nothing. He came back and slumped into his booth. The manager came up.

"Sir, you can't beg at Denny's," he said. I have to say, that seems like a good policy, although unevenly enforced. I've seen plenty of customers going into the 'come on, honey, let's have some post-Grand Slam Breakfast sex 'begging for at Denny's at 3 a.m. I'd never actually seen anyone begging for money or food.

The homeless man got up and trudged out into the miserably cold night I went back to my puzzle. Twenty minutes later, however, the man returned.

He stood by the host stand, just standing there, trying to get warm. All of a sudden he began moaning loudly and grabbing his chest. And then he collapsed and began to shake. I called the waitress over and she and the manager came running up and he looked to be near death: ashen-face, gasping for breath, writhing in pain, slipping into unconsciousness. The manager called 911, and moments later an ambulance and a team of EMTs arrived and began work on him.

They brought in a gurney and gently lifted him onto it. It was time to rush him to the hospital. As they lifted the gurney up to take him out of the Denny's, I looked at the man.

He winked at me and gave me a slight smile. They wheeled him out and he closed his eyes and rested.

The vast, cold and indifferent universe had been outwitted on this one night.

Chapter 37: "What You Can't Get at the Trader Joe's in Berkeley"

I was in the Trader Joe's in Berkeley. You know, the one there at the intersection of MLK and University. Yeah, that one.

Oddly enough, I have had that exact exchange with people in Berkeley about forty or fifty times. Which is fairly ridiculous because there is only one Trader Joe's in Berkeley.

And it's located at MLK and University. So why would anyone have to identify its particular location? Anyway, it appears to be part of the conversation that occurs in Berkeley when you mention that you went to the Trader Joe's in Berkeley. You mention that you went to the Trader Joe's in Berkeley and then they say, 'You mean the one at MLK and University?' and then you say, 'Yeah, that one', and then those eleven seconds are gone from your life forever.

I went there every morning and bought two or three bananas because I read somewhere that bananas are the perfect food. And then I told that to someone and they didn't believe it so I said I would prove it and googled 'bananas are the perfect food' and the second link was headlined: 'Bananas are not the perfect food.'

Which didn't really deter me from continuing to buy two or three of them every morning.

Anyway, I had picked out my bananas and was looking at some hummus when a guy came up to the Trader Joe's employee standing next to me restocking the cheese, and the following conversation ensued.

Confused Guy: "Yeah, I'm looking for where you have coffee by the cup."

Trader Joe's Employee: "What do you mean?"

Confused Guy: "I just want a cup of coffee and I can't find where you have that."

Trader Joe's Employee: "We don't sell cups of coffee."

Confused Guy: "Oh."

We all went back to our business, then:

Confused Guy: "Could you make me a cup of coffee?"

Trader Joe's Employee: "We don't really do that."

Confused Guy: "Just this once?"

Trader Joe's Employee: "We don't even have an urn here."

Confused Guy lets out a long and very aggrieved sigh.

Confused Guy: "Wow."

He walked off. I did a little more shopping and got in line, and Confused Guy was two people ahead of me. Another conversation ensued with the clerk at the register.

Confused Guy: "Do I have to buy something to get cash back?"

Trader Joe's Clerk: "Yup."

Confused Guy: "Wow. This store. Lot's of rules."

He walked off and returned moments later with one large apple and got in line behind me.

I was putting my stuff in my backpack as he did his transaction.

Trader Joe's Clerk: "Minimum $5 purchase for cash back, sir."

Confused Guy: "What?!"

Trader Joe's Clerk: "Sorry."

Confused Guy: "You know what? Trader Joe's is just bullshit. This is a bullshit store!"

And he walked out. Of the Trader Joe's in Berkeley. The one at MLK and University. Which is neither a coffeehouse nor a bank. Just a Trader Joe's.

Chapter 38: "The $30 Bicycle Adventure, Part One"

Coco came down to Berkeley for a week at Thanksgiving, 2011. It was time for a father-son adventure in San Francisco.

For reasons not entirely clear to me now, I decide to buy a cheap bicycle and fix it up. I was focused on buying a French or English bicycle built in the 1970s. Manufacturing of bicycles now is almost entirely done in Taiwan. Virtually every bicycle company in the world designs their bicycles in their own studios and then uses one of several large bicycle factories in Taiwan for the manufacture of the bikes.

But, back up until the early 1980s, a French bike was made in France, an English bicycle was made in England, an American bicycle was made in America.

English and French bicycle frames from the 1970s were made to a high standard of quality and, well, coolness. These are the classic ten-speed bicycles of my college days. Raleigh, Motobecane, Peugeot.

The frames were made of steel, which is heavier, obviously, than the alloys used today. So to keep them light, the tubing is narrow. The bikes have a decidedly delicate or "skinny" look to them. Plus they have curves. The front fork (the part that holds the front wheel) is arched outward, not thrusting straight down, the way they sensibly and brutishly do nowadays.

I look at these bikes now and I can just picture myself wearing short shorts, knee high basketball socks, adidas running shoes, singing "Stir It Up" by Bob Marley and the Wailers to myself and wondering how in the world I will ever get up the nerve to talk to the red-haired girl who always smiled at me at Wilson Library on the West Bank campus of the University of Minnesota.

One plan I came up with in the fall of 1976 was to mention to her that I was working on Eugene McCarthy's third party bid for the Presidency and we were looking for volunteers. That seemed like a fool-proof opening: Gene McCarthy was still somewhat cool, and what could be more appealing to a beautiful, tall red-haired girl working in a library than a politically-committed leftist boy?

Probably a lot of things. One girl I was madly smitten with in college stunned me one day when she went on a rant against Communist infiltration of American society and how Joe McCarthy had been on to something. She sounded like she'd been talking to my grandmother, who used to drive me nuts with her "Joe McCarthy was on to something" rants. Since you could never be too sure about someone's politics, best not to open with that. I figured it would be best to ask them what they thought of Richard Nixon after making out had occurred, not before.

Wait until after I get her shirt off and then hear her accuse the Catholic church of betraying Cardinal Mindszenty?

I don't think so, I decided. It was too risky.

Politics was out.

How about a fun activity? Maybe I'll ask her if she wants to go shoot pool sometime. I was awfully good at shooting pool in those days, and could run a table every once in a while. Nah, then she'd be standing there holding her cue thinking: 'What a jerk. He's running the table just to show off. I should have stayed home and watched "Three's Company."'

Then there was the: 'Hey, I'm doing a paper on Schopenhauer's aesthetics, and I can't find one of the books I was looking for on the shelf' scheme.

Okay, I'd say that... and then what? She'd look and see that it's checked out and... and... I'd say thanks and walk away. I mean, the whole Schopenhauer's aesthetics was a great opener, but I had nothing after that.

What was I supposed to say after she told me somebody else had checked the book?

'Oh, that's too bad. Say, would you like to join me for a plate of rice and veggies at the New Riverside Cafe after you get off work?'

Or: 'Hey, did you hear they're showing "Triumph of the Will" over at the Varsity? I'm thinking of going over there and organizing some chants against fascism and propaganda. Wanna join me?'

Nah, forget the whole Schopenhauer's aesthetics book ruse.

Wait, wait. How about this? I get two tickets to University of Minnesota hockey game and walk up to her and ask her if she wanted to go with me to a hockey game and... what if she hates hockey? Why would a girl who works in a library be interested in hockey? She'll probably tell me that hockey is a proto-thug sport and disgusts her in every way, and what was I supposed to say?

'Yeah, but I like hockey. Hockey is fun.'

Oh, that's a good response. And then she'd just roll her eyes and look disdainfully at me.

In fact, in every version of how I would start talking to this girl, it ended up in my mind with her saying 'no', then rolling her eyes and looking disdainfully at me.

Thus, unsurprisingly, I never did work up the nerve to talk to her, and I have operated under the assumption her life was marked by a great sorrow and longing over that ever since.

It's certainly not true, but just go with me on this one. I don't have a lot else to hang my hat on right now.

Anyway, Coco was coming down to Berkeley for a week for Thanksgiving and we needed an adventure. So I found a 1973 Motobecane road bike for sale on Craigslist. It was at a guy's apartment in the Outer Richmond neighborhood of San Francisco. But we wouldn't go there directly. We would wander through the City before arriving at the guy's apartment. It would be an adventure.

He came down from Humboldt State on Saturday. Sunday morning dawned and there was a misty rain coming down on the San Francisco that November morning.

"Wake up, Coco," I said. "It's time to go on The $30 Bicycle Adventure!"

He rolled his eyes and looked disdainfully at me.

"Okay," he said. "I'll go."

The Bicycle Adventure was my version of being a middle class father. After we lost everything several years earlier, a problem arose: how do I maintain being a middle class father when I can't feed, or house, or clothe my children? My children, particularly the middle two -- Saskia and Coco -- had borne the brunt of the instability of our economic lives. They lost their home, their little sisters and their parents, to some extent, in the middle of high school. Their mother and two younger sisters had moved to another continent and country that provided a more benevolent safety net, and their father was homeless and, often, starving.

The Friday afternoon question of 'Hey, dad, can I have twenty bucks and the car tonight to go out with my friends' wasn't even asked.

I couldn't give them money, or a home, or even food. Or shoes. Or a sense of faith in their father as a source of strength and stability.

So what could I give them?

I could give them a Bicycle Adventure. A Bicycle Adventure is a journey into your city to get what you need from it. You will go to unusual corners of your city and end up in places you normally wouldn't go and meet people you normally wouldn't meet because you cannot afford to walk into a bicycle store and buy a new bicycle. You are building a bicycle out of parts you are scrounging up where you can: a bicycle seat here, a frame there, a crankset from this guy and a wheelset from that.

A Bicycle Adventure is about being resourceful and unafraid of making mistakes and fearless about going to parts of the city you do not know or feared before you entered them. Life is a Bicycle Adventure. That's what I was giving them. Since I could not give them anything else, I was giving them this: an improvised, unexpected guide on how to make something out of nothing from your life.

It was a hot Saturday afternoon in Oct., 2008, and Coco and I got off the Blue Line at the Vernon Station in South LA, and crossed the street to catch a 105 bus to Vernon and Western.

I had a bicycle, and Coco had a bicycle frame. Across the street from us was an immense flea market, and behind us a strip mall filled mainly with shops catering to the Hispanic customers in the area. It is a not a particularly scenic part of Los Angeles. In fact, an argument could be made that it is a particularly ugly part of Los Angeles.

But it is lively. Hundreds of people walking around, shopping, idling, or screaming into portable loudspeakers about Jesus. The whole area smells like cooking and food, hot corn oil and burning peppers and sizzling onions, and there is plenty of shouting and music.

And on this day, two white guys: me and Coco. I think I can confidently say that we were the only white people in this neighborhood on this morning and probably on hundreds of morning on either side of this particular day.

In fact, we were so obviously out of place that a 30ish, nerdy-looking black guy came up to us and said: "Hey, are you guys going to Primo's?"

"Yes," I said. "How did you know?"

"Well, why else would two white guys be standing here with bikes, waiting for a bus?"

He made an excellent point. The ONLY good reason for two white guys with bicycles (or, more accurately, parts of a bicycle) was to catch the 105 bus and ride it a couple miles to the intersection of Vernon and Western, right there in the messy, violent and lively heart of South Los Angeles, was to go to Primo's.

I have to admit, Coco was a little nervous about the adventure I had taken him on. And I don't really blame him. It wasn't the most relaxing place in the world to be. I mean, I'm pretty sure that street preacher behind us screaming into the portable loudspeaker said something about the end of the world coming soon. And by the looks of this neighborhood, he had pretty good evidence that it wasn't far off.

What had led us to Primo's was a bit convoluted. In 2007, my older son Cristian had done a conversion on an old ten speed bicycle frame to a fixed gear. A fixie conversion. It was a cutting edge move in San Marino at the time. While fixie conversions were relatively common in hipster-infested neighborhoods in San Francisco, Brooklyn, the east side of Los Angeles, and other similar type locales, they were virtually unheard of in sedate San Marino.

Many kids drove to school in $50,000 SUVs.

Cristian had been turned on to the fixie conversion idea from his older sister, Claire, who rode a fixie conversion from her apartment in the Mission District in San Francisco to the University of San Francisco where she was studying economics and African Studies. Why African Studies? Don't ask. We raised our children to pursue what interested them. Claire got interested in Africa for some reason. Ended up living there for a year even, travelling throughout East Africa on her own. taking trains and buses, living in the Kibera slum in Nairobi, and partying on the beach in Mozambique. She lives in Brooklyn, runs a coffeehouse and is working on her Master's in Education and is just a tremendous person in every way imaginable.

Back to Cristian. He started riding his fixie conversion to school and the retro appeal of it caught on and suddenly dozens of San Marino kids turned over the keys to the Audi Q7 and got a fixie, skinny jeans, checkered belts and flannel shirts. Just like Cristian. Except he hadn't chosen the look as a pose. He found these clothes at thrift stores and they fit his budget.

Coco went on Craigslist and found a fixie himself. I taught him how to haggle with the guy and eventually he bought it for $150, a significant discount off the $400 the guy originally was asking.

And six months later, it was stolen.

It was an intensely depressing experience for all of us.

Coco had no other transportation. This was how he got to school. Now he had to walk.

Let's do a fixie conversion, I suggested. See if you can find somebody who does them cheap and get a frame and we'll do it.

He did -- Primo of Primo's Bike Shop at Vernon and Western in South Central Los Angeles. Coco found him on Craigslist. He also found a 1983 Peugeot frame for $40. Primo said he would do the conversion for $273. Okay, I said, this we can afford. And Primo said he would do it while we waited.

So, we got on the Gold Line and took it to Union Station in downtown LA. Then the Red Line over to the 7th and Metro Station, and then the Blue Line to the Vernon Station. From here we would have to take a bus. I had my bike, Coco was carrying his frame.

I want to stop here for just a moment and point out that everyone in San Marino I told this story to is astonished that I took my son on this trip. Not because of the neighborhoods we journeyed through but because of the mode of transportation: train and bus. It just isn't done, according to these people.

And many people outside of Los Angeles are astonished to hear that the city actually has a buses and trains. Well, in fact, it does. An immense system. The average daily ridership on the buses and trains in Los Angeles is 1.48 million. That's right, nearly a million and a half people are riding buses, trains and subways (yes, Los Angeles has a subway) every single day.

There? See? You learned something surprising about L.A. Why? Because it is a relentlessly surprising place. Every time you think you have your hands around it, another metamorphosis occurs and you don't.

The bus came and we rode to Primo's Bike Shop. And we were definitely the only white guys on the bus. It was Coco's journey into the other side of Los Angeles -- the dirty, run-down, crime-ridden, lively and amusing and desperate part of Los Angeles. We arrived at Primo's and came in with the frame.

Primo is a short, fat, Hispanic guy, of undetermined age. He sits at the counter, and holds court. You can get anything you want at Primo's Bike Shop, provided Primo decides to sell it to you. And he seems to operate his business on another motto: the customer is occasionally right, but Primo is always right.

He forgot we were coming. "Oh, man," he said. "I don't think I can do it."

"Oh, sure you can," I said. "We came all the way here from Pasadena on the train and bus to have you do this."

"You came here on the train and bus?" he said, incredulously. "A couple of white guys came here on the bus?"

"Yup," I said. "We don't have a car."

Primo looked at me. "You don't have a car and you came all the way here to have me make you a bike?"

"Yup," I said. "Don't really want to go back without one, either."

"Well, let me see what I can do," he said.

So he started barking orders to the four guys who work for him, and who appear to be the constant source of his dismay. An hour later, he had taken a bare frame and built a bicycle: wheels, tires, handlebar stem and handlebars, seat post and seat, brackets, and chain. All he had to work with was a frame. In the end, he gave us a bicycle. $273.

All the while, an endless stream of customers came in and out. Guys looking for new inner tubes, hipster fixie riders from Culver City looking for a drink of water, a guy selling white socks, somebody who needed a basket, and on and on. And the basic rule we discovered about Primo's is this: Primo is right and you are wrong. On any given topic.

"I want to get that bike seat?"

"For that bike?"

"Yeah."

"No. It would look terrible. I'm not gonna sell it to you."

"But I like it."

"Too bad. It's not a good seat for you."

This would be a typical exchange between Primo and a customer. And he wasn't trying to sell something more expensive. He just sized the situation up, and if he decided he wasn't going to sell you something for whatever reason, you were not going to be able to buy it. So just move along, my friend. Move along. Primo has bigger fish to fry.

He and his assistants finished the bike in about an hour. We paid him, got on the bus and then the train and rode back to Pasadena.

And then Coco was king. Anybody in San Marino could go over to Jones Bicycle and buy a manufactured fixie. Coco had bought a frame off Craigslist. He then took the train and bus to the heart of South Los Angeles and had one built for him and then came back with it.

Go ahead, go over to Jones Bicycles in San Marino and have your mom drop $1,500 on a fixed gear bicycle. It'll never have the cred this one does. This one we got from Primo.

Coco still has the bike that Primo built nearly four years later. Parts have had to be replaced, upgrades made here and there. But it's still the bike that Primo made.

He hated Los Angeles and Southern California growing up and wanted to leave it as soon as possible. He graduated from high school two years later, went off to the University of Vermont, but did not like northern New England at all. He has since transferred to Humboldt State in northern California, and is now spending a year studying in South Africa. He plans on one day becoming a farmer and growing tea, and I couldn't guess where he will end up in his life, and neither can he.

But I do know one thing, and I told him this that day as we were riding home from Primo's through Los Angeles, the convulsing, violent, improvisational and breathtaking city he had grown up in.

"You know what, Coco? You're an Angeleno. No matter where you go for the rest of your life, this city is part of what you are."

He looked out the window of the train.

"And I got a pretty cool bike today," he said.

Chapter 39: "He Was Calling from Paris to Let Heather Know

He Was Cool With It"

I have children living in Germany, New York City, Washington, D.C., Minnesota and Northern California. So I keep my phone on all the time. Because you just never know when one of them might call to tell you they love you.

Or something like that.

During the winter of 2011, I lived in a room in a cold and worn-out house a few blocks south of the UC-Berkeley campus. The furnace didn't work, and the stove wasn't much and the shower usually worked like this: five minutes of ice cold water, suddenly face-melting hot water for about 40 to 45 seconds, then back to cold water.

The other woman living in the house was in law school and I saw her maybe six times in the nearly three months I lived there.

A few weeks later, I was home alone, as always, sleeping in the wee small hours of the morning. Which is unusual for me at that time of day. Normally, I am up at 2 in the morning. I sleep in shifts. Usually I fall asleep at around 10 p.m., then wake up around 1:30 or so in the morning, and then fall back asleep at around 3 or 4 in the morning and sleep fitfully until 7 a.m. If I'm lucky.

I read an article in the BBC online magazine that claimed in the pre-Industrial Revolution era, this was a normal sleep pattern. People regularly awoke in the middle of the night and prayed, or visited their neighbors or had sex. Even though I seem to have a medieval sleep pattern, I can tell you honestly that I don't do any of the above during these waking hours. Mainly, I read and get nervous.

Anyway, at 2:37 on this particular night, I was sleeping. And my phone rang. And I answered it without looking at the number.

Me: "Hello?"

Guy On The Other End: "Heather?"

Me: "Wrong number."

Guy On The Other End: "Look, I just want to know if she's there."

Me: "Dude, you've got a wrong number. There is no Heather here."

Guy On The Other End: "Look, I'm cool with guys. I just want to know if she's there."

Me: "You have a wrong number! And it's 2:30 in the morning."

Guy On The Other End: "Oh, sorry. I'm calling from Paris..."

Me: "Well, I'm awake now. What are you doing in Paris?"

We talked for about ten minutes. He was a junior in college. Fall semester in France. Studying French. Likes Paris quite a bit. I told him I wasn't much for Paris. Talked a bit about Paris and then I said I wanted to go back to sleep.

Guy On The Other End: "Right. Sorry about that."

Me: "No big deal. Hey, and good luck with the whole Heather thing."

Guy On The Other End (sighing): "Whatever."

And then we hung up. I suppose I could have told him he'll get over Heather. There's better women out there for him. But I never believed anyone when they told me that. I just let him go. I was awake now. And it was almost noon in Paris, and time for lunch. So I went into the kitchen and had some cottage cheese.

Chapter 40: "Play the Accordion, Go to Jail"

In 1993, we were living in a lovely rented house in the Chevy Chase canyon neighborhood of Glendale, CA. I was entering my second season on "Roseanne" and Marina was pregnant with our sixth child (and fourth daughter), Saskia.

"Roseanne" was produced at the CBS Studio Center lot on Radford Avenue in the Studio City section of Los Angeles. By car, the trip is 12.8 miles. We only had the one car -- 1991 Toyota Landcruiser. It seats eight. Marina was opposed to purchasing a second car -- I'm not exactly clear why. She had her reasons. So, every morning, I would load my bike into the back of the car and she would drive me (along with the three kids not in school) over to Studio City.

Then at night when we finished work (usually around two in the morning, for some reason), I would hop on my bicycle and ride back to Glendale. It took a little over an hour to get home.

It was not a good situation. It was a long ride and the last half mile was up a winding canyon road. I would regularly pass coyotes wandering along Chevy Chase Drive, as I pumped my way up the hilly road.

Late that fall, I sold my first episode script on the show (split with another writer) and got a check for about $11,000.

So, naturally, I took that money and bought... a piano.

It was the piano I had always wanted: a 6-foot, ebony black Yamaha G2 grand piano. It cost about $9,500.

With the remaining $1,500 or so, I bought a 13 year-old used Mercedes diesel sedan from a Mexican guy in Los Feliz who seemed awfully happy to see that car go. It was a crummy car -- the seats were bad, the engine sputtered, and it had some rust. The kids refused to ride in it, and I don't blame them.

But at least I had the piano I wanted and I didn't have to ride my bicycle past lean and hungry-looking coyotes at 3:30 in the morning on Chevy Chase Dr.

Most of the children took piano lessons, although those got hard to pay for in the last few years of our time in San Marino. I grew up playing the piano, and after I got the Yamaha, I spent many a happy hour relearning pieces I had studied in high school when I was a good piano player.

One of the worst days of my life was the day we sold the piano. It was the summer of 2006, and we listed it on Craigslist. I had Marina handle the transaction because I was too sad about the whole thing. Every once in a while (okay, twice a month), I go on Craigslist and look for an ebony Yamaha G2, and imagine myself one day buying another one. That will be a happy day.

She sold it to a Filipino family in San Gabriel, CA, who had a daughter who was a serious pianist and was applying to Juilliard and seemed likely to get in. She came to our house to try the piano, and played an Etude by Liszt. She was spectacular. It was a piece of music I would never be able to play. This girl deserves a great piano, I thought. She hasn't hit the limit of her talent yet.

I remember the exact day I hit the limit of my talent on the piano. I was a senior in high school and was taking lessons from a teacher named David Viste at a music school in downtown Minneapolis. He decided I should take on a Sonata by Beethoven. Technically, I had learned more difficult pieces in my life. But I remember one afternoon I was working on a passage from the third movement, and it hit me.

You know what? I will be able to master this piece in terms of actually being able to play it, but I don't understand it. There are ideas in this music that a way beyond me. Beethoven is way, way, way smarter than me.

I took lessons for a couple more years in college, but eventually gave it up when I couldn't afford lessons anymore.

This girl, however, was well beyond my level. She was the kind of girl who might understand Beethoven.

"Well, at least it went to a family that will appreciate it," Marina said, as the piano was lugged out of the house.

"Yeah, I guess," I said. "But I appreciated the piano." I thought.

I am years away from another piano, but after I settled in Berkeley this spring I got my tax refund and I had a few hundred bucks burning a hole in my pocket and I decided to take up the accordion.

It would be sort of like having a piano.

Sort of.

It was an idiotic idea, I'll admit it.

Seriously? An accordion?

I told myself it would be like having a handheld piano.

It's really not, though. It's an accordion. It's a goofy instrument.

I had talked myself out of the idea of getting an accordion until one day I was walking along Solano Avenue in Berkeley and a busker was sitting outside the Bank of America playing the accordion and it was pretty to listen to. He was playing "Imagine" by John Lennon.

That's it, I decided, I'm going to get an accordion.

I found an accordion on Craigslist. It was offered at $400, and I hammered the guy down to $240. We agreed to meet on a Sunday afternoon at a Trader Joe's in Oakland.

Annie and I had spent the weekend together and were blissfully happy. We had had our ups and downs, but things seemed to have achieved a certain kind of equilibrium. She had come to believe in the relationship and in me. At one point, a couple days earlier, we were in a Wells Fargo office to discuss a refinancing of her mortgage and she had brought me along because she believed that bankers take men more seriously than women.

She introduced me to the banker as "my life partner" and I didn't really say anything to the banker other than it was nice to meet him. The two of them discussed a refinance that he had intended to contact her about, and it was a great deal. I didn't say a word. Mainly, I sat there and was thinking about soccer and not really paying attention.

After the meeting was over, Annie thanked me profusely.

"For what?" I asked. "I didn't do anything. I didn't even say anything."

"I just appreciated you being there," she said. "It was really helpful. I just felt like the guy took me more seriously."

I shrugged. Hey, if me sitting in a chair thinking about Barcelona's chances in the Champions League that year while she and a banker talked about her mortgage was a big help to her, I'm good with that. She had earlier in the week taken me to meet with an adviser to her pension fund. I can do calculations quickly in my head, and had done them as quickly as the woman's calculator and then was looking out the window at a car while the two of them talked about her pension.

"How does that sound?" Annie asked me about a certain point in the discussion of her pension.

"Oh, sorry," I said. "I wasn't paying attention. I was looking at that car out there." Annie let out a bemused but frustrated sigh.

Still, she was happy with me. I seemed like a good partner. We had gone through some ups and downs, but things were good now. This was a man she could trust.

And then came the accordion.

It was the President's Day holiday weekend. On Sunday morning, Annie said she wanted to make pork chops for dinner that night. I said I had to go over to Oakland to pick up an accordion so I would be gone for a while.

"You're getting an accordion?" she asked.

Uh-oh. Now I'm going to have to explain that not only am I picking up an accordion, I'm actually BUYING an accordion. What a stupid idea this was! Why was I buying an accordion? This had to be the most idiotic purchase of my life.

"Uh, yeah," I said. "I'm picking one up."

"Well, I can take you over there," she said.

"It's no problem," I said. "I was just planning on taking BART over to the Lake Merritt Station and then riding my bike over to Trader Joe's and meeting the guy."

"The Trader Joe's is not that close," she said. "I'll take you over there."

What I should have done at this point is one of two things:

A. Admit I was actually purchasing an accordion.

Or

B. Just go over to the Trader Joe's in Oakland by myself and handle the whole transaction on my own and just not involved her in this whole embarrassing business of me buying an accordion.

What I shouldn't have done is:

C. Have Annie give me a ride over there and come up with an intricate and completely implausible set of lies designed to cover up the fact that I was actually buying an accordion. And then once she knew I was lying about the fact that I was actually buying an accordion and not picking one up, as I was falsely claiming, and had concocted an increasingly fanciful set of lies to cover this fact up until she realized I was a lying liar and she couldn't be with me anymore because I wasn't a person she could trust.

So, naturally, I chose C.

The entire transaction was the perfect illustration of Mark Twain's adage of "Always tell the truth because there's less to remember."

Suffice to say, Annie watched me buy the accordion for $240, which I denied to her face that I was doing. And then got increasingly angry about her confronting me about this lie on the way back to my house in Berkeley.

The whole sordid adventure ended with Annie pulling up in front of my house and turning to me and saying this:

"Okay, David, this is it. I want you right now to admit to me the truth about this accordion. Just tell me what's going on. And I don't want to hear some ridiculous story about how you're picking it up for your roommate Nicholas because I saw you pay the guy and I saw the guy showing you how it works. If you would just be honest and tell me you bought this accordion and apologize for lying to me, then you can drop it off and we can go back to my house and have pork chops and a nice evening together."

I took a deep breath... and stuck with my stupid, implausible, utterly false story.

As I stepped out of the car, Annie looked at me.

"If you leave now, I want you to know it is over between us," she said. "If you stick with this lie, then I know I can't trust you and it's over."

I stuck with the lie.

Why?

I think the best answer is: I am an idiot. Who cares if I was buying an accordion? I guess I did. I was embarrassed about the whole purchase and couldn't admit to myself that I was doing something as stupid as buying an accordion.

That's really all I've got for an explanation.

Things were never the same between us after that. Annie decided that I wasn't the kind of person who she could trust as a life partner. If I would lie about something as stupid as an accordion, what else would I lie about?

I came in the house with my accordion. I opened the case once, pressed a few buttons, and then the next day decided that the accordion was a curse.

I ran an ad on Craigslist and sold it for $100 to a guy who collects accordions.

There is a music store in downtown Berkeley that has a sticker in the window: "Play the accordion, go to jail."

I never actually played the accordion. But I did lose $140 on the deal. And a life partner.

To be completely fair to Annie, it wasn't just the accordion. There were a number of things that bothered her about me. I was hot-headed. I liked to argue. I was a wise-ass too many times and she is a serious and sweet-natured person who doesn't take to sarcasm and arguing, which I take to like an addict.

Marina and I had talked about Annie many months earlier.

"She'll leave you, David," Marina said.

And so she did. Annie did leave me. It wasn't the accordion. It was everything else about my messy and difficult life.

Chapter 41: "The Fog Rolls In"

"You've said that you have problems with anger," the therapist at a free clinic said to me.

"Yes," I said.

"I'd like to explore that a little bit," she said.

"Okay," I said.

"Could you describe to me what has happened when you feel you've had a problem with anger?" she said.

"I've exploded," I said. "Yelling, screaming, completely losing control."

"Who have you exploded at?" she asked.

"Usually the people I love," I said.

She looked at me impassively.

"And how did that make you feel?" she asked.

"Afterwards, you mean?" I asked.

"Yes, afterwards."

"Ashamed," I said.

"Ashamed? Why?"

I sat silently in the chair. She didn't say anything. I looked out the window. It was a chilly late winter afternoon in San Francisco. The fog was starting to roll in from the Pacific.

"I don't know," I said. "Maybe because I felt like I betrayed them or something."

"How did you feel betrayed them?" she asked. That, oh woman in this small quiet room, would be a long list indeed.

Chapter 42: "A Good Time to Feel Sorry For Yourself"

I was riding my bicycle on the Ohlone Parkway in Berkeley running an errand. It's a bicycle and pedestrian pathway that follows the BART from El Cerrito to the edge of downtown Berkeley.

I was gloomy.

This hadn't been a particularly good week. Woes a'plenty. Really feeling sorry for myself.

And then the chain slipped off my gearing.

No big deal, really. I can fix that in a few seconds. But not something you really want to be doing when you have bike baskets loaded with stuff -- a gallon of milk, a couple of books, and a sweater and a pair of penny loafers I had just bought at a thrift shop. Take the bike baskets off, flip the bike over, slip the chain back on, flip the bike back over, put the baskets back on...

As I was going through this, I was thinking to myself: "You know what would be great? It would be great if I could get a frickin' break. Just something good. Anything!"

As I was fixing the chain and muttering to myself, a severely disabled woman in a motorized wheelchair came up. She had extremely short legs that didn't reach more than a few inches past the seat and arms that clung to the side of her twisted body. She drove the wheelchair by manipulating a knob on the left armrest, using nearly paralyzed hands.

"Hey, do you need some help?" she asked me.

"Me?" I asked.

"Don't see anyone else around here," she snapped back.

"No, I'm okay," I said. "Just the chain slipped off."

"I've got bike tools if you need them," she said.

"You've got bike tools?" I said. "Why would you have bike tools?"

She looked at me.

"Uhh, for this," she said, indicating her wheelchair.

"It's not really a bike," I said. "How would bike tools help you?"

"Look, if you're gonna be a smartass..." she said.

"I'm not trying to be a smartass," I said. "It's just you're not using a bike. What bike tools would you find applicable to your chair?"

"For flat tires," she said.

"How would you fix a flat tire?" I asked.

"Well, I slide out of this thing, take the tire off, replace the tube, put the tire back on, pump the tire back up, and then get back in," she said.

"Wow," I said. "That is badass!"

"Oh, I'm badass, alright," she said.

My bike was all fixed up and ready to go.

"Well, thanks for the offer," I said. "You have a good day."

She shrugged.

"Eh," she said.

I rode off and the thought occurred to me: You know when's a good time to feel sorry for yourself?

Not today.

Chapter 43: "Hey, Kid, Being 21 Sucks. 56 Is Where It's At"

Albany, CA, is a small prosperous suburb of Berkeley. It was known many, many years ago as "the Northern Gateway to Western Alameda County." Which, in the annals of accolades, ranks considerably below "Paris of the Orient" (Saigon) but significantly above "Armpit of Indiana" (and I think we all know which town named Gary, Indiana, we are talking about here.)

Anyway, I was over at the Albany Public Library at lunch one day, and came up to the Reference Desk, where there was no Reference Librarian and a kid sitting on one of the chairs with his Razor Scooter on the other.

I stood there for a while, and he did nothing.

"Could you move your scooter so I can use this chair?" I said to him, finally, when glaring at his scooter didn't seem to have the impact I was looking for.

"Oh, sure," he said, and moved his scooter.

I sat down.

"Sheesh," I said.

"What?" he said.

"I shouldn't have had to ask you to move your scooter," I said. "You should have offered me the chair."

"Well, I gave you the chair, so..."

"Whatever," I grunted.

We sat there silently for a few moments, then I looked around.

"Where's the reference librarian?" I said to the kid. "I'm kind of in a hurry."

"Why? What do you have to do?"

"I need to borrow their flash drive to download something --"

"They have a flash drive here they let you borrow?" he said, excitedly.

"Yup," I said. "All you need is to give them your driver's license. You have a driver's license, right?"

"No. I'm 13," he said.

"Hah-hah," I said, cackling. "No flash drive for you."

He grunted.

"I can hardly wait until I'm 16," he said. "I'm getting my driving license right away then."

"Driving license?" I said, mockingly.

"Yeah. When I'm 16."

"It's not called a driving license," I said. "It's called a driver's license."

"Same thing," he snapped back.

"No," I said. "One thing is the right name for it and the other -- which is the one you're using -- is the wrong name."

"Whatever."

"Look, kid," I said. "I'm just trying to spare you massive amounts of mockery when you use the wrong word, but whatever."

(It turns out both of us were wrong. It's actually called a "driver license." So that's a big old 'whatever' to the two of us.)

"What I'm really waiting for is when I turn 21," he said. "That's the perfect age. I'm gonna turn 21 and then I'm gonna stop aging."

"21 sucks, kid," I said. "21 is for losers."

"Oh, really."

"Yes, really," I said. "You know what's the perfect age? 56."

"Why 56?" he asked.

"Because I'm 56 and look at me," I said. "I'm awesome."

The kid looked at me for a moment.

Kid: "No comment."

The Reference Librarian came up, and asked who's first.

"Obviously me," he said to her.

He had a long list of things he needed her to check on for him. I sat there. It was okay, however, because I'm 56. And that's the perfect age.

You'll see, Mr. Wisenheimer 13 year-old Razor Scooter Kid. One day when you're 56, you're gonna realize that 56 is the pinnacle of awesomeness. Okay? Got that?

He finally finished with what he wanted from the Reference Librarian, and then looked at me and sneered. I sneered back.

Chapter 44: "The Counter Girl at the Bagelteria Offers Her Views"

In February, 2012, I was in New York City. Not the best time of the year to be there, but it does beat August.

I was visiting two of my daughters, Sasha and Claire, who share an apartment in the Williamsburg section of Brooklyn. The part of Williamsburg they live in isn't the hipster-y part, nor is it in the Hasidim-y part either. Both of those parts are nearby, but they live in a section of large old apartment buildings that are mainly Dominican.

I had come out to help Claire move in with Sasha. Claire had lived for the prior year on Putnam Avenue in Bed-Stuy. When she had originally told me she had gotten an apartment in Bed-Stuy, she was excited: "My place is four blocks from where Notorious B.I.G. grew up!"

That's great, I said, weakly. Say, isn't he the guy who was shot to death and most of his music was about growing up in a violent, drug-infested neighborhood?

Just wanted to make sure we were talking about the same Notorious B.I.G. here. Oh, we are? Okay, then...

Claire decided to move in with Sasha, which I was happy about. Marisa came up from Washington, D.C., to help with the move. We rented a UHaul moving truck, and Sasha and Claire joined Marisa in the front seat while Sasha's friend Jason and I sat, locked up, in the darkened back of the van. We each sat on kitchen table chairs and held on for dear life.

Marisa had never driven a truck before. And she was outstanding at it. But I think we can all agree that sitting on a kitchen table chair in the pitch dark back of a locked moving van while Marisa rambles along from Bed-Stuy to Williamsburg on a Saturday morning can be a bit on the hair-raising side. Not completely hair-rising. Just sufficiently hair-raising to warrant several shots of Jameson once you get to Williamsburg. That's all I'm saying.

Every morning I was there, I walked from their apartment to a bagel joint a block away. It is called Bagelteria. Run by a Dominican family. They used to call me "Irish" because I am white and have white hair.

As in, "Hey, Irish, whaddya want today?"

I enjoyed talking to the young woman behind the counter because, it turned out, she has more opinions that she freely expresses than I do. Which is saying something.

"You got a woman in your life?" she asked me one day.

"Yes, I do," I said.

"How's it goin'?" she said.

"Ehh." I said. "I'm crazy in love with her, but sometimes it doesn't go so good."

"It's probably mainly your fault," she said.

"Yeah," I said. "Probably it is."

I smiled at her. She nodded, knowingly.

"What about you?" I asked. "Is there a man in your life?"

"I got a boyfriend," she said. "But he's trouble too. Men are trouble. But..."

And then she smiled a sly, knowing smile.

"Annie says the same thing, I'm sure," I said.

"Oh, her name is Annie?" she asked. "Is she Irish too?"

"I'm not Irish!" I said. "I've told you that!"

"Whatevah, Irish," she said.

One morning while she was toasting my bagel, she said she was thinking about me and wanted to offer me this advice.

So here it is: Romance Advice from the Counter Girl at the Bagelteria

1. It's okay to kiss and make out at work, provided the store isn't busy and you go in the back and not out front where the customers are.

2. If you're mad at him, write down what you're mad about on your iPhone and show it to him three days later when you're both calmed down.

3. No Inter-borough dating. It just never works. It's late, you've had a fight at his apartment up in Harlem and now you have to go home to Brooklyn. That's gonna be two transfers, and do you really want to be on the subway at 1 in the morning, mad at him? I don't think so.

Oh, and one other thing:

Rihanna could do much better than Chris Brown.

Any other questions?

Chapter 45: "Dancing With the Stars"

My time in Berkeley has been unsettled at best. I have been mostly unhappy here. Things did not go well with me and Annie, and finally we agreed to end it. Her view was that we were "mismatched." Which was true. Annie is orderly, quiet, mindful and settled. I am not. She is precise, and I round everything to the nearest thousand.

I suppose that was charming to her for a while, but as time went on, my heedless approach to life wore on her in ways that ultimately made her feel happier away from me than with me.

It was devastating. I was flattened by it. But I had been flattened by things before, and had stood back up, brushed myself off and moved on. Not in the sense of finding someone else or even falling out of love with her. I don't quite see that passing away or moving on. Or at least not for a very long time. I don't fall out of love. And I don't shed people. They stay in my life like clothes in a closet. You open the door and are digging around and there it is: that shirt you loved in high school.

I never quite close any doors and Annie will always be there, just as Marina still is.

Marina will always be there, sitting across from me at our long dining room table, talking to her late while the children slept or standing in the dawn, smiling at me on the deck of a creaky ship sailing up the Dalmatian coast.

And Annie will always be there too. There will always be that sound of her voice in my head, talking about her novel, or feeling the smooth skin of her back, pulling her close to me in a dark and quiet bedroom.

I moved on in the sense that, well, life always moves on, whether you want it to or not.

When I picture my life going forward now, it has a shape not unlike my current life.

"Hey, you wanna watch 'Dancing With the Stars' on OnDemand?" my housemate, Nicholas, asked me one night. "I downloaded season five."

I didn't really want to, but Nicholas clearly did. It just seemed like another silly, insubstantial show about nothing. But Nicholas wanted me to watch it with him. So I did.

And I loved it.

Loved everything about it. Loved the dancing and the music and the costumes and exaggerated dramas and the bad singing and the screaming "judges" who had nothing really to say about the dancing. It was transporting. A spectacle that meant absolutely nothing.

About an hour into it, Nicholas turned to me.

"So, what do you think?" he asked.

"You know what?" I said. "I love 'Dancing With the Stars.'"

Night settled in and I wasn't alone. I was with Nicholas. We watched the show and chatted and time passed quietly and without sorrow. I was happy thinking about how large my life has been.

And how I fell in love so greatly with two remarkable women.

With Marina, we lived a passionate and meteoric marriage that produced eight children.

And with Annie, well, I think of her often and when I do, I think of the lines from that old Bob Dylan song:

> *"Twas in another lifetime*
>
> *One of toil and blood*
>
> *When blackness was a virtue*
>
> *And the road was full of mud*
>
> *I came in from the wilderness*

A creature void of form

'Come in,' she said,

'I'll give you shelter from the storm.'

"Dancing With The Stars" ended and we went out and sat on the stoop of our rented house. It was a rare cloudless night in the Bay Area. Nicholas was smoking and I looked up at the sky.

"Wow," I said. "Look at that. Clear sky at night."

"You can even see stars," he said. "That almost never happens around here."

We sat quietly for a while, and Nicholas took a long drag on his cigarette and then turned to me.

"It's beautiful," he said.

"What is?" I asked. "The stars?"

"No, everything," he said. "Just everything."

We then were quiet for a long time and looked up at the night sky.

I thought of all my children. They were all in their beds now, sleeping, and safe and making lives for themselves and finding happiness in their own way. At an age when most men are firmly settled in homes with families and careers and looking forward to retirement and travel, I was living in a rented house with a guy I had met only months earlier.

Not that it was bad. Nicholas is good company and the house was pleasant.

I started thinking about what I wanted now. And this is what I want: a nice two bedroom apartment somewhere in San Francisco that has big windows that look out at the bay and the Berkeley Hills in the distance where Annie lives. One bedroom for me and one for visitors.

It will have a small but useful kitchen and in the dining room will be a big table for when my children visit.

When I go down to the street, a block away will be a joint that serves strong coffee and wine and has TV sets that show soccer matches and a crowd that knows what's going on in the game.

I don't have any desire anymore to own a house or to fall in love again.

All I really want now is that apartment, this cup of coffee and that game on the television set in the joint down the street. Maybe Barcelona will be playing Real Madrid, or it will be Boca Juniors vs River Plate. It will be some large, passionate match, and I will be there with people I know, smiling and screaming and content.

And a piano. I also want a piano.

An ebony G2 Yamaha grand piano with a metronome so I can sit down on a winter afternoon and play. And then when the sun is setting, I can put on a sweater and walk down the street and see the people I know.

San Francisco was my home now. It would be the final city I live in. I had grown up in Minneapolis, lived for eight years outside of Boston, and then a couple of decades in Los Angeles.

I miss Los Angeles deeply every day, miss its chaos and energy and ambition. But that part of my life is over now. Those years have come to an end. I am in the Bay Area now, and this is where I will remain.

San Francisco is a quieter place, a softer, more elegant city, a bit more artful and much more self-deluded. And I don't mind that. It is shabbier than it thinks of itself, sweeter than it knows.

What had all of this been about? All of this. The end of my career, the loss of my marriage and family, the homelessness, the Rideshares, the soaring and crashing romance.

What had all of it been about?

Maybe it was just like the show. A vast and ornate spectacle, full of drama and comedy, bad singing, mistakes, colors, lights, screaming people with funny accents, cheers and boos, disasters, and triumph.

But in the end, it was all just a spectacle that didn't mean anything. It meant nothing at all.

It was just all of us, and we were all just dancing with the stars.

Chapter 46: "Something Is Going to Happen"

I was on the phone to my youngest daughter, Juliette, one morning. It was afternoon in Germany and she was home from school.

I call there often, usually every day. Just chit-chat. How was school? What is happening around the house? What's the weather like?

The kinds of things you talk about when you come home from work and they are home from school.

Except we live 5,000 miles apart.

I was feeling particularly bleak this morning. Things were not working out as I had hoped. The distance between me and my daughters -- physically and psychologically and emotionally -- seemed to be expanding.

"What's wrong, Daddy?" she asked me all of a sudden.

"Nothing," I lied. "Why?"

"You don't seem like yourself," she said. "You seem kinda sad or something."

"I am very sad," I said.

"Why?"

"Because I don't know why things are so hard or when I'll see you," I said.

"Oh, that," she said.

"Yup, that," I said.

"I miss you and Mari so much and sometimes I feel a bit overwhelmed by everything," I said.

"Well, don't worry," she said. "Something's gonna happen."

"What do you mean, something's gonna happen?" I asked.

"Just that," she said. "Something's going to happen. Something's always happening with you."

"Oh, really?" I said. "Well, it's nice to hear you say something like that."

"It's the way you are," she said. "Something is going to happen. I'm confident."

Juliette is confident. Do you hear that, universe? Juliette is confident something is going to happen!

Chapter 47: "The Girl In the Florescent Pink Dress in Garberville"

Garberville, California, was first settled in 1853, and was called Dogtown. About 20 years later, the town's first Postmaster, Jacob Garber, decided to upgrade the name of the town and changed it from Dogtown to Garberville. Naturally.

It actually isn't even a town. It's what called a "census-designated place." Which means the 913 residents of Garberville lived in a place that has people in it, but doesn't have any of the other niceties that make a town, stuff like municipal government. In other words, Garberville looks like a town, but actually isn't.

A report by the BBC in May, 2011, called Garberville "the marijuana heartland of the U.S."

I was in Garberville on Friday on a trip up to Arcata, CA, to visit Coco, who attends Humboldt State University there. Garberville is 204 miles north of Berkeley and 75 miles south of Arcata. It is surrounded by a vast redwood forest, and the main feature of the town for the visitor appeared to be, on this particular Friday, a festival of noisy trucks and motorcycles rumbling through town. In other words, a typical Northern California Census-Designated Place.

Northern California can be judged to start at several places.

For Angelenos, Northern California starts once you leave Santa Barbara headed north. They would be wrong about this, of course, but don't confuse them. Everything north of Santa Barbara is described as "scenic" or "nice to visit" or "it's great up there." The general sense that most Angelenos have of Northern California -- and San Francisco, in particular -- is positive. It's cleaner, better organized, less crime-ridden and quieter. I don't know that any of this is particularly true, but nevertheless, Angelenos think quite highly of any part of the state north of Santa Barbara.

A solid argument could be made that Northern California starts around Watsonville, just south of San Jose and extends northward to the Oregon border. This would be the designation chosen by most people in the Bay Area. People who live in the Bay Area -- especially lifelong residents -- have a deep antipathy toward Southern California and Los Angeles in particular.

In their minds it is a disgustingly large megalopolis whose mere existence proves that human beings are a depraved and unsalvageable species. Oh, and they're stealing all our water.

They might be right in both of these assessments.

Angelenos are always surprised to hear that a big rivalry exists between the two cities. Sure, there's the Dodgers-Giants rivalry in baseball, but that's about it as far as the awareness that Angelenos have of the explosive animosity that apparently exists between the two cities.

Since I moved up here, I've had numerous conversations with Bay Area natives who sneer at L.A. and congratulate me on moving out of, well, the worst place on earth. "But I love L.A.," I'll say. And they'll look at me as if I've just told them that I love festering boils or something like that. "Really?" they'll say. "What do you like about it?"

"It's great," I'll say. "It's a great, great city. I think it's one of the most remarkable places on earth."

Then there will a long uncomfortable silence followed by: "Okay, then." And they quickly move away.

For me, however, having made the drive to Arcata twice now, Northern California starts considerably north of the Bay Area. Northern California to me is a place of small towns dependent on three commodities: lumber, fish, or marijuana. If your town is north of San Francisco and the economy limps along on any or all of these three commodities, you're in Northern California. If your town is north of San Francisco and has scenic vineyards with wine tasting rooms, oops, sorry: you're not really in Northern California.

And another thing: in my geography of northern California, people wear brown. I challenge anyone to show me a woman in a white mini skirt or a man in a cream-colored seersucker suit anywhere between the Oregon border and the Napa County line. It's a land of muted earth tones on the residents.

At one point in the late 1930s and early 1940s, parts of northern California and southern Oregon had a secessionist movement and wanted to form their own state. It was going to be called the State of Jefferson. (This name won out in a newspaper contest over other names, among them Discontent.)

The state capital was going to be Yreka, California. And its largest city would have been Redding, California, which 70 years later has managed to nearly hit 90,000 residents.

Things were moving forward toward secession after Thanksgiving, 1941, when group of young men armed with rifles blocked US 99 highway and handed out a "Proclamation of Independence" to people driving through. And then a couple weeks later the Japanese bombed Pearl Harbor and the whole fun of making a new state just sort of went out the window.

Regardless, to this day, this part of California has remained a profoundly rural and profoundly different area. And anyone driving along the 101 from San Francisco to the Oregon border will notice that... along with a relentless parade of people loitering around the small towns along the way, "living off the grid".

Which is the new way of saying that you're actually just a hobo. And an awfully grimy one at that.

I had stopped in Garberville to take a break on the drive, and was in a coffeehouse and a noisy diesel-powered pickup truck pulled up. It was originally white, but was covered in dust and caked mud.

The driver got out, and he was pretty much what you'd expect him to be: mid-30s, wearing a grimy, sweat-caked and dusty fedora with a frazzled pony tail hanging out the back, a dirty t-shirt, dirt-covered brown denim work pants, and boots. He was missing a front tooth.

He came around to the passenger door and opened it up and a complete miracle emerged.

It was a girl, about six years old. She was wearing a fluorescent pink sun dress, florescent green flip-flops and a headband that was striped in bands of florescent pink and green. Her hair was cut in little girl bob. She stood briefly on the sidewalk, looked around in a completely pre-possessed manner of a girl who knew exactly how a girl should look on a hot, late summer day when going to town.

She took her father's hand.

"Come on, Daddy," she said. "Let's get ice cream."

They walked off and he smiled.

Where did this girl come from? At what point did she acquire the knowledge that neon pink and electric green work together, but only in carefully plotted ways? It sure didn't look like an outfit her dad picked out. And if the woman who found that guy attractive enough to mate with was still in this little girl's life, she probably wasn't scanning the H & M website for something fun to wear to get ice cream.

Where DID this little girl figure this out?

Plato tried to deal with this exact same question: how do we know about things we do not experience? For instance, we know that justice exists despite the fact that we have never experienced it. Plato postulated the existence of something he called the world of Forms.

In this world of Forms, the pure version of a thing exists and it is perfect and without time or space.

We humans somehow -- dimly and imperfectly -- understand the form of each thing and comprehend a thing in its relationship to the Form.

I always thought that this theory of Plato's was a huge pile of crap. And then I had daughters. Six of them.

Marina and I didn't raise them to be girlie girls, and they certainly aren't. They are each and all of them full-blooded women, the end result of a style of parenting my late mother would have called "raised by wolves."

And yet each of them, when they were girls, somehow knew stuff that little girls seem to almost innately know: what shoes look fun with that dress, how to wear sunglasses, how to walk down the street with your sister and complain about the mean girl. I never taught any of my daughters that sort of thing. And they certainly didn't pick it up from Marina, either.

And yet they all had some knowledge of the Form called Little Girl. Just like that little girl did who got out of the filthy truck in a town once known as Dogtown, and walked down the street in a florescent pink sundress and matching flip flops and headband on a mission to get an ice cream.

Chapter 48: "The 5:19 Going North Out of Menlo Park"

Let's see, I thought to myself, as I checked the Caltrain schedules. I want an express train that leaves Menlo Park, CA, sometime after 5 p.m. Oh, here's one. There's a 5:19 train that gets into the downtown San Francisco Caltrain station at 6:02.

There's a seven block walk over to the Powell St. BART station. That's not a bad walk. About 15 or 20 minutes. I'll walk past the Moscone Center and into the heart of the Financial District in downtown San Francisco. The City is beautiful this time of year. It's a nice time of the year to walk in San Francisco.

Actually, it's not bad to walk any time of the year in San Francisco because it's a beautiful city.

At Powell St., I can catch the Pittsburg/Bay Point train to the MacArthur Station in Oakland, and then transfer to the Richmond train. That will get me to North Berkeley BART at about 7 p.m.

Then I can walk be home by about 7:15.

And I can do that every day. I can read on the train, make phone calls, do a crossword puzzle. I'm a commuter now.

Juliette was right. Something did happen. I got a job.

Chapter 49: "Juan Carlos Tells Us Of His Life"

In April, 2011, before we both left Los Angeles, Saskia and I made our last Rideshare together up to the Bay Area. And this one ride was the fitting coda for both us about the years we endured, together and apart, as a father and a daughter.

"Who is this guy we're riding up with?" Saskia asked, as we sat at the Universal City Red Line station waiting for our ride up to San Francisco. Saskia—who was heading to college in the fall—was joining me because her big sister, Sasha, my eldest, was coming from New York to visit friends in San Francisco, and this probably would be the last time Saskia and I would ever make this trip.

"His name is Juan Carlos," I said.

"Juan Carlos what?" she asked.

"I don't know," I said. "That's all I got."

"Why is he going up to San Francisco?"

"I don't know," I said.

"You don't know his last name, you don't know why he's going up to San Francisco," she said. "Good job, David."

"He sounded nice."

"Great," she said. "He's probably a gang-banger. And he's probably going up for a gang meeting."

And then she laughed.

Joking about a man named Juan Carlos was something that came easily for Saskia because she was fluent in Spanish and had grown up in Los Angeles. The stew of languages and cultures that she swam in every day was normal for her.. Virtually everyone she knew was bilingual, and not just in Spanish: Mandarin, Armenian, Russian, Arabic, and on and on.

She was being ridiculous about Juan Carlos, of course, but she did point out one of the basic problems with Rideshare: you really have no idea who you're going to end up spending the next six hours with. For all you know, it could be Charles Manson. Or an Amway distributor, which is its own special form of torment.

When I talked with him on the phone, Juan Carlos hadn't sounded like a serial killer, or a gang banger, or dangerous at all. He sounded like a very happy person, fun-loving, blithe, the sort of typical type of person the rest of the world imagines living in sunny Southern California: young, vaguely foreign. I liked him because on the phone he laughed easily at most things I said, funny or not.

But I really didn't know much about him. Which would be no big deal were I making this trip alone. On my own, I always figured if the ride sucked, I could get out anywhere and figure things out from there. After a year of homelessness I had discovered resourcefulness that I did not know I possessed. I now knew that I could be proverbially and literally dropped in the middle of nowhere and figure my way home. In whatever form that home might take. It felt somewhat like freedom.

But Saskia was joining me, and wasn't really all that keen on the trip anyway. She would see her sister again in a few weeks anyway when the eldest three girls would come from the East Coast for her high school graduation, plus the trip meant she would miss two days of school near the end of her senior year, and, finally, the whole idea of ride-sharing with her father must have irritated the hell out of her. Simply saying "Trust me, Saskia," to a girl who had seen her father lose her childhood home, I'm sure pushed her normally trusting nature to the outer reaches of its elasticity.

I tried another approach.

"Saskia," I said in my well-practiced father-knows-best tone, "Some day, maybe when you're in your thirties or forties, you're going to tell your children about the Rideshare trips you took to San Francisco with your father. And your kids and everyone else you tell are going to think they're such incredibly cool stories and they're going to love hearing about it."

"Somehow I doubt it," she said, and then scowled and curled up the right side of her upper lip.

A moment later, Juan Carlos pulled up in a three year-old Hyundai subcompact that had not been packed with the greatest of care. The left side of the back seat area was stacked high with clothes, books, shoes, a guitar, and the other clutter of a life lived casually. There was room for Saskia and possibly room for her backpack if we just rearranged things a bit. "There we go! Plenty of room," he said. Saskia stared blankly at him.

"Sorry it's a little crowded, but you're slender," he said to her with a goofy smile. That got her to smile.

He had on a tee shirt and track pants and wore his hair long and looked to be about twenty-five. I bet he's from Argentina, I thought, because I love Argentine soccer, and many Argentine soccer players have long hair. I have wanted to go to Argentina since before I was born. But I probably never would, so getting a ride from an Argentine was about as close as I would ever get to the country I had dreamed of visiting since watching the 1978 World Cup and deciding it was my true homeland, the way a dreamy twenty-two-year-old English and philosophy major from Minneapolis might do.

I looked back at Saskia. She glared at me, the way an angry seventeen-year-old girl whose father had completely screwed up her life might do.

"So," I said to Juan Carlos once we were on the freeway, "Tell me about yourself."

Maybe he could get that upper lip to unsnarl. I was long past capable of that.

Juan Carlos was not twenty-five, as I had guessed; he was thirty-eight. He was originally from a village in the Michoacán state of Mexico, but he had lived in the United States since he was fourteen. His village was outside the big Mexican city of Morelia, and his had been a happy childhood. His parents owned farmland and raised sugar cane, and he lived in a nice house on the edge of the village. They had horses and twenty-five head of cattle (whom he knew, each of them, by name.)

The family had three dogs: two Chihuahuas and an unspotted, all-black Dalmatian. I'd never heard of an all-black Dalmatian. Maybe it was just a big black dog that he had decided was an extremely rare all-black Dalmatian because people like to make things up about their lives sometimes to make them seem more interesting. The Dalmatian's name was Negro.

Negro, he told us, lived to be twenty years old. Or maybe he wasn't. You never know how old a dog is, he said. They live their lives the way they want to.

In Mexico, he said, we think about dogs differently than in America. In America, people think about dogs as members of their families. Americans have to raise the dog, train him, teach him, feed him and care for him, as if he were a baby joining the family. In Mexico, he said, dogs are our best friends. They may live with you, but they can take care of themselves. They find their own food, they wander around all day with their other dog friends, and at night, they come to visit you, like a friend would.

In the mornings, the dogs would leave the house, sometimes anticipating where Juan Carlos and his father and brothers would go during the day, and the dogs would come along. He said at nights, after working in the fields, when it was time to bring the cattle in, his grandfather would whistle and the Chihuahuas and Negro would come up to the men on their horses. His grandfather or his father would tell the dogs it was time to bring the cattle in. And off they would go.

"Wait a minute," I said. "You used Chihuahuas for herding cattle?"

"Yes," he said. "They are very good at it. Dogs can do anything. They don't just do what you think they can do, they can do much more."

I looked at Saskia and she was smiling. Juan Carlos' beguiling tales of village life in Mexico were softening her. The idea of Chihuahuas herding cattle seemed particularly amusing.

It was a good morning for a ride. We were coming up to the Tejon Pass and the sky was clear and the hillsides were still green from the winter rains and snow. It was sunny, but it wasn't yet summer. The air was still cool, and when I rolled down the windows it was fresh and smelled good. This was going to be a happy ride.

"Do you have brothers and sisters?" I asked, wanting to expand the conversation, wanting Juan Carlos to tell us more about his life.

"There were five boys and then my sister came."

I smiled, thinking of my six girls and two boys. "Oh, man, your sister must be the princess of the house." I laughed a fatherly laugh.

"Well, actually, my sister passed away," he said.

"Oh, that's terrible," I said. "What happened?"

He got quiet for a moment, and I looked back at Saskia, who suddenly had a concerned look. I rolled up the window because I didn't want the noisy sound of rushing air to interrupt. He took a deep breath.

"When I was twelve years old, my sister, my mother, my father and two of my brothers were killed in a car accident. My thirteen-year-old brother and my seven year-old brother and I weren't in the car; we weren't there when it happened."

Saskia had a stricken look on her face. This just seemed so wrong. Silly, light-hearted Juan Carlos with the cattle-herding Chihuahuas and the twenty year-old Dalmatian, suddenly seemed to both of us to be a different sort person all together.

"I just... I just can't imagine that," I said.

Juan Carlos stared ahead at the road. We drove for a moment, and I started to feel bad for pressing the point. But he continued.

"It was hard," he said. "I mean, I was just a kid."

"How did you come to grips with it? I mean, how do you get through something like that?"

"There were two moments," he said, "that sort of pushed me through it. The first was when my uncle told my two brothers and me what had happened. I felt a strong rush through my body, like I was high on the most powerful drug possible. I just felt so light, like I was flying."

"It must have been adrenaline," I said.

"I don't know," he said. "Maybe it was adrenaline. Or maybe it was their spirits moving through me. I just don't know."

The way he said this made me believe the second guess was correct.

"The second moment happened on the morning of the funerals. I was showering and, when I finished, I reached out for a towel." He took a hand off the steering wheel and made a grabbing motion. "But there wasn't one there." He paused. "That's one of the things my mother always did. She was always making sure there were towels in the bathroom and soap and little things like that."

"And then I realized that this was the rest of my life. No one would take care of me. I was alone in the world. I would have to take care of myself. And no matter what happened to me, good or bad, I would have no one to share it with. I couldn't come home and say: 'oh, listen to what happened to me.' Because there now was no one there to listen. No mother. No father. No older brothers. No little sister."

We took this in, and it felt as if the car moved silently through the mountains for a while.

"Juan Carlos," I said finally. But my voice trailed off. "It's hard to survive bad things, isn't it?" I said.

"But you have to do it," he said. "You just have to go on."

And he did. Two years after the crash that killed his family, when he was fourteen, he left for America. He said he just had to leave the village, with its herding Chihuahuas and Negro, the black Dalmatian, and sugar cane fields and the smell of cooking coming out of the windows in the late afternoon as he walked home from school.

He went to stay with an aunt who lived in Long Beach. He didn't speak a word of English. He was an illegal alien. One of the seemingly endless sea of illegal aliens that some believe are clogging the schools, streets, hospitals, restaurant kitchens, construction sites, auto repair garages and strawberry fields of California. Juan Carlos taught himself English, took up skateboarding and the piano and the guitar. He read novels in English and became a musician. He drove for Fedex for ten years, then worked his way into television production, one of those guys on the stage dressing the set. He was gradually becoming someone new. I have become, he said, some kind of an American.

"I am Mexican in my soul," he said. "But I have become American in my soul, too.

"My brothers came a year after me, but they left," he said. "They couldn't take it here. But I wanted to be here. I wanted to make a life here. And I did."

"Do you ever go back?" I asked.

"I couldn't for a long time because I was, you know, illegal. But when I was nineteen I went back for the first time."

He described returning to his village. It looked as it did when he'd left: small, familiar, dusty and warm. He walked along the streets for a time, looking into shops and greeting people. He turned a corner and in the near distance saw a dog. It was Negro. They both stopped and appraised each other, and then Negro trotted up to him, wagged his tail, and leaned against Juan Carlos, waiting for him to scratch behind his ears.

"I bent over and whispered his name, and he leaned closer to me. 'Negro,' I said. The old dog leaned even closer to him, pushing his chest against Juan Carlos' legs, lifting up his head and looking at the boy who was now a man with a deep voice and different clothes.

The image of that scene, Juan Carlos and Negro standing on a street corner, best friends reunited after many years, silently leaning against each other, felt like I'd just watched the climactic scene from a movie. In the backseat, Saskia was crying quietly, and I rubbed my eyes as well.

"You survived," I said softly, not wanting to break the spell of his story.

"Yes, I did," he said. He looked at me and smiled. "I am overqualified when it comes to survival."

For the rest of the drive, Juan Carlos and I talked non-stop, about agriculture in Mexico, about the Revolution and Zapata and Pancho Villa, about books he had read, and the woman he loved, now waiting for him in northern California. We listened to music he composed and recorded. Several days later, he would email me links to two of the songs. I asked Saskia to translate them but she told me she didn't want to. They were too sad, she said. They were about losing someone and not being able to find them.

But I have to say, the Juan Carlos we met in that cramped Hyundai was a happy person. He smiled most of the way, had a dozen projects he intended to pursue, was in love with a woman, and wanted some day to marry her. "I live my life the way I want to," he'd said. "The past is always there, but I wouldn't be who I am without it."

He'd also told us a story about going for a run several years earlier. It was a rainy morning in Los Angeles, and he was running through a park. Suddenly, he said, he felt overcome with sorrow, so he stopped and leaned against a tree. "I felt like they were all there, in the tree, he said. My mother, my father, my brothers and my little sister. I could feel them saying to me, 'Go on, Juan Carlos, we are here with you. Just keep going on.'

"And so I do," he said. "That's what I do."

We arrived in Oakland about six hours later. He dropped us off at the Grand Lake Theater in Oakland where we were to meet Annie. Saskia and I stood for a moment and watched him drive away, not saying anything.

Finally, she looked at me. "That was a wonderful ride," she said.

"Yes it was," I said. And I put my arm on her shoulder and we stood together.

Chapter 50: "Everyone is Good"

In late October, 2012, Nicholas and I were watching a baseball game and it was a tremendous game and I suddenly felt so full of life.

I walked over to Nicholas' computer and started an email to Annie. The subject line: "Goddamn it, I miss you."

The text of the email: "I'm sorry, but it's true."

A few minutes later she wrote back.

"I miss you, too."

We exchanged short notes to each other for a day or so, and then I wrote her: "If it is possible, I would like to meet you, you know, for coffee or something, and just talk."

"I think that's possible," Annie wrote back. "Where?"

"How about the Peet's above Shattuck in North Berkeley."

It was the place we had first had coffee three years earlier.

She was bemused, and we agreed to meet a week later.

I was as nervous as I had been the first time we met. I ordered a coffee, she had some kind of mysterious chai tea latte thing that she always orders and is never quite satisfied with. We sat down outside and chatted nervously for a bit. Then she said it.

"So, what have you been up to?" she said. "I miss hearing your stories."

"Would you like to hear one?" I asked.

"Yes," she said.

So I started to tell about my new job and the commute and the people I meet on BART and the trains and the homeless guy I have a running feud with at the Powell BART station and how we yell at each other over a now-forgotten grievance, and the nervous guy who left his Bichon Frise and five pounds of marijuana on the Caltrain.

I went on and on, and as I talked she slowly slid her hand across the small table and put it in mine and she looked at me and smiled.

"What is it?" I said.

"Just keep talking," she said. "I like listening to you talk."

***

Annie and I gave it one more try. And it was wonderful for months and months. And then it wasn't. The job in Menlo Park ended when the company failed. I feel into a deep, immobilizing sadness and it was more than she could take. We ended it once again, this time probably for good.

But Annie had given me one great gift: this story I have told you. Were it not for her, I would have never written it, would have never tried to take the tangled cords of my life and tried to unfurl them and lay them out for you, dear reader, as honestly as I could. She helped me remember and feel and try to understand what it is that I have lived.

***

For years and years I have awakened in the middle of the night and been up, usually for a couple of hours or longer, and then gone back to sleep. This is the time of day I usually do a lot of writing. I also think about my children and the people I love -- what they are doing at this particular moment: Coco probably is having lunch in South Africa, Mari and Juliette are in school in late morning classes in high school in Germany, my daughters, Alexandra, Marisa and Claire, in Brooklyn and Washington, D.C., are just getting up to go to work at their office, or hospital or classroom. The rest -- Saskia at college in Minnesota, Cristian on the Cheyenne River Indian Reservation in South Dakota where he is working as a nurse, and Annie in her house overlooking the San Francisco Bay -- are asleep in their rooms, maybe it's raining or windy where they live out there and maybe it's just a quiet, calm and foggy night up there in the Berkeley Hills.

It's such an ingrained part of my life that I can't even say I'm irritated about it. What's nice about it on this particular night is noticing the little noises of the house -- the dryer humming downstairs, the cat walking through the kitchen, the refrigerator whirring quietly.

I'll make a pot of espresso soon and that will help me sleep (I have an odd brain -- this works for me), but for now I don't mind being up. I'm in a house. It's a small house, but I'm not alone in the night. There's a dryer downstairs humming, a cat walking through the kitchen and a refrigerator whirring and my housemates sleeping.

Everyone is good. I miss them all very much and love them even more. And they should all know that their David is doing alright. He's awake, he's writing and he carries them in his heart.

Printed in Great Britain
by Amazon.co.uk, Ltd.,
Marston Gate.